Bibliovores

Contains *Unshelved* comic strips originally published on the *Unshelved* website from December 5, 2011 to March 28, 2013. *Conference Tips* originally published in *ALA CogNotes* newspapers in January 2012, June 2012, and January 2013. *WWDD@ BEA* originally published as a downloadable comic on April 17, 2007. *Unshelved Secret Origins: Dewey* originally published in the *Reading With Pictures* anthology on August 18, 2010.

ISBN-13: 978-1-937914-04-2

First printing: June 2013

Printed in China.

Bibliovores

an **UNSHELVED** collection
by Gene Ambaum & Bill Barnes

Eat up!

**OVERDUE
MEDIA**
Seattle

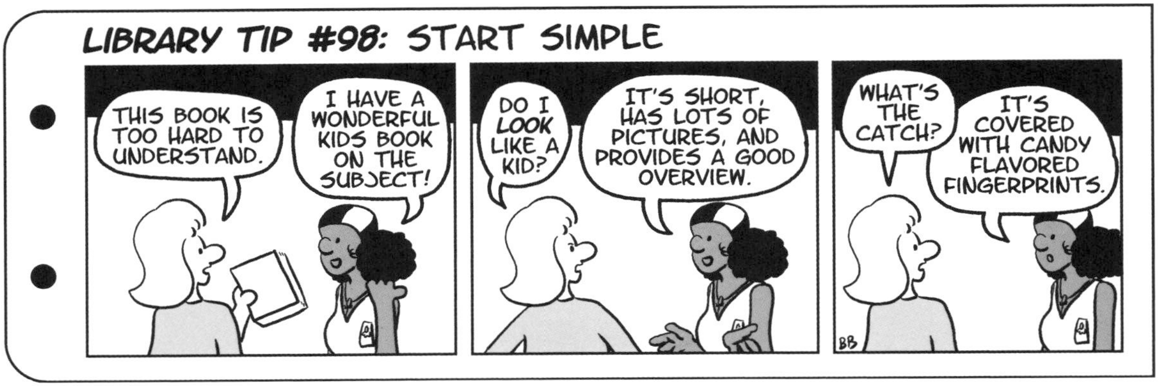
LIBRARY TIP #98: START SIMPLE
THIS BOOK IS TOO HARD TO UNDERSTAND.
I HAVE A WONDERFUL KIDS BOOK ON THE SUBJECT!
DO I LOOK LIKE A KID?
IT'S SHORT, HAS LOTS OF PICTURES, AND PROVIDES A GOOD OVERVIEW.
WHAT'S THE CATCH?
IT'S COVERED WITH CANDY FLAVORED FINGERPRINTS.
BB

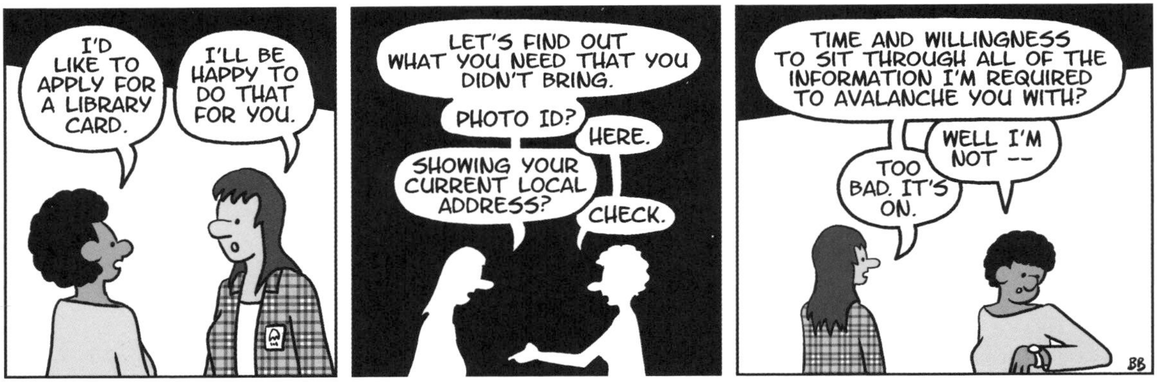
I'D LIKE TO APPLY FOR A LIBRARY CARD.
I'LL BE HAPPY TO DO THAT FOR YOU.
LET'S FIND OUT WHAT YOU NEED THAT YOU DIDN'T BRING.
PHOTO ID?
HERE.
SHOWING YOUR CURRENT LOCAL ADDRESS?
CHECK.
TIME AND WILLINGNESS TO SIT THROUGH ALL OF THE INFORMATION I'M REQUIRED TO AVALANCHE YOU WITH?
WELL I'M NOT --
TOO BAD. IT'S ON.
BB

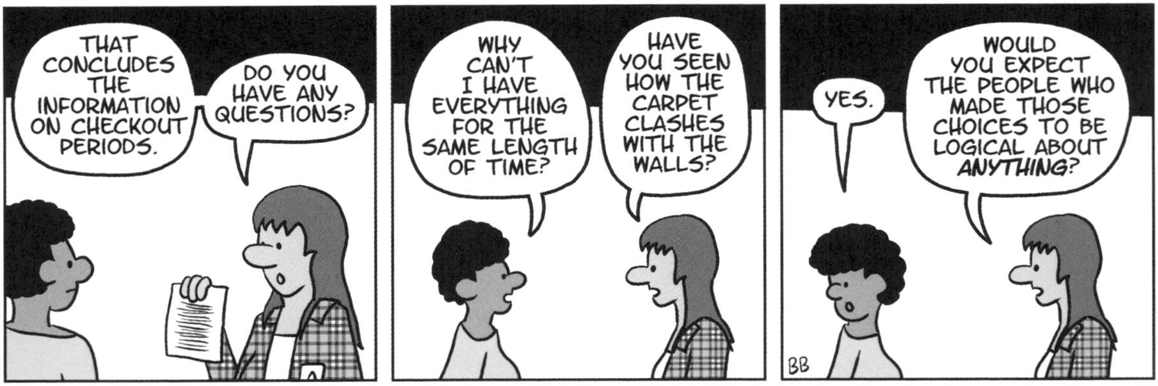
THAT CONCLUDES THE INFORMATION ON CHECKOUT PERIODS.
DO YOU HAVE ANY QUESTIONS?
WHY CAN'T I HAVE EVERYTHING FOR THE SAME LENGTH OF TIME?
HAVE YOU SEEN HOW THE CARPET CLASHES WITH THE WALLS?
YES.
WOULD YOU EXPECT THE PEOPLE WHO MADE THOSE CHOICES TO BE LOGICAL ABOUT ANYTHING?
BB

Bibliovores

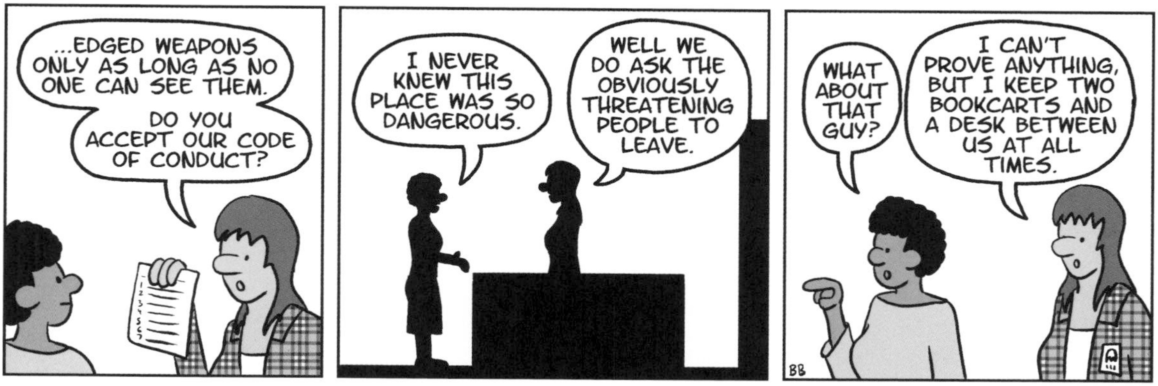

...EDGED WEAPONS ONLY AS LONG AS NO ONE CAN SEE THEM.
DO YOU ACCEPT OUR CODE OF CONDUCT?
I NEVER KNEW THIS PLACE WAS SO DANGEROUS.
WELL WE DO ASK THE OBVIOUSLY THREATENING PEOPLE TO LEAVE.
WHAT ABOUT THAT GUY?
I CAN'T PROVE ANYTHING, BUT I KEEP TWO BOOKCARTS AND A DESK BETWEEN US AT ALL TIMES.
BB

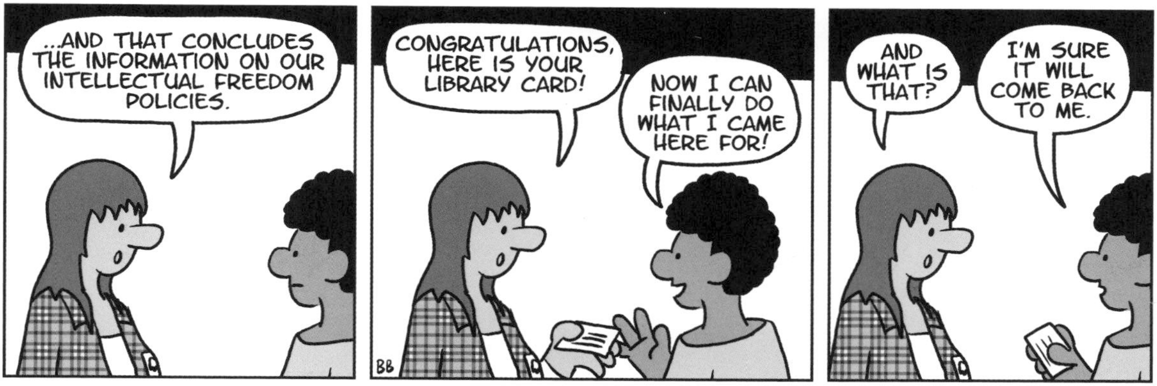

...AND THAT CONCLUDES THE INFORMATION ON OUR INTELLECTUAL FREEDOM POLICIES.
CONGRATULATIONS, HERE IS YOUR LIBRARY CARD!
NOW I CAN FINALLY DO WHAT I CAME HERE FOR!
BB
AND WHAT IS THAT?
I'M SURE IT WILL COME BACK TO ME.

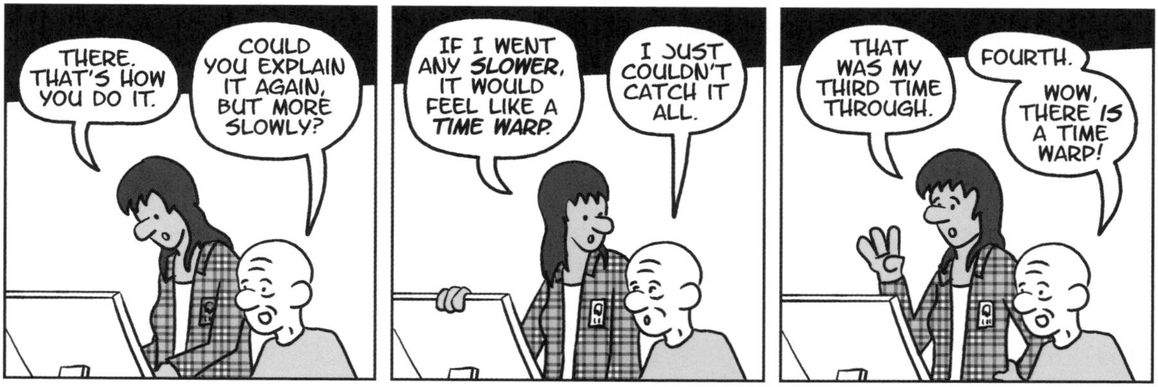

THERE. THAT'S HOW YOU DO IT.
COULD YOU EXPLAIN IT AGAIN, BUT MORE SLOWLY?
IF I WENT ANY SLOWER, IT WOULD FEEL LIKE A TIME WARP.
I JUST COULDN'T CATCH IT ALL.
THAT WAS MY THIRD TIME THROUGH.
FOURTH.
WOW, THERE IS A TIME WARP!

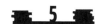

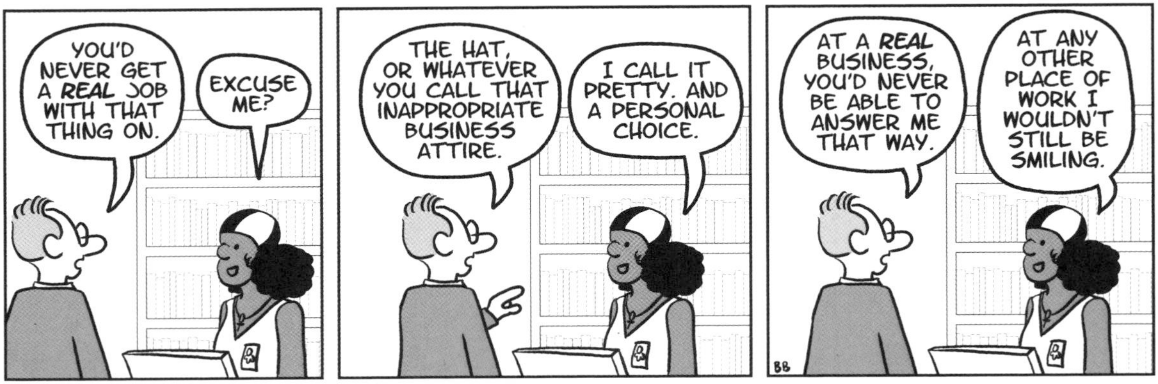
YOU'D NEVER GET A **REAL** JOB WITH THAT THING ON.
EXCUSE ME?
THE HAT, OR WHATEVER YOU CALL THAT INAPPROPRIATE BUSINESS ATTIRE.
I CALL IT PRETTY. AND A PERSONAL CHOICE.
AT A **REAL** BUSINESS, YOU'D NEVER BE ABLE TO ANSWER ME THAT WAY.
AT ANY OTHER PLACE OF WORK I WOULDN'T STILL BE SMILING.
BB

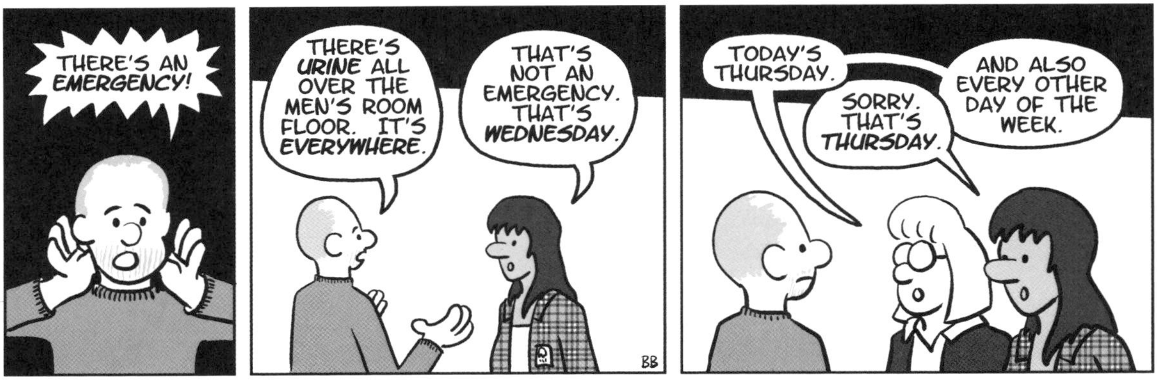
THERE'S AN ***EMERGENCY!***
THERE'S ***URINE*** ALL OVER THE MEN'S ROOM FLOOR. IT'S ***EVERYWHERE***.
THAT'S NOT AN EMERGENCY. THAT'S ***WEDNESDAY***.
BB
TODAY'S THURSDAY.
SORRY. THAT'S ***THURSDAY***.
AND ALSO EVERY OTHER DAY OF THE WEEK.

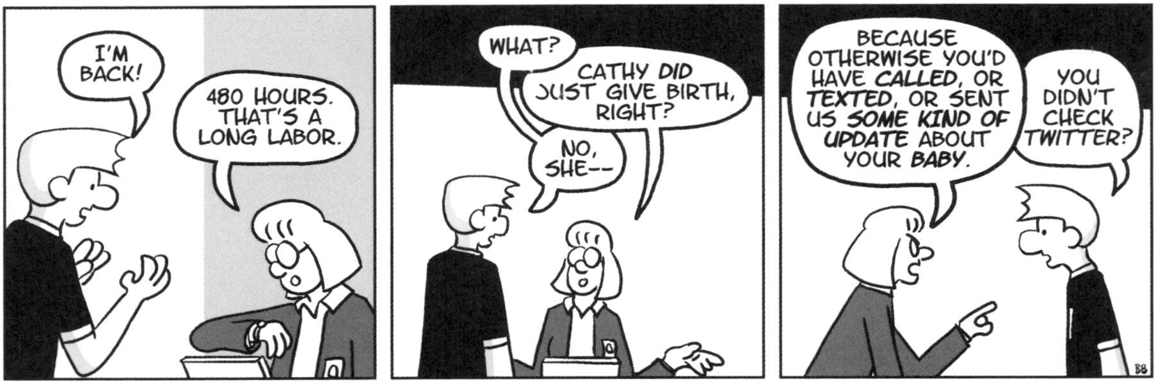
I'M BACK!
480 HOURS. THAT'S A LONG LABOR.
WHAT?
CATHY ***DID*** JUST GIVE BIRTH, RIGHT?
NO, SHE--
BECAUSE OTHERWISE YOU'D HAVE ***CALLED***, OR ***TEXTED***, OR SENT US ***SOME KIND OF UPDATE*** ABOUT YOUR ***BABY***.
YOU DIDN'T CHECK ***TWITTER***?
BB

Bibliovores

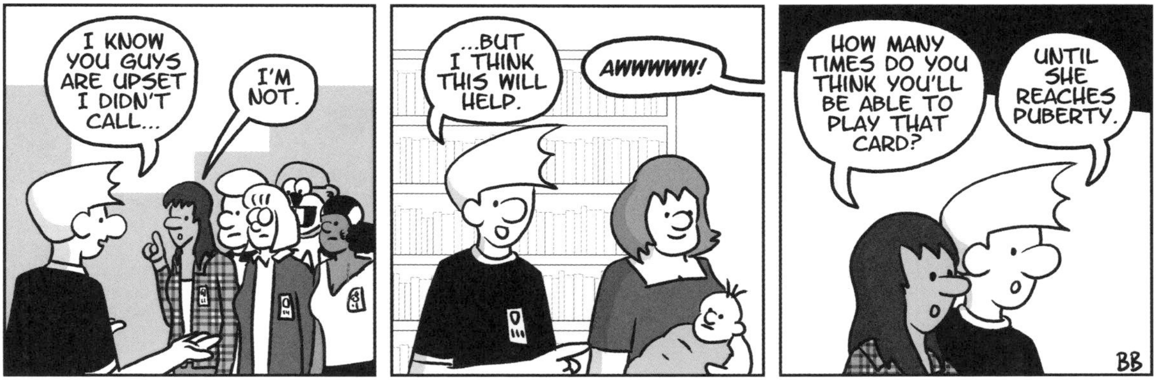
I KNOW YOU GUYS ARE UPSET I DIDN'T CALL...
I'M NOT.
...BUT I THINK THIS WILL HELP.
AWWWWW!
HOW MANY TIMES DO YOU THINK YOU'LL BE ABLE TO PLAY THAT CARD?
UNTIL SHE REACHES PUBERTY.
BB

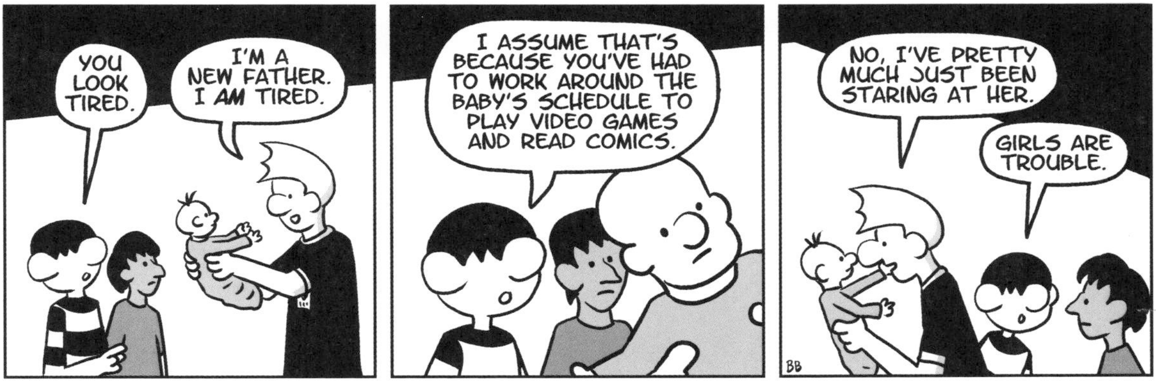
YOU LOOK TIRED.
I'M A NEW FATHER. I *AM* TIRED.
I ASSUME THAT'S BECAUSE YOU'VE HAD TO WORK AROUND THE BABY'S SCHEDULE TO PLAY VIDEO GAMES AND READ COMICS.
NO, I'VE PRETTY MUCH JUST BEEN STARING AT HER.
GIRLS ARE TROUBLE.
BB

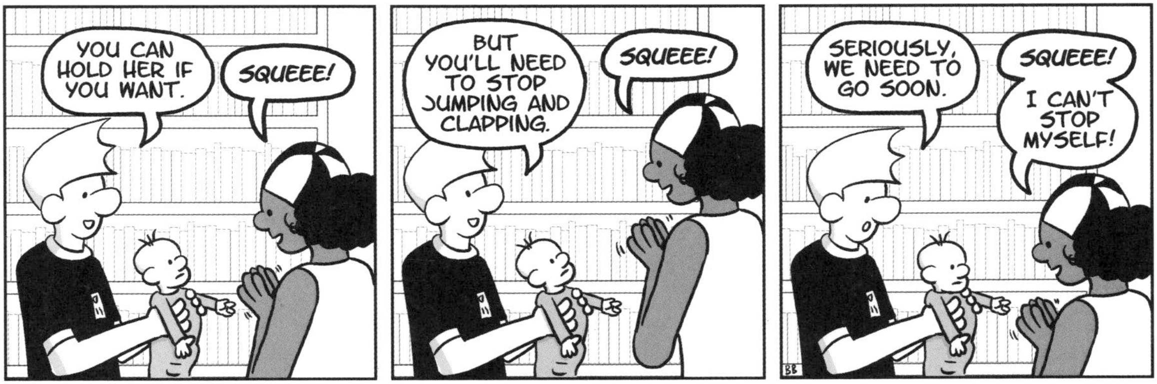
YOU CAN HOLD HER IF YOU WANT.
SQUEEE!
BUT YOU'LL NEED TO STOP JUMPING AND CLAPPING.
SQUEEE!
SERIOUSLY, WE NEED TO GO SOON.
SQUEEE!
I CAN'T STOP MYSELF!
BB

HOW WAS THE BIRTH?
I CAN SEE THE HEAD!
NOW IT'S GONE.
I CAN SEE IT AGAIN!
MAYBE IT'S HAVING TOO MUCH FUN BUNGEE JUMPING TO COME OUT YET.
ARE YOU SURE YOU CAN'T SEDATE MY HUSBAND?
BB

HOW DID YOU DECIDE ON HER NAME? IT'S SO UNUSUAL!
WE DEBATED FOR MONTHS BEFORE SHE WAS BORN.
LEIA.
NO.
UHURA.
NO.
BUFFY.
NO.
THEN, ON THE WAY TO THE HOSPITAL...
I'M NOT HAVING THIS BABY ON YOUR MOTORCYCLE!
SPEED 42 LIMIT
DON'T PANIC!
BB
I DON'T GET IT.
THAT'S OKAY, ISN'T IT, TRILLIAN?

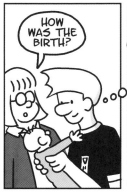

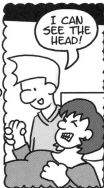

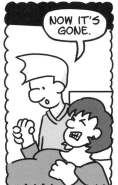

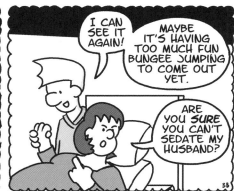

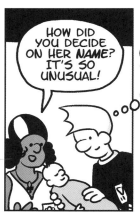

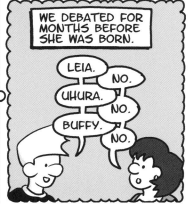

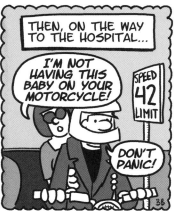

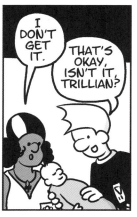

This depicts our actual process in trying to name Dewey and Cathy's baby. We went through all of our favorite works of science fiction before settling on *The Hitchhiker's Guide to the Galaxy* by Douglas Adams. Tamara, of course, is a stand-in for every reader who didn't catch the reference(s). Sometimes you just have to write from your heart.

Bibliovores

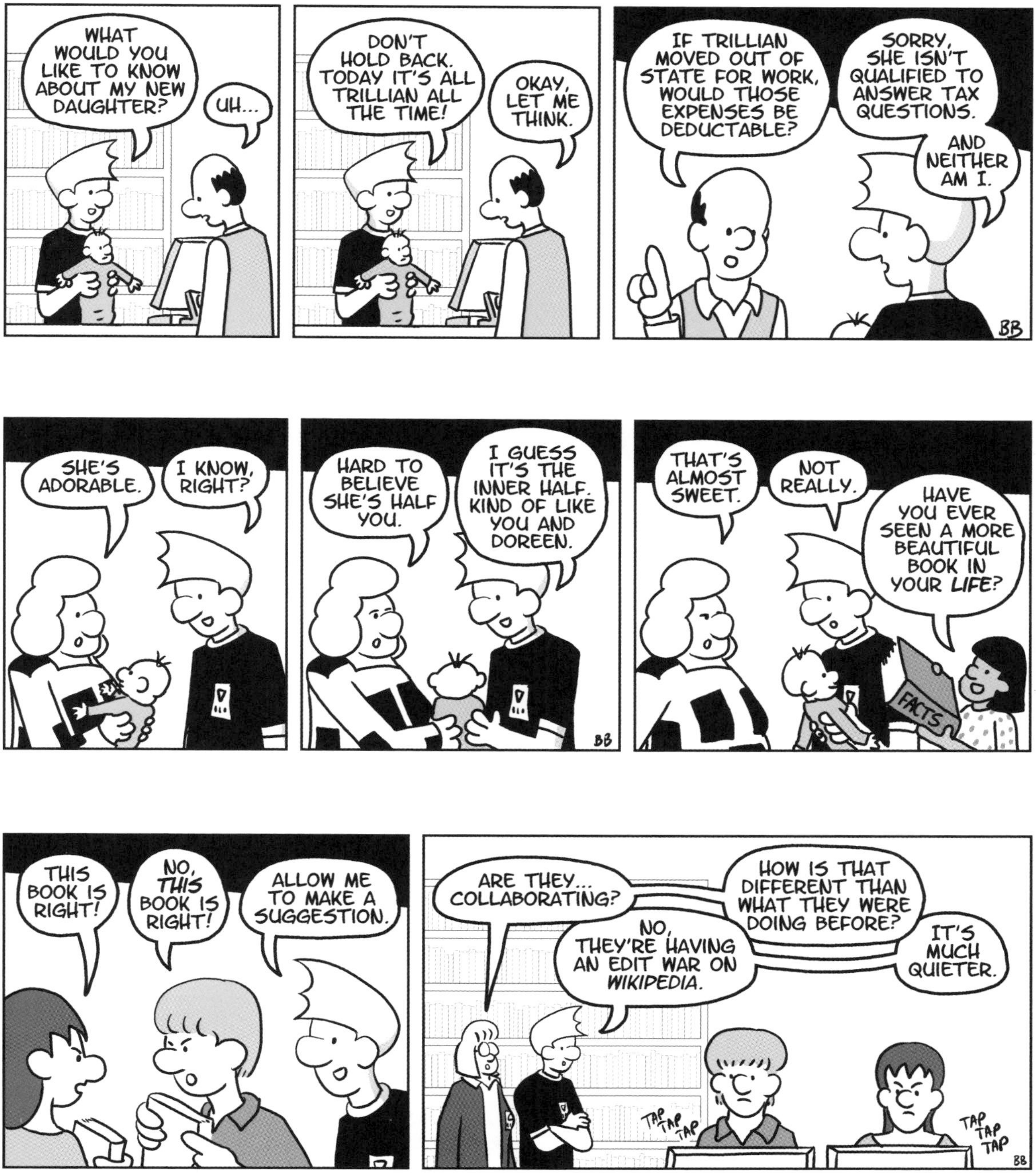
WHAT WOULD YOU LIKE TO KNOW ABOUT MY NEW DAUGHTER?
UH...
DON'T HOLD BACK. TODAY IT'S ALL TRILLIAN ALL THE TIME!
OKAY, LET ME THINK.
IF TRILLIAN MOVED OUT OF STATE FOR WORK, WOULD THOSE EXPENSES BE DEDUCTABLE?
SORRY, SHE ISN'T QUALIFIED TO ANSWER TAX QUESTIONS.
AND NEITHER AM I.
BB
SHE'S ADORABLE.
I KNOW, RIGHT?
HARD TO BELIEVE SHE'S HALF YOU.
I GUESS IT'S THE INNER HALF. KIND OF LIKE YOU AND DOREEN.
BB
THAT'S ALMOST SWEET.
NOT REALLY.
HAVE YOU EVER SEEN A MORE BEAUTIFUL BOOK IN YOUR *LIFE*?
FACTS
THIS BOOK IS RIGHT!
NO, *THIS* BOOK IS RIGHT!
ALLOW ME TO MAKE A SUGGESTION.
ARE THEY... COLLABORATING?
NO, THEY'RE HAVING AN EDIT WAR ON *WIKIPEDIA*.
HOW IS THAT DIFFERENT THAN WHAT THEY WERE DOING BEFORE?
IT'S MUCH QUIETER.
TAP TAP TAP
TAP TAP TAP
BB

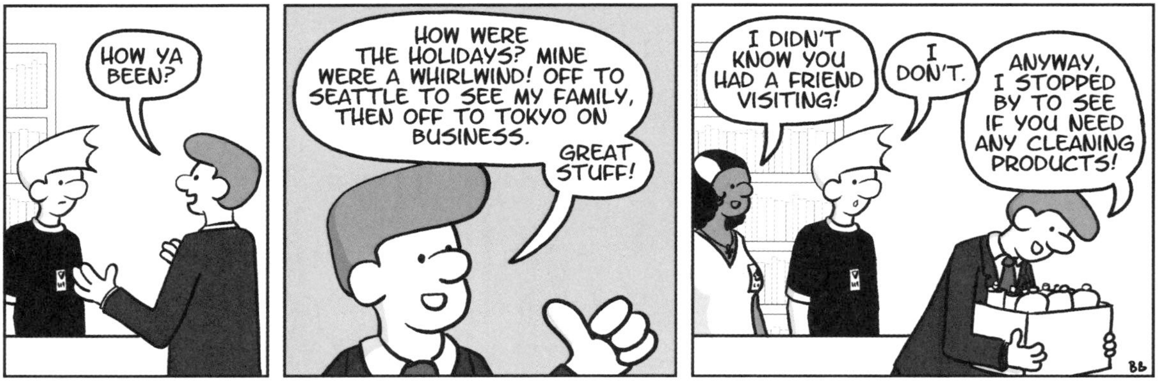
HOW YA BEEN?
HOW WERE THE HOLIDAYS? MINE WERE A WHIRLWIND! OFF TO SEATTLE TO SEE MY FAMILY, THEN OFF TO TOKYO ON BUSINESS.
GREAT STUFF!
I DIDN'T KNOW YOU HAD A FRIEND VISITING!
I DON'T.
ANYWAY, I STOPPED BY TO SEE IF YOU NEED ANY CLEANING PRODUCTS!
BB

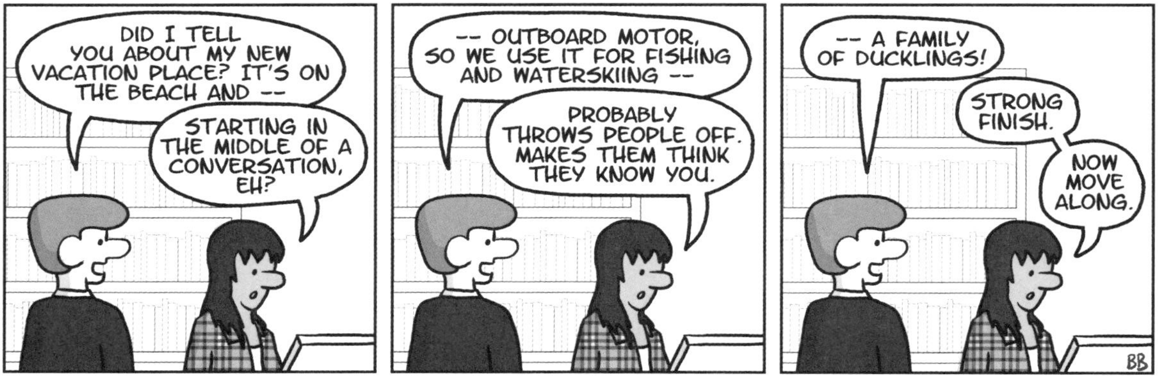
DID I TELL YOU ABOUT MY NEW VACATION PLACE? IT'S ON THE BEACH AND --
STARTING IN THE MIDDLE OF A CONVERSATION, EH?
-- OUTBOARD MOTOR, SO WE USE IT FOR FISHING AND WATERSKIING --
PROBABLY THROWS PEOPLE OFF. MAKES THEM THINK THEY KNOW YOU.
-- A FAMILY OF DUCKLINGS!
STRONG FINISH.
NOW MOVE ALONG.
BB

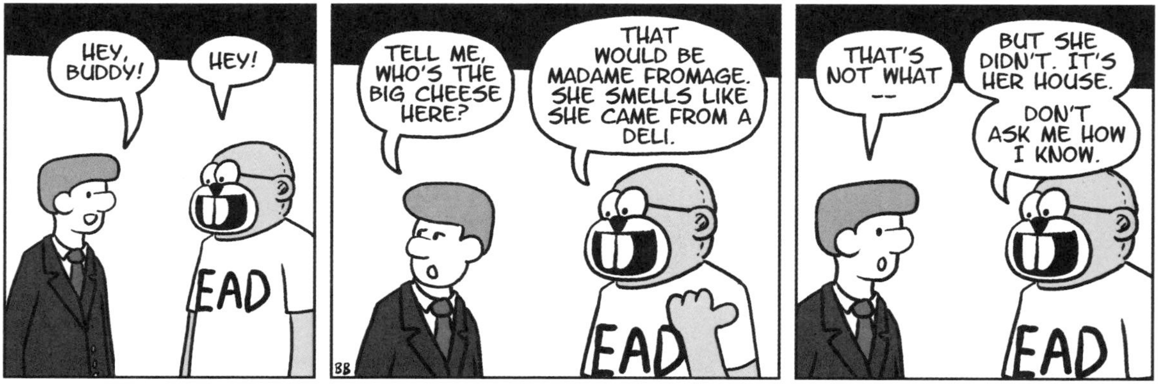
HEY, BUDDY!
HEY!
EAD
TELL ME, WHO'S THE BIG CHEESE HERE?
THAT WOULD BE MADAME FROMAGE. SHE SMELLS LIKE SHE CAME FROM A DELI.
BB
EAD
THAT'S NOT WHAT --
BUT SHE DIDN'T. IT'S HER HOUSE.
DON'T ASK ME HOW I KNOW.
EAD

Bibliovores

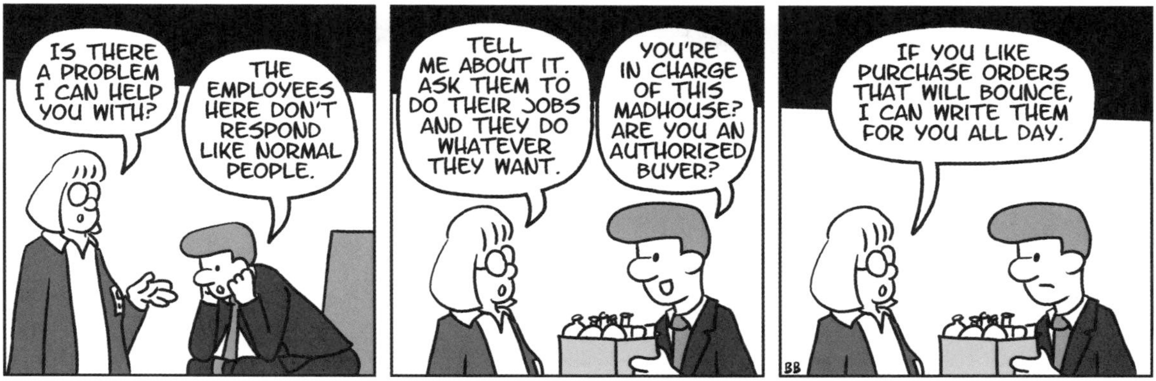
IS THERE A PROBLEM I CAN HELP YOU WITH?
THE EMPLOYEES HERE DON'T RESPOND LIKE NORMAL PEOPLE.
TELL ME ABOUT IT. ASK THEM TO DO THEIR JOBS AND THEY DO WHATEVER THEY WANT.
YOU'RE IN CHARGE OF THIS MADHOUSE? ARE YOU AN AUTHORIZED BUYER?
IF YOU LIKE PURCHASE ORDERS THAT WILL BOUNCE, I CAN WRITE THEM FOR YOU ALL DAY.
BB

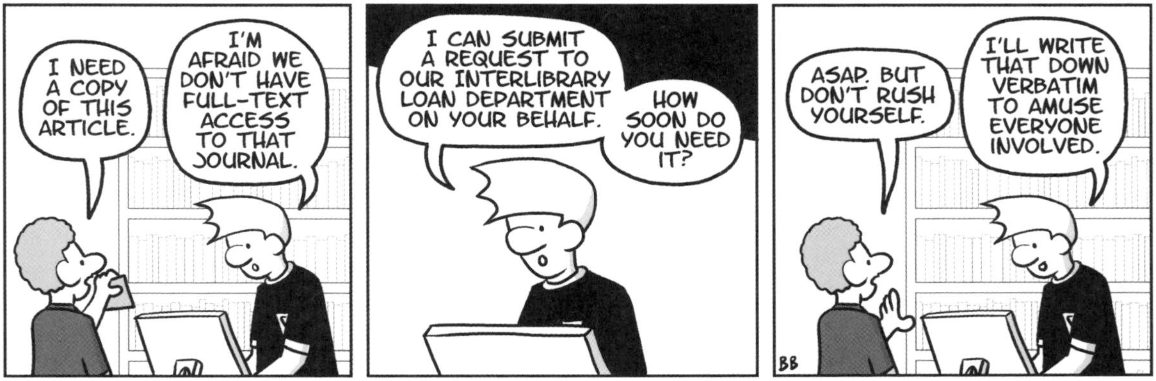
I NEED A COPY OF THIS ARTICLE.
I'M AFRAID WE DON'T HAVE FULL-TEXT ACCESS TO THAT JOURNAL.
I CAN SUBMIT A REQUEST TO OUR INTERLIBRARY LOAN DEPARTMENT ON YOUR BEHALF.
HOW SOON DO YOU NEED IT?
ASAP. BUT DON'T RUSH YOURSELF.
I'LL WRITE THAT DOWN VERBATIM TO AMUSE EVERYONE INVOLVED.
BB

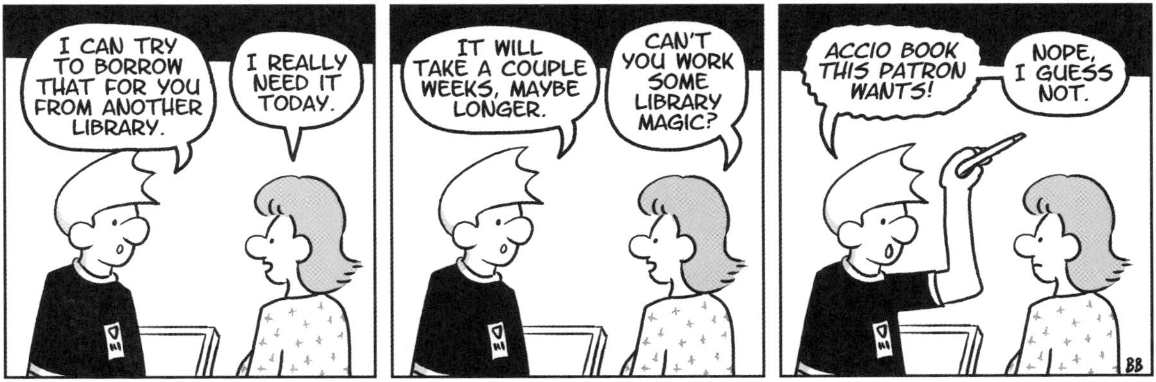
I CAN TRY TO BORROW THAT FOR YOU FROM ANOTHER LIBRARY.
I REALLY NEED IT TODAY.
IT WILL TAKE A COUPLE WEEKS, MAYBE LONGER.
CAN'T YOU WORK SOME LIBRARY MAGIC?
ACCIO BOOK THIS PATRON WANTS!
NOPE, I GUESS NOT.
BB

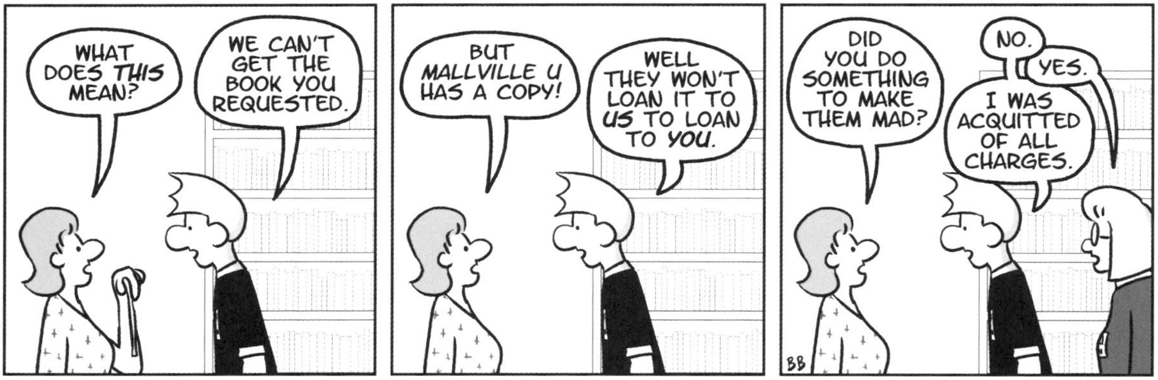
WHAT DOES THIS MEAN?
WE CAN'T GET THE BOOK YOU REQUESTED.
BUT MALLVILLE U HAS A COPY!
WELL THEY WON'T LOAN IT TO US TO LOAN TO YOU.
DID YOU DO SOMETHING TO MAKE THEM MAD?
NO.
YES.
I WAS ACQUITTED OF ALL CHARGES.
BB

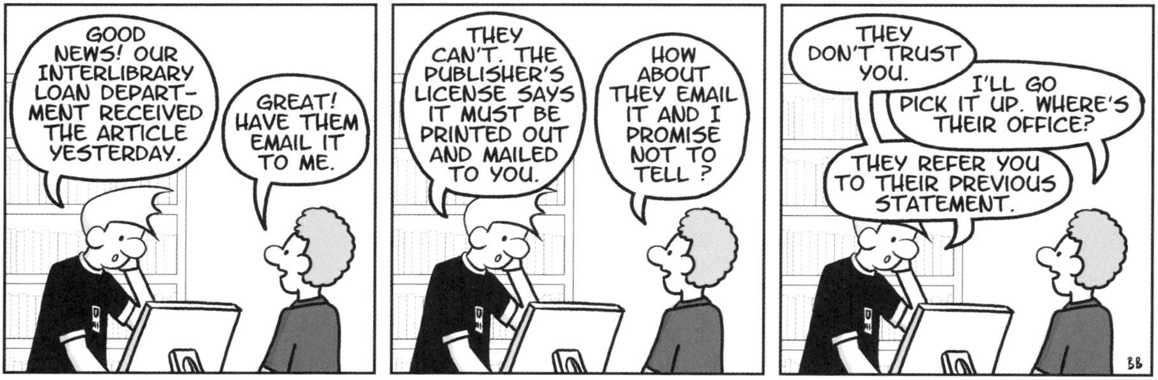
GOOD NEWS! OUR INTERLIBRARY LOAN DEPART-MENT RECEIVED THE ARTICLE YESTERDAY.
GREAT! HAVE THEM EMAIL IT TO ME.
THEY CAN'T. THE PUBLISHER'S LICENSE SAYS IT MUST BE PRINTED OUT AND MAILED TO YOU.
HOW ABOUT THEY EMAIL IT AND I PROMISE NOT TO TELL ?
THEY DON'T TRUST YOU.
I'LL GO PICK IT UP. WHERE'S THEIR OFFICE?
THEY REFER YOU TO THEIR PREVIOUS STATEMENT.
BB

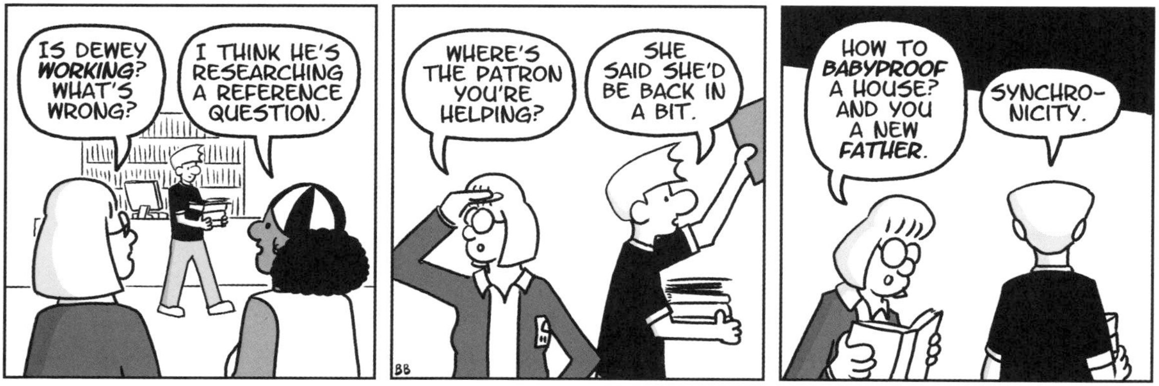
IS DEWEY WORKING? WHAT'S WRONG?
I THINK HE'S RESEARCHING A REFERENCE QUESTION.
WHERE'S THE PATRON YOU'RE HELPING?
SHE SAID SHE'D BE BACK IN A BIT.
HOW TO BABYPROOF A HOUSE? AND YOU A NEW FATHER.
SYNCHRO-NICITY.
BB

Bibliovores

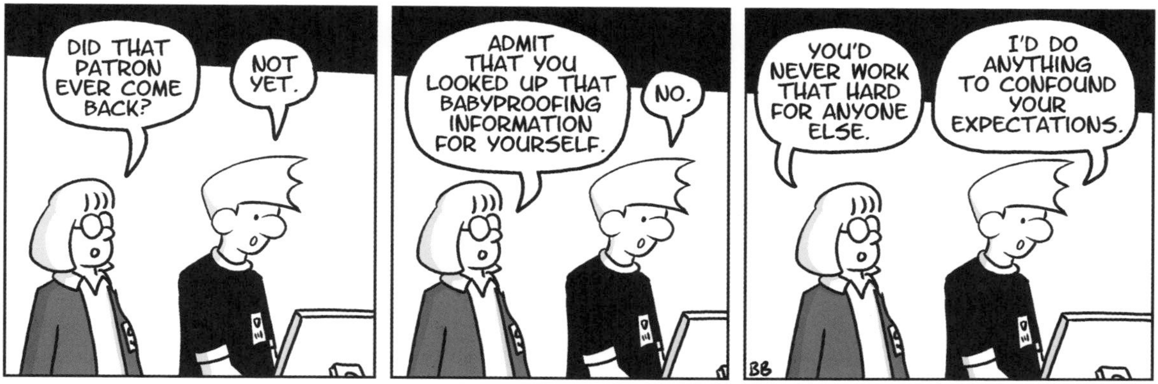
DID THAT PATRON EVER COME BACK?
NOT YET.
ADMIT THAT YOU LOOKED UP THAT BABYPROOFING INFORMATION FOR YOURSELF.
NO.
YOU'D NEVER WORK THAT HARD FOR ANYONE ELSE.
I'D DO ANYTHING TO CONFOUND YOUR EXPECTATIONS.
BB

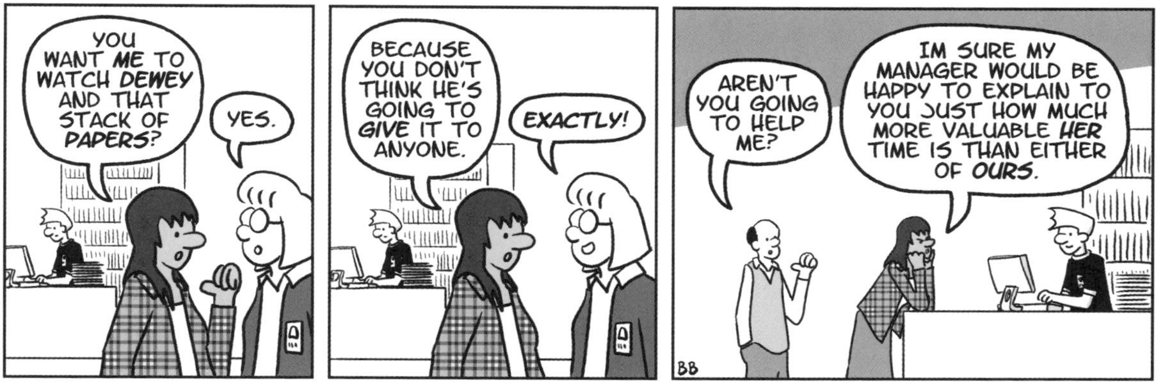
YOU WANT ME TO WATCH DEWEY AND THAT STACK OF PAPERS?
YES.
BECAUSE YOU DON'T THINK HE'S GOING TO GIVE IT TO ANYONE.
EXACTLY!
AREN'T YOU GOING TO HELP ME?
IM SURE MY MANAGER WOULD BE HAPPY TO EXPLAIN TO YOU JUST HOW MUCH MORE VALUABLE HER TIME IS THAN EITHER OF OURS.
BB

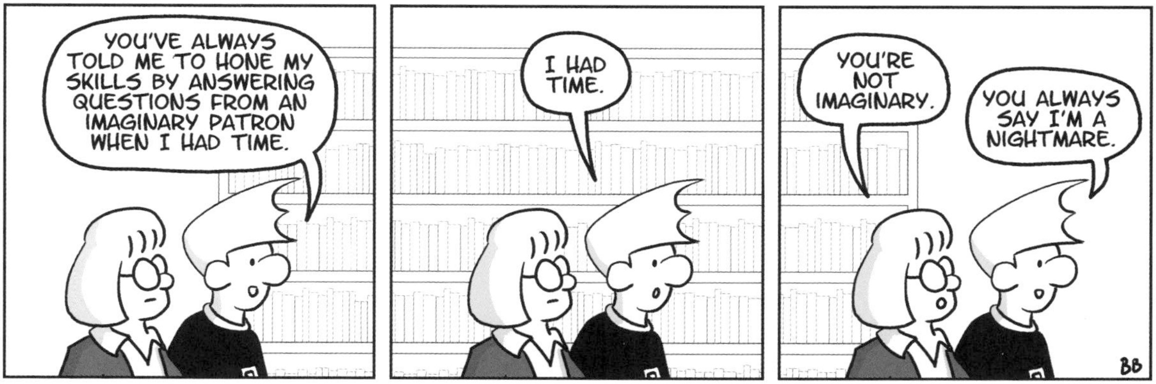
YOU'VE ALWAYS TOLD ME TO HONE MY SKILLS BY ANSWERING QUESTIONS FROM AN IMAGINARY PATRON WHEN I HAD TIME.
I HAD TIME.
YOU'RE NOT IMAGINARY.
YOU ALWAYS SAY I'M A NIGHTMARE.
BB

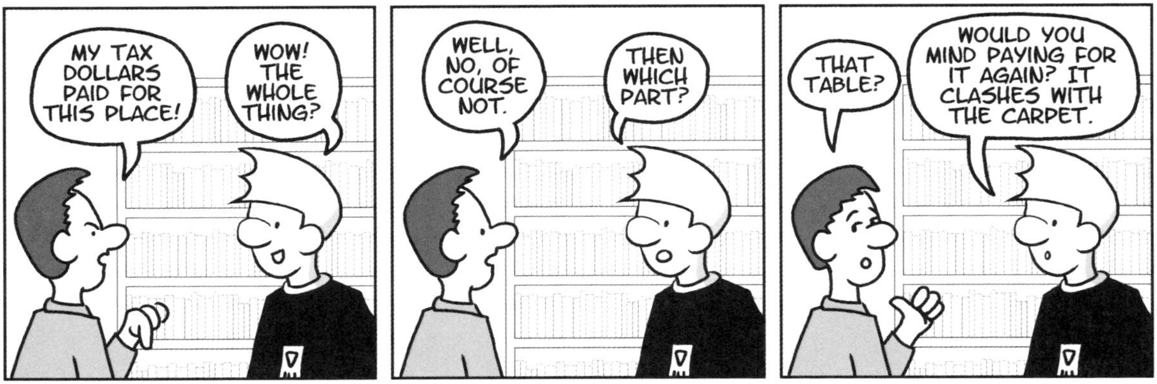
MY TAX DOLLARS PAID FOR THIS PLACE!
WOW! THE WHOLE THING?
WELL, NO, OF COURSE NOT.
THEN WHICH PART?
THAT TABLE?
WOULD YOU MIND PAYING FOR IT AGAIN? IT CLASHES WITH THE CARPET.

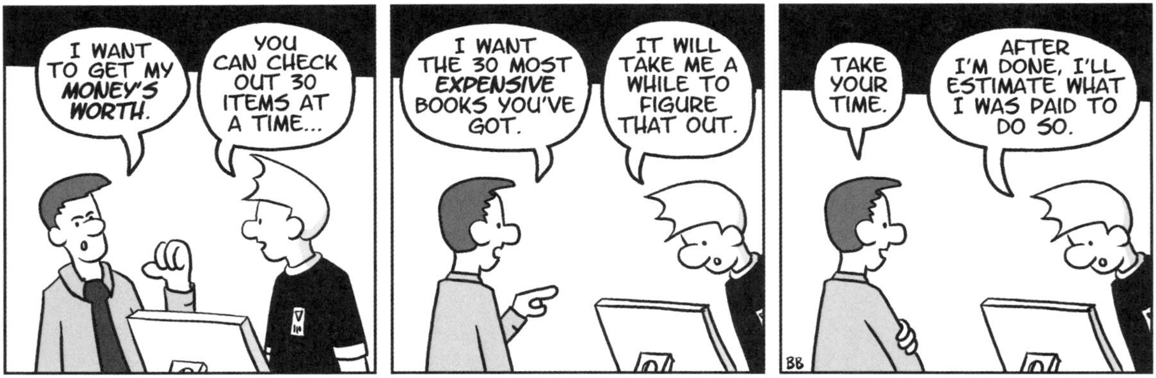
I WANT TO GET MY *MONEY'S WORTH*.
YOU CAN CHECK OUT 30 ITEMS AT A TIME...
I WANT THE 30 MOST *EXPENSIVE* BOOKS YOU'VE GOT.
IT WILL TAKE ME A WHILE TO FIGURE THAT OUT.
TAKE YOUR TIME.
AFTER I'M DONE, I'LL ESTIMATE WHAT I WAS PAID TO DO SO.
BB

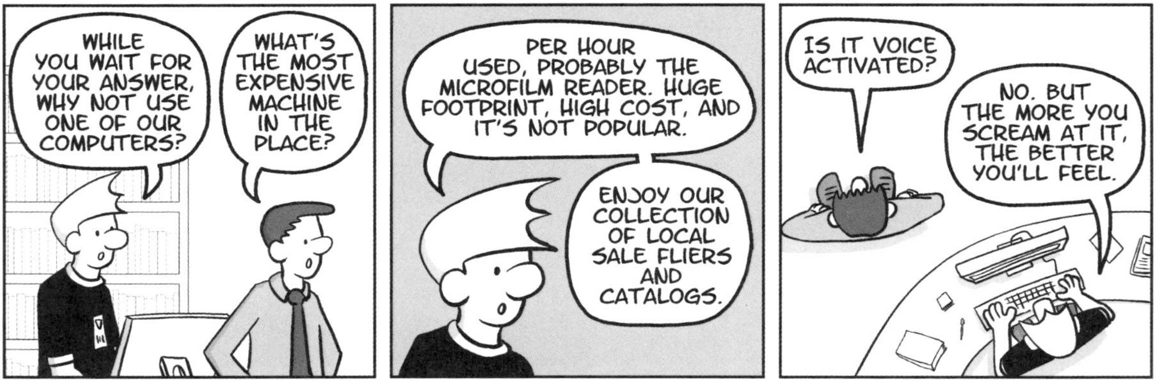
WHILE YOU WAIT FOR YOUR ANSWER, WHY NOT USE ONE OF OUR COMPUTERS?
WHAT'S THE MOST EXPENSIVE MACHINE IN THE PLACE?
PER HOUR USED, PROBABLY THE MICROFILM READER. HUGE FOOTPRINT, HIGH COST, AND IT'S NOT POPULAR.
ENJOY OUR COLLECTION OF LOCAL SALE FLIERS AND CATALOGS.
IS IT VOICE ACTIVATED?
NO. BUT THE MORE YOU SCREAM AT IT, THE BETTER YOU'LL FEEL.

Bibliovores

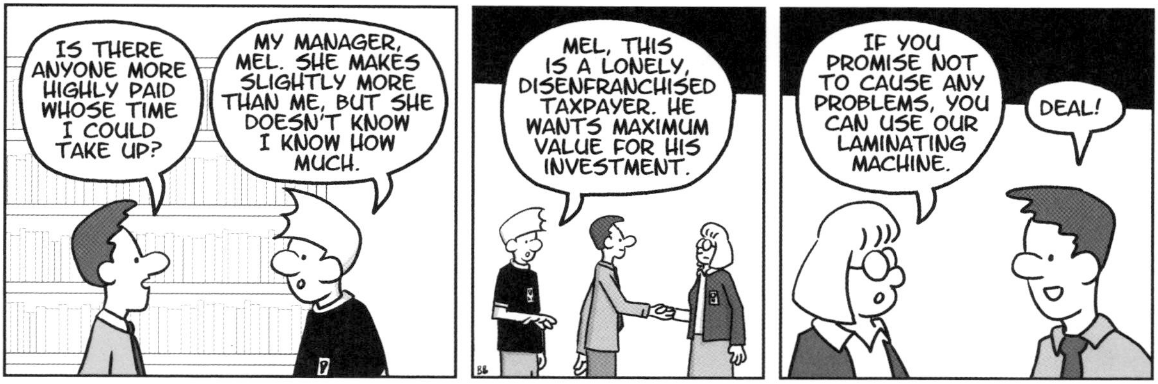

IS THERE ANYONE MORE HIGHLY PAID WHOSE TIME I COULD TAKE UP?
MY MANAGER, MEL. SHE MAKES SLIGHTLY MORE THAN ME, BUT SHE DOESN'T KNOW I KNOW HOW MUCH.
MEL, THIS IS A LONELY, DISENFRANCHISED TAXPAYER. HE WANTS MAXIMUM VALUE FOR HIS INVESTMENT.
BB
IF YOU PROMISE NOT TO CAUSE ANY PROBLEMS, YOU CAN USE OUR LAMINATING MACHINE.
DEAL!

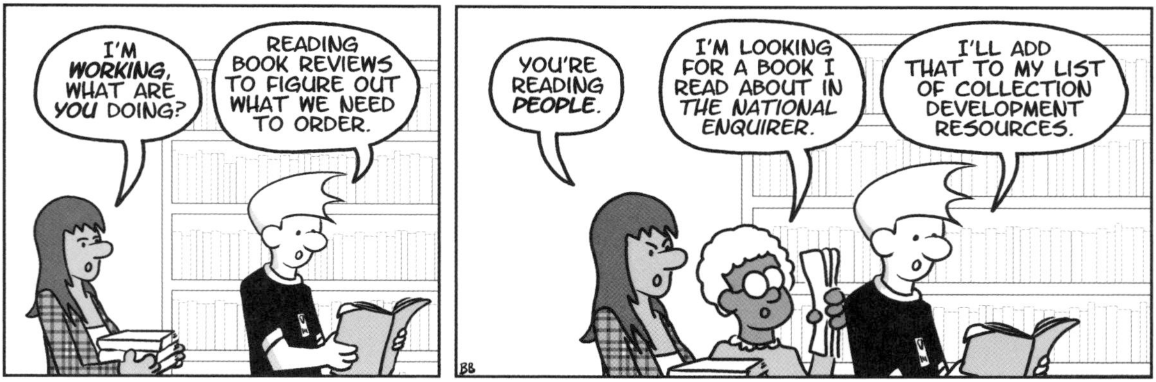

I'M WORKING, WHAT ARE YOU DOING?
READING BOOK REVIEWS TO FIGURE OUT WHAT WE NEED TO ORDER.
YOU'RE READING PEOPLE.
I'M LOOKING FOR A BOOK I READ ABOUT IN THE NATIONAL ENQUIRER.
I'LL ADD THAT TO MY LIST OF COLLECTION DEVELOPMENT RESOURCES.
BB

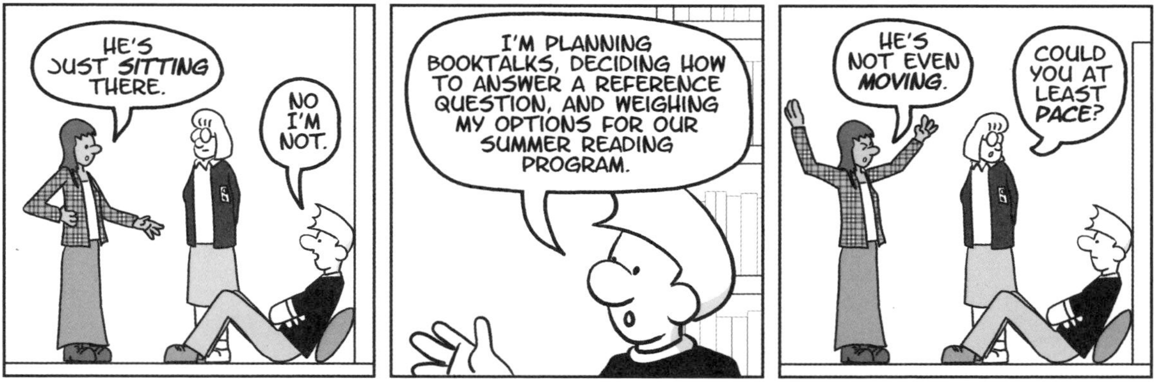

HE'S JUST SITTING THERE.
NO I'M NOT.
I'M PLANNING BOOKTALKS, DECIDING HOW TO ANSWER A REFERENCE QUESTION, AND WEIGHING MY OPTIONS FOR OUR SUMMER READING PROGRAM.
HE'S NOT EVEN MOVING.
COULD YOU AT LEAST PACE?

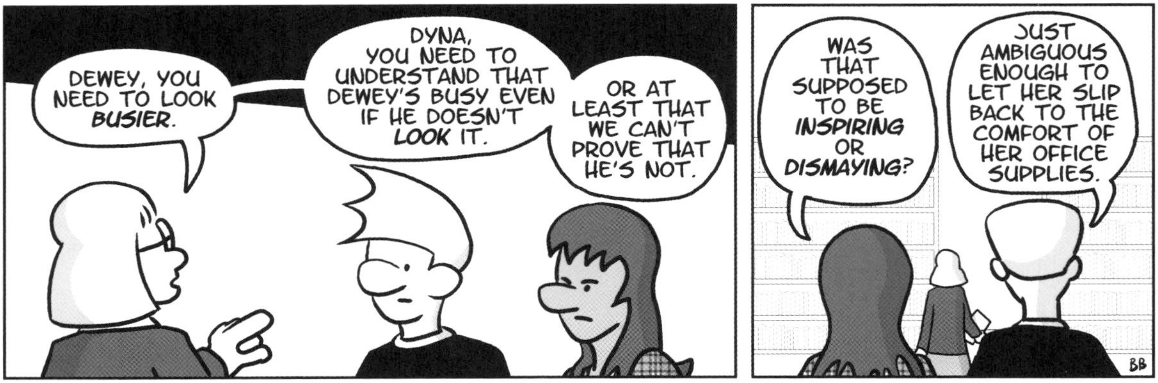
DEWEY, YOU NEED TO LOOK BUSIER.
DYNA, YOU NEED TO UNDERSTAND THAT DEWEY'S BUSY EVEN IF HE DOESN'T LOOK IT.
OR AT LEAST THAT WE CAN'T PROVE THAT HE'S NOT.
WAS THAT SUPPOSED TO BE INSPIRING OR DISMAYING?
JUST AMBIGUOUS ENOUGH TO LET HER SLIP BACK TO THE COMFORT OF HER OFFICE SUPPLIES.
BB

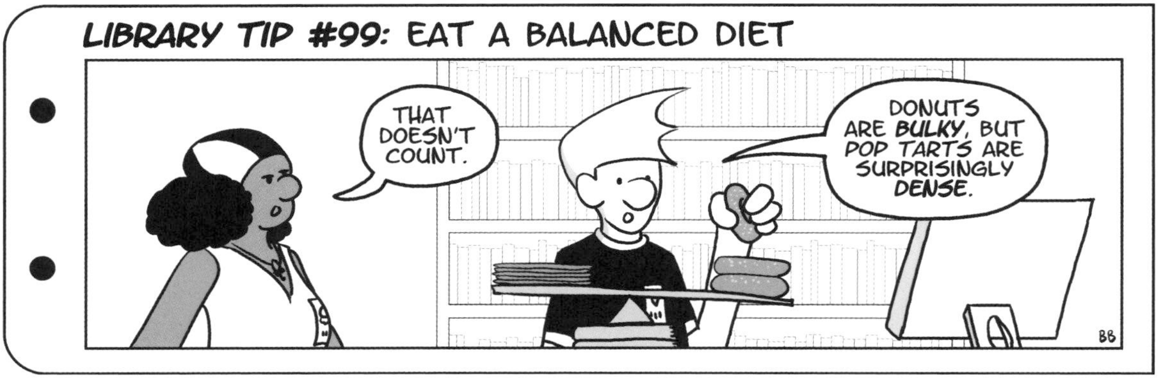
LIBRARY TIP #99: EAT A BALANCED DIET
THAT DOESN'T COUNT.
DONUTS ARE BULKY, BUT POP TARTS ARE SURPRISINGLY DENSE.
BB

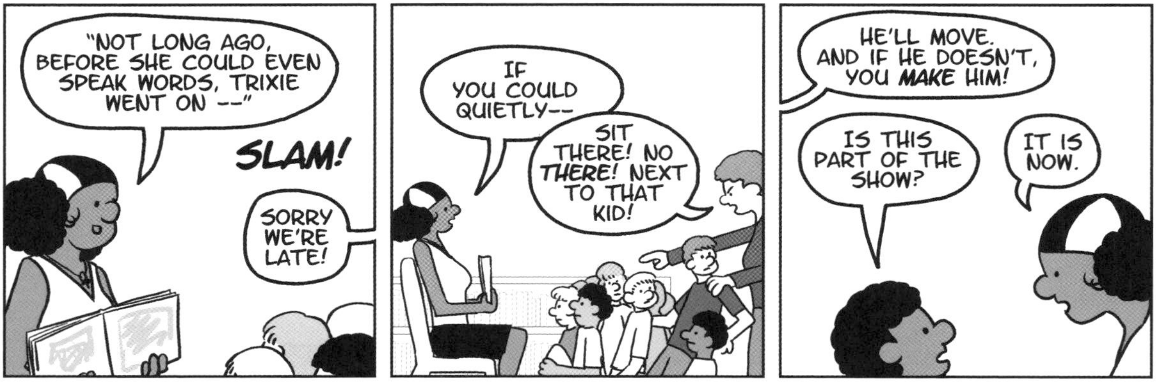
"NOT LONG AGO, BEFORE SHE COULD EVEN SPEAK WORDS, TRIXIE WENT ON --"
SLAM!
SORRY WE'RE LATE!
IF YOU COULD QUIETLY--
SIT THERE! NO THERE! NEXT TO THAT KID!
HE'LL MOVE. AND IF HE DOESN'T, YOU MAKE HIM!
IS THIS PART OF THE SHOW?
IT IS NOW.

Bibliovores

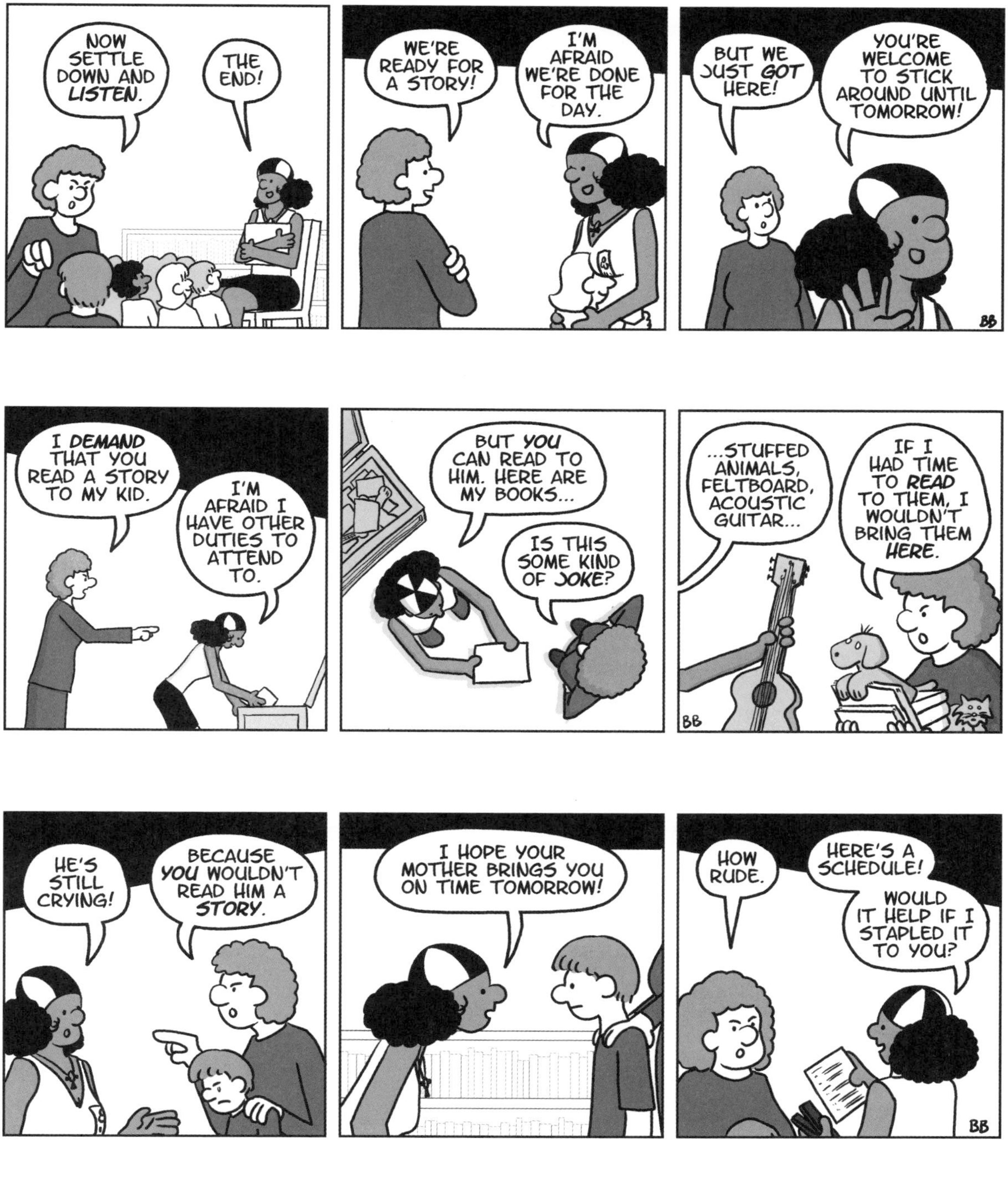
NOW SETTLE DOWN AND LISTEN.
THE END!
WE'RE READY FOR A STORY!
I'M AFRAID WE'RE DONE FOR THE DAY.
BUT WE JUST GOT HERE!
YOU'RE WELCOME TO STICK AROUND UNTIL TOMORROW!
BB
I DEMAND THAT YOU READ A STORY TO MY KID.
I'M AFRAID I HAVE OTHER DUTIES TO ATTEND TO.
BUT YOU CAN READ TO HIM. HERE ARE MY BOOKS...
IS THIS SOME KIND OF JOKE?
...STUFFED ANIMALS, FELTBOARD, ACOUSTIC GUITAR...
IF I HAD TIME TO READ TO THEM, I WOULDN'T BRING THEM HERE.
BB
HE'S STILL CRYING!
BECAUSE YOU WOULDN'T READ HIM A STORY.
I HOPE YOUR MOTHER BRINGS YOU ON TIME TOMORROW!
HOW RUDE.
HERE'S A SCHEDULE!
WOULD IT HELP IF I STAPLED IT TO YOU?
BB

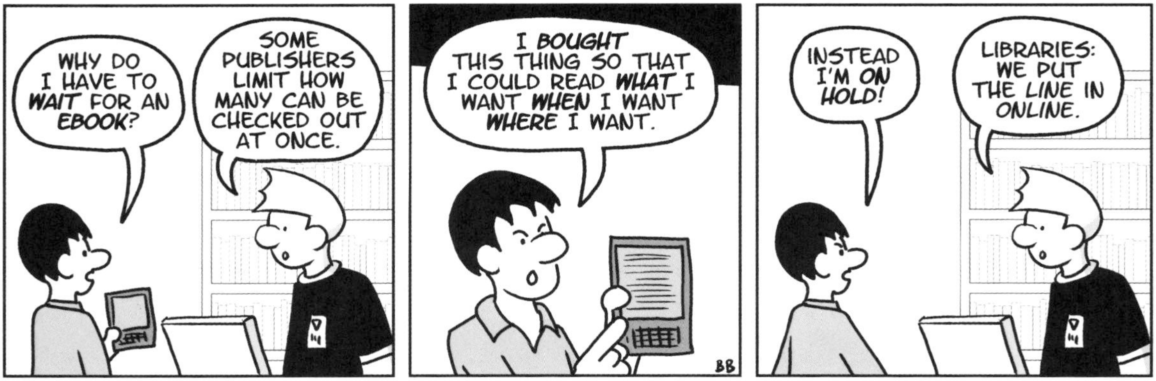
WHY DO I HAVE TO **WAIT** FOR AN **EBOOK**?
SOME PUBLISHERS LIMIT HOW MANY CAN BE CHECKED OUT AT ONCE.
I **BOUGHT** THIS THING SO THAT I COULD READ **WHAT** I WANT **WHEN** I WANT **WHERE** I WANT.
INSTEAD I'M **ON HOLD**!
LIBRARIES: WE PUT THE *LINE* IN ONLINE.
BB

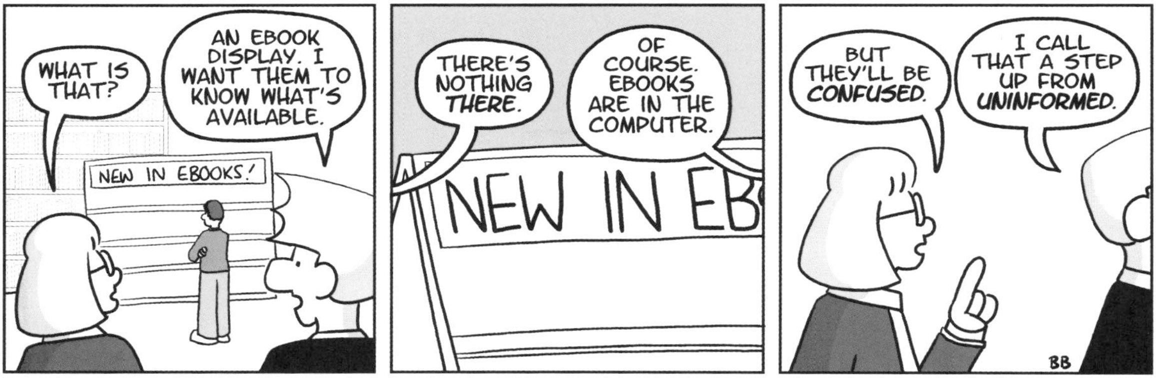
WHAT IS THAT?
AN EBOOK DISPLAY. I WANT THEM TO KNOW WHAT'S AVAILABLE.
NEW IN EBOOKS!
THERE'S NOTHING **THERE**.
OF COURSE. EBOOKS ARE IN THE COMPUTER.
NEW IN EB
BUT THEY'LL BE **CONFUSED**.
I CALL THAT A STEP UP FROM **UNINFORMED**.
BB

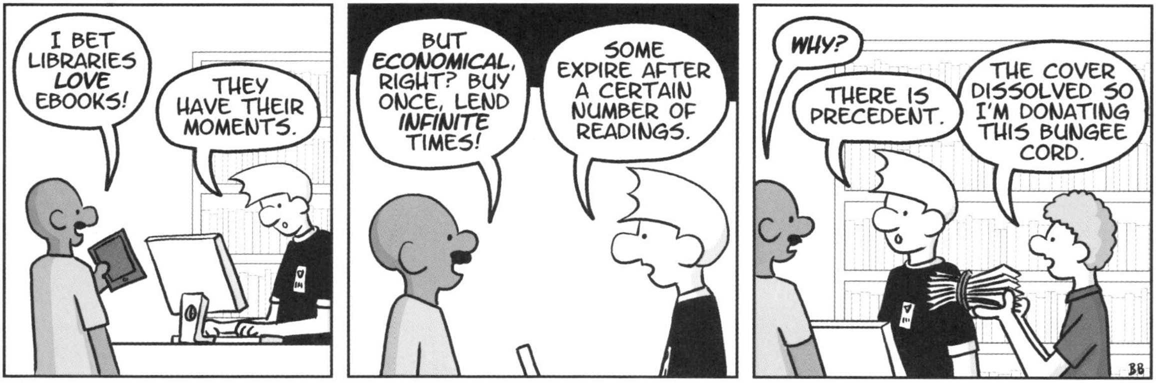
I BET LIBRARIES **LOVE** EBOOKS!
THEY HAVE THEIR MOMENTS.
BUT **ECONOMICAL**, RIGHT? BUY ONCE, LEND **INFINITE** TIMES!
SOME EXPIRE AFTER A CERTAIN NUMBER OF READINGS.
WHY?
THERE IS PRECEDENT.
THE COVER DISSOLVED SO I'M DONATING THIS BUNGEE CORD.
BB

Bibliovores

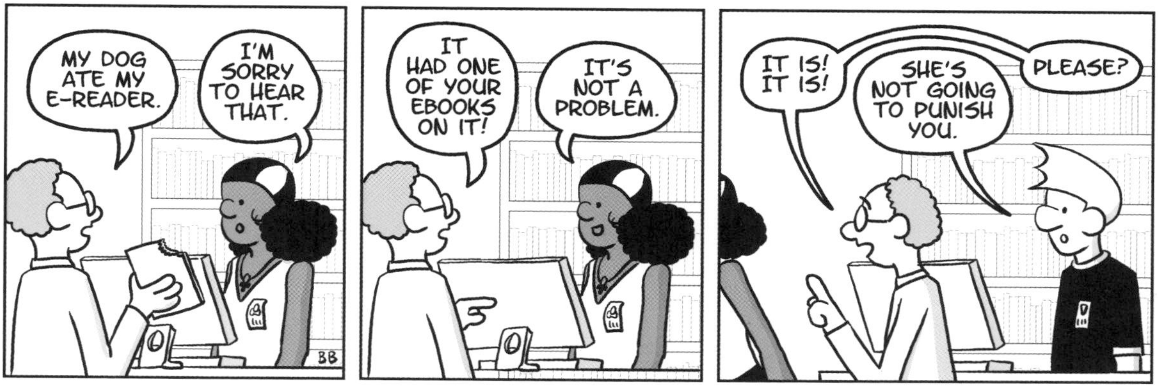

MY DOG ATE MY E-READER.
I'M SORRY TO HEAR THAT.
IT HAD ONE OF YOUR EBOOKS ON IT!
IT'S NOT A PROBLEM.
IT IS! IT IS!
SHE'S NOT GOING TO PUNISH YOU.
PLEASE?
BB

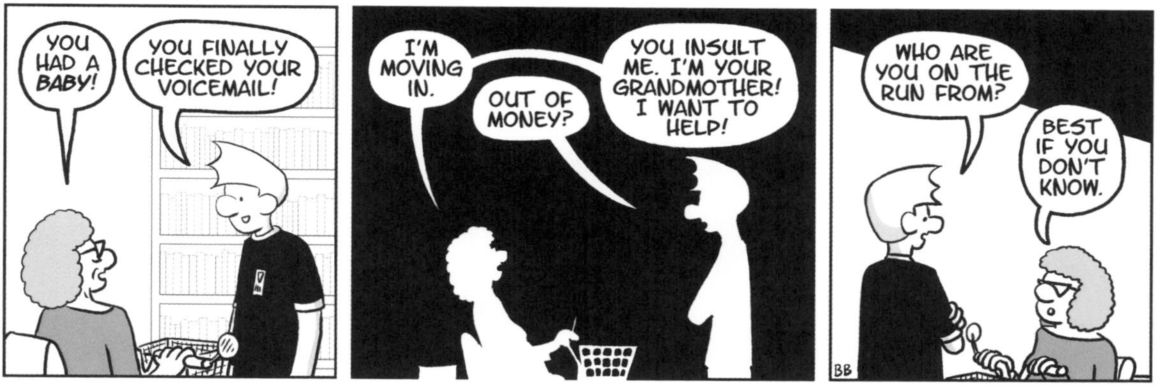

YOU HAD A *BABY*!
YOU FINALLY CHECKED YOUR VOICEMAIL!
I'M MOVING IN.
OUT OF MONEY?
YOU INSULT ME. I'M YOUR GRANDMOTHER! I WANT TO HELP!
WHO ARE YOU ON THE RUN FROM?
BEST IF YOU DON'T KNOW.
BB

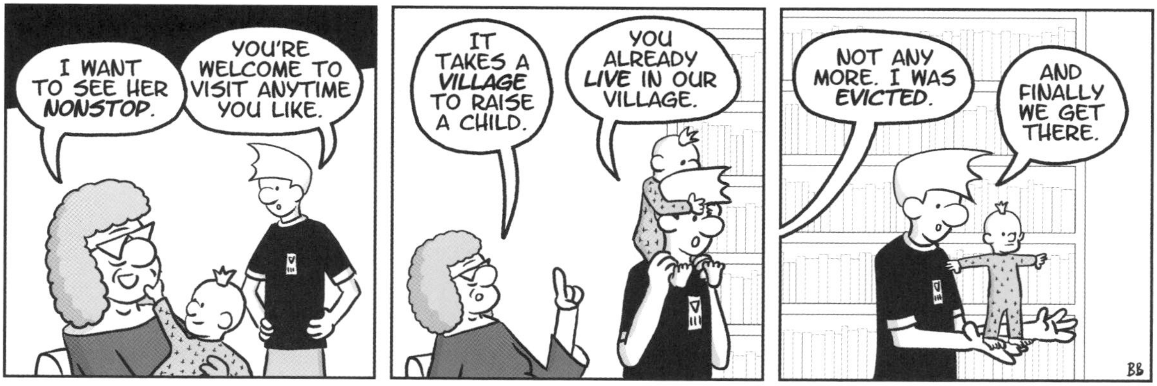

I WANT TO SEE HER *NONSTOP*.
YOU'RE WELCOME TO VISIT ANYTIME YOU LIKE.
IT TAKES A *VILLAGE* TO RAISE A CHILD.
YOU ALREADY *LIVE* IN OUR VILLAGE.
NOT ANY MORE. I WAS *EVICTED*.
AND FINALLY WE GET THERE.
BB

UNSHELVED

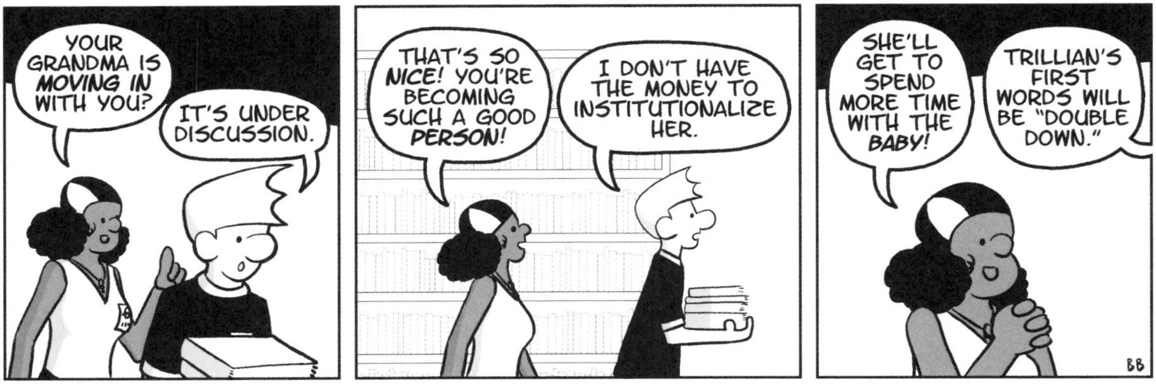
YOUR GRANDMA IS MOVING IN WITH YOU?
IT'S UNDER DISCUSSION.
THAT'S SO NICE! YOU'RE BECOMING SUCH A GOOD PERSON!
I DON'T HAVE THE MONEY TO INSTITUTIONALIZE HER.
SHE'LL GET TO SPEND MORE TIME WITH THE BABY!
TRILLIAN'S FIRST WORDS WILL BE "DOUBLE DOWN."
BB

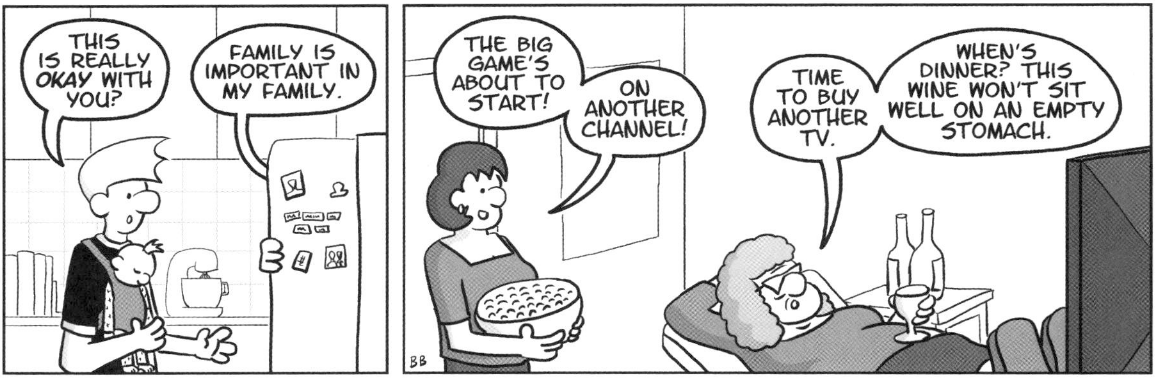
THIS IS REALLY OKAY WITH YOU?
FAMILY IS IMPORTANT IN MY FAMILY.
BB
THE BIG GAME'S ABOUT TO START!
ON ANOTHER CHANNEL!
TIME TO BUY ANOTHER TV.
WHEN'S DINNER? THIS WINE WON'T SIT WELL ON AN EMPTY STOMACH.

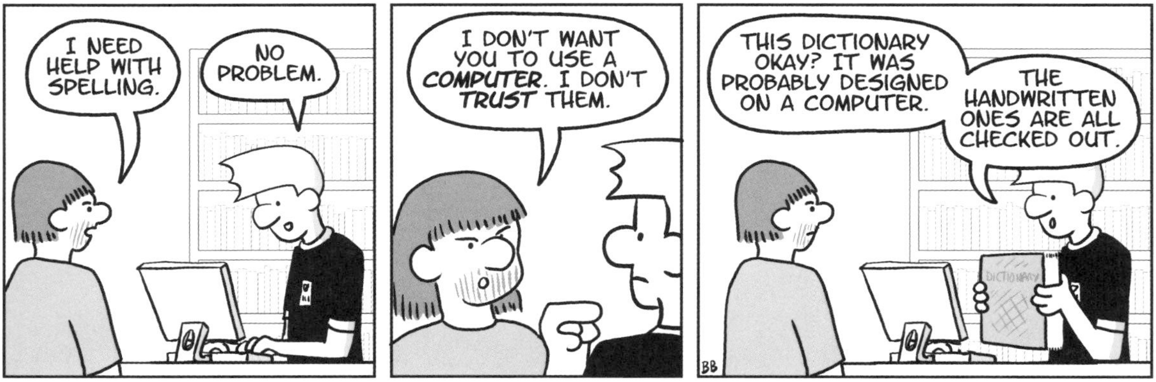
I NEED HELP WITH SPELLING.
NO PROBLEM.
I DON'T WANT YOU TO USE A COMPUTER. I DON'T TRUST THEM.
THIS DICTIONARY OKAY? IT WAS PROBABLY DESIGNED ON A COMPUTER.
THE HANDWRITTEN ONES ARE ALL CHECKED OUT.
DICTIONARY
BB

Bibliovores

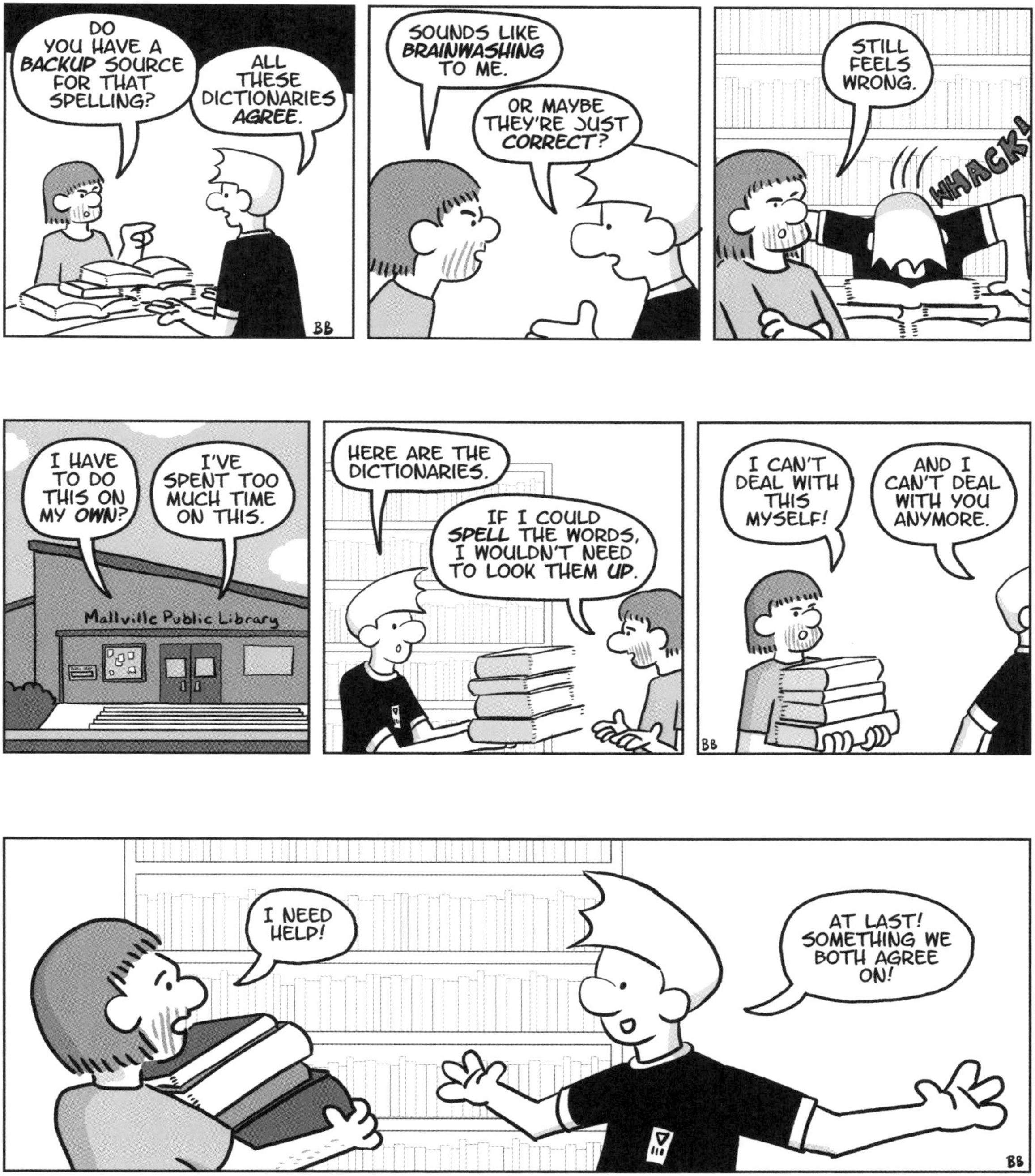

DO YOU HAVE A BACKUP SOURCE FOR THAT SPELLING?
ALL THESE DICTIONARIES AGREE.
BB
SOUNDS LIKE BRAINWASHING TO ME.
OR MAYBE THEY'RE JUST CORRECT?
STILL FEELS WRONG.
WHACK!
I HAVE TO DO THIS ON MY OWN?
I'VE SPENT TOO MUCH TIME ON THIS.
Mallville Public Library
HERE ARE THE DICTIONARIES.
IF I COULD SPELL THE WORDS, I WOULDN'T NEED TO LOOK THEM UP.
BB
I CAN'T DEAL WITH THIS MYSELF!
AND I CAN'T DEAL WITH YOU ANYMORE.
I NEED HELP!
AT LAST! SOMETHING WE BOTH AGREE ON!
BB

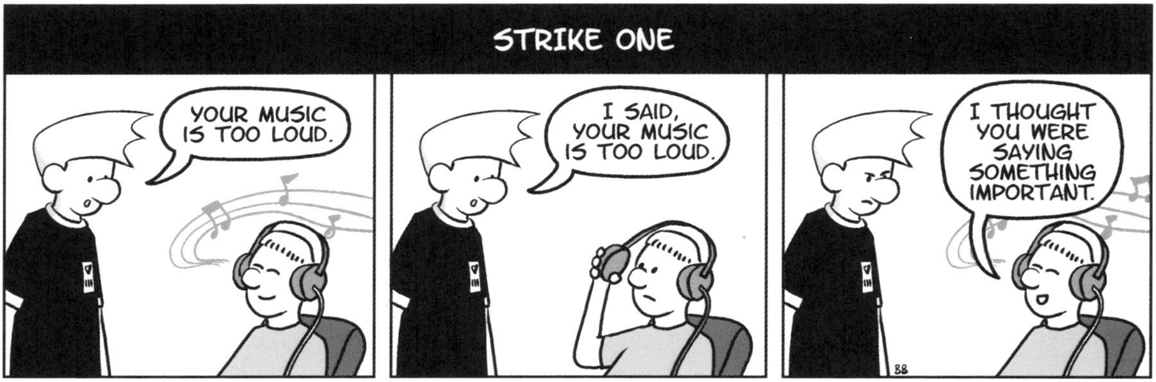
STRIKE ONE
YOUR MUSIC IS TOO LOUD.
I SAID, YOUR MUSIC IS TOO LOUD.
I THOUGHT YOU WERE SAYING SOMETHING IMPORTANT.
BB

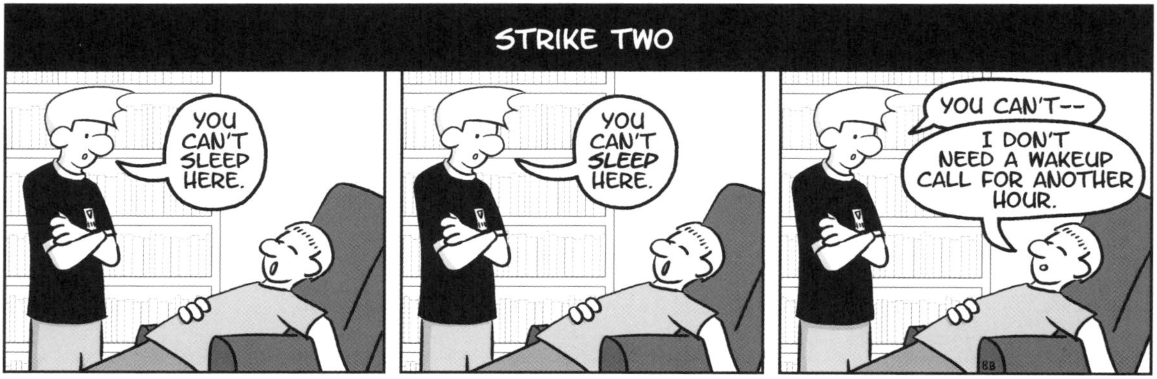
STRIKE TWO
YOU CAN'T SLEEP HERE.
YOU CAN'T **SLEEP** HERE.
YOU CAN'T--
I DON'T NEED A WAKEUP CALL FOR ANOTHER HOUR.
BB

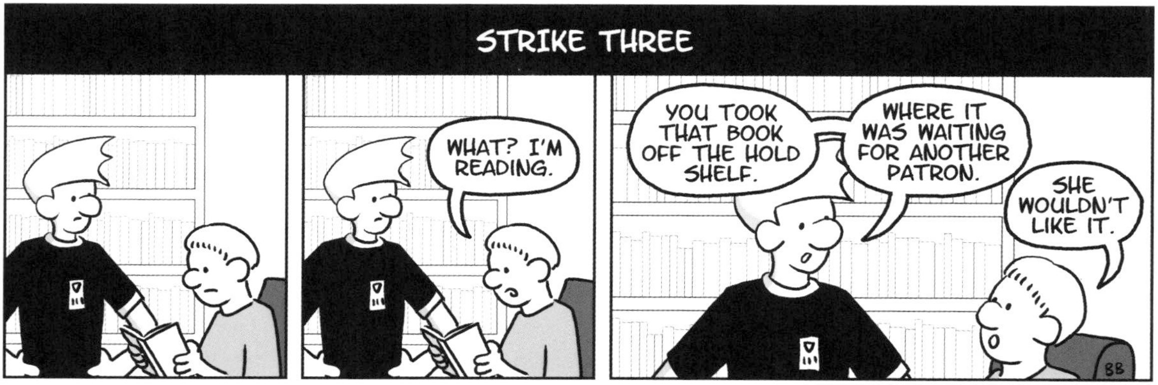
STRIKE THREE
WHAT? I'M READING.
YOU TOOK THAT BOOK OFF THE HOLD SHELF.
WHERE IT WAS WAITING FOR ANOTHER PATRON.
SHE WOULDN'T LIKE IT.
BB

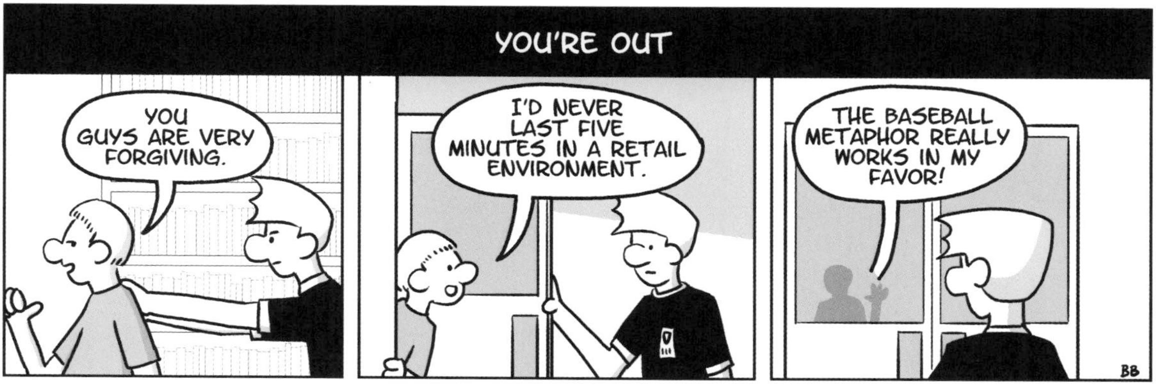
YOU'RE OUT
YOU GUYS ARE VERY FORGIVING.
I'D NEVER LAST FIVE MINUTES IN A RETAIL ENVIRONMENT.
THE BASEBALL METAPHOR REALLY WORKS IN MY FAVOR!
BB

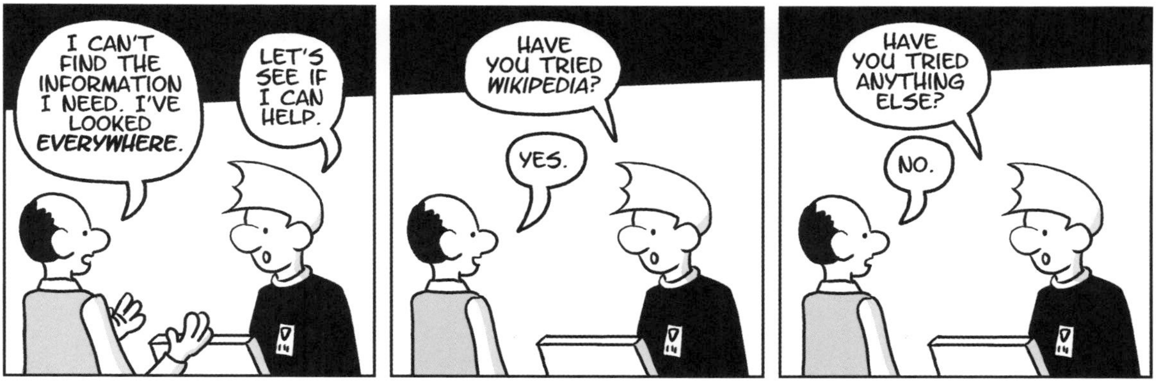
I CAN'T FIND THE INFORMATION I NEED. I'VE LOOKED **EVERYWHERE**.
LET'S SEE IF I CAN HELP.
HAVE YOU TRIED *WIKIPEDIA*?
YES.
HAVE YOU TRIED ANYTHING ELSE?
NO.

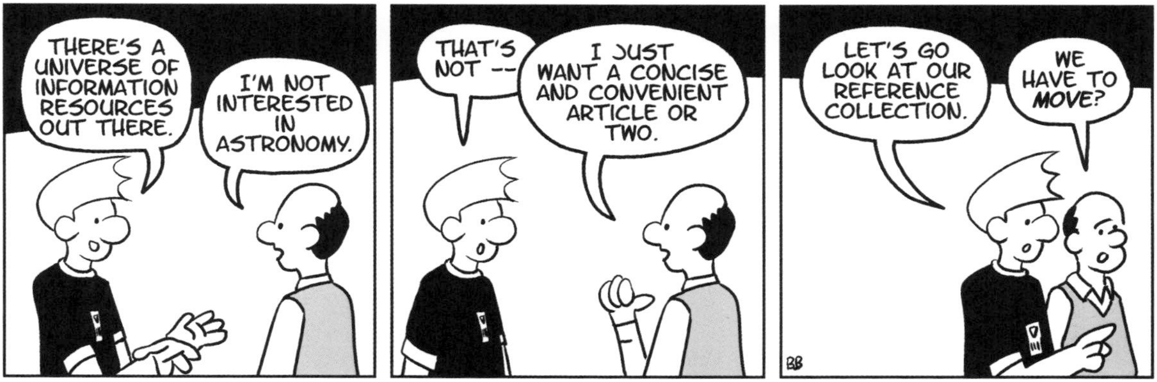
THERE'S A UNIVERSE OF INFORMATION RESOURCES OUT THERE.
I'M NOT INTERESTED IN ASTRONOMY.
THAT'S NOT --
I JUST WANT A CONCISE AND CONVENIENT ARTICLE OR TWO.
LET'S GO LOOK AT OUR REFERENCE COLLECTION.
WE HAVE TO *MOVE*?
BB

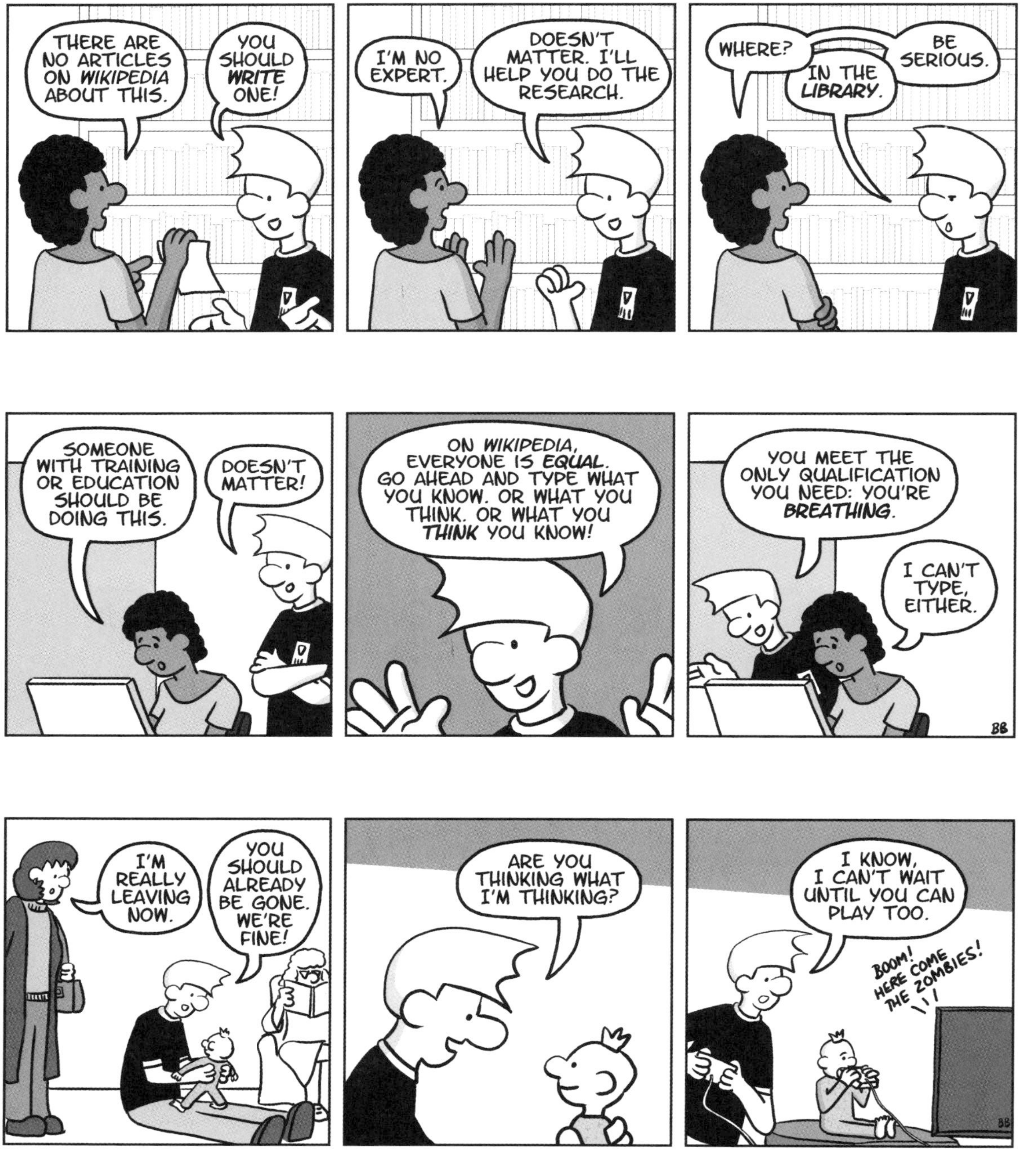

THERE ARE NO ARTICLES ON *WIKIPEDIA* ABOUT THIS.
YOU SHOULD *WRITE* ONE!
I'M NO EXPERT.
DOESN'T MATTER. I'LL HELP YOU DO THE RESEARCH.
WHERE?
IN THE *LIBRARY*.
BE SERIOUS.
SOMEONE WITH TRAINING OR EDUCATION SHOULD BE DOING THIS.
DOESN'T MATTER!
ON *WIKIPEDIA*, EVERYONE IS *EQUAL*. GO AHEAD AND TYPE WHAT YOU KNOW. OR WHAT YOU THINK. OR WHAT YOU *THINK* YOU KNOW!
YOU MEET THE ONLY QUALIFICATION YOU NEED: YOU'RE *BREATHING*.
I CAN'T TYPE, EITHER.
BB
I'M REALLY LEAVING NOW.
YOU SHOULD ALREADY BE GONE. WE'RE FINE!
ARE YOU THINKING WHAT I'M THINKING?
I KNOW, I CAN'T WAIT UNTIL YOU CAN PLAY TOO.
BOOM! HERE COME THE ZOMBIES!
BB

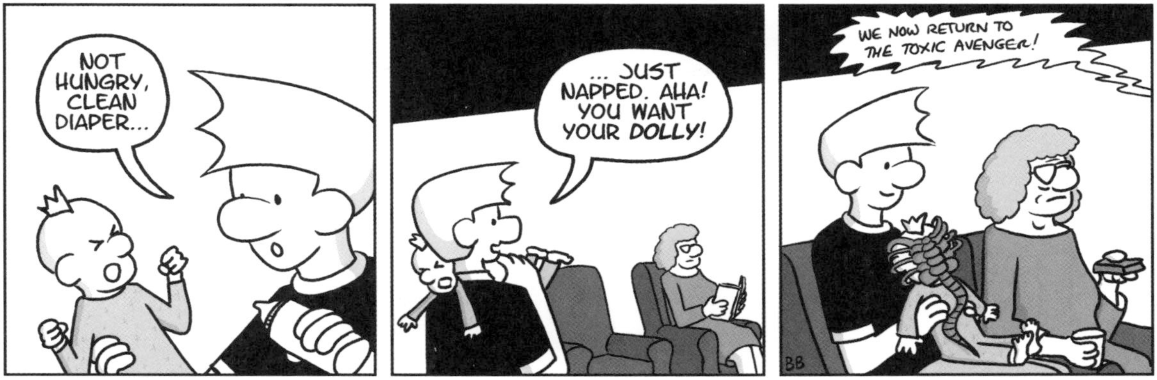
NOT HUNGRY, CLEAN DIAPER...
... JUST NAPPED. AHA! YOU WANT YOUR DOLLY!
WE NOW RETURN TO THE TOXIC AVENGER!
BB

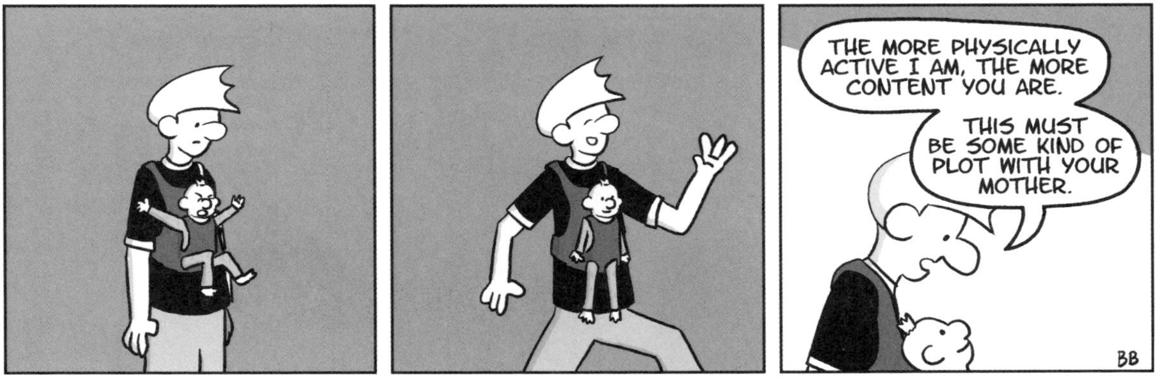
THE MORE PHYSICALLY ACTIVE I AM, THE MORE CONTENT YOU ARE.
THIS MUST BE SOME KIND OF PLOT WITH YOUR MOTHER.
BB

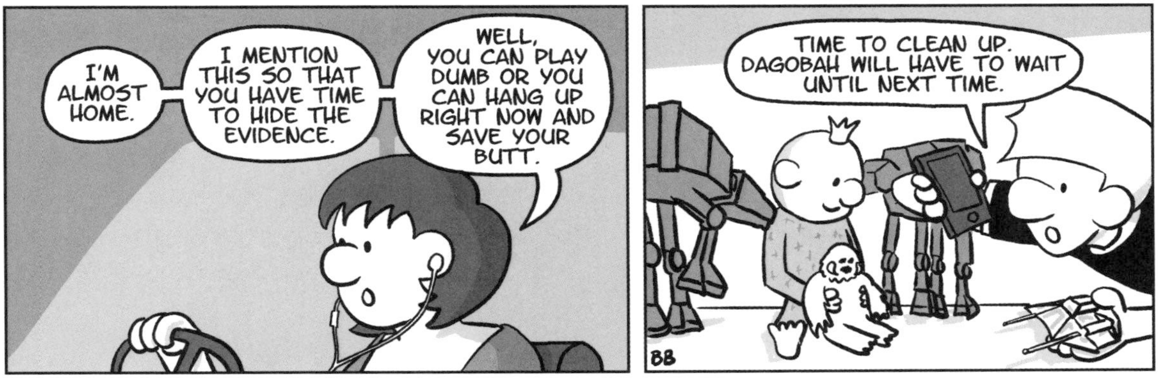
I'M ALMOST HOME.
I MENTION THIS SO THAT YOU HAVE TIME TO HIDE THE EVIDENCE.
WELL, YOU CAN PLAY DUMB OR YOU CAN HANG UP RIGHT NOW AND SAVE YOUR BUTT.
TIME TO CLEAN UP. DAGOBAH WILL HAVE TO WAIT UNTIL NEXT TIME.
BB

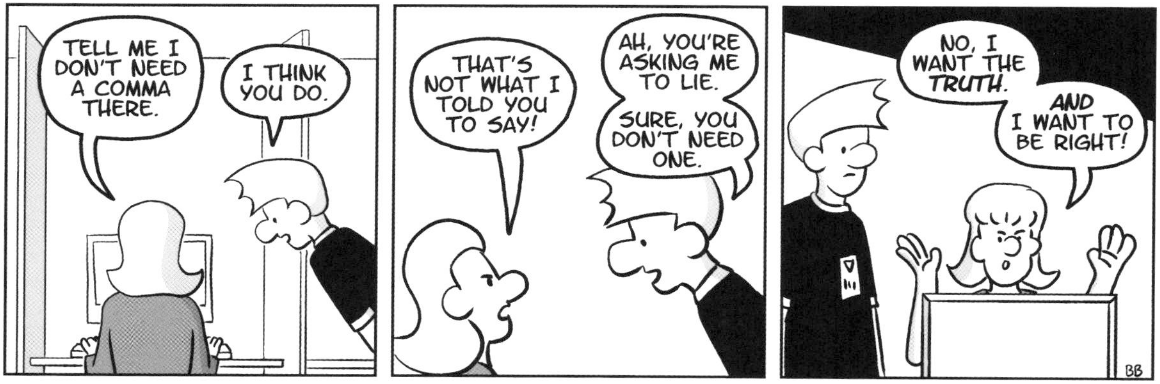
TELL ME I DON'T NEED A COMMA THERE.
I THINK YOU DO.
THAT'S NOT WHAT I TOLD YOU TO SAY!
AH, YOU'RE ASKING ME TO LIE.
SURE, YOU DON'T NEED ONE.
NO, I WANT THE *TRUTH*.
AND I WANT TO BE RIGHT!
BB

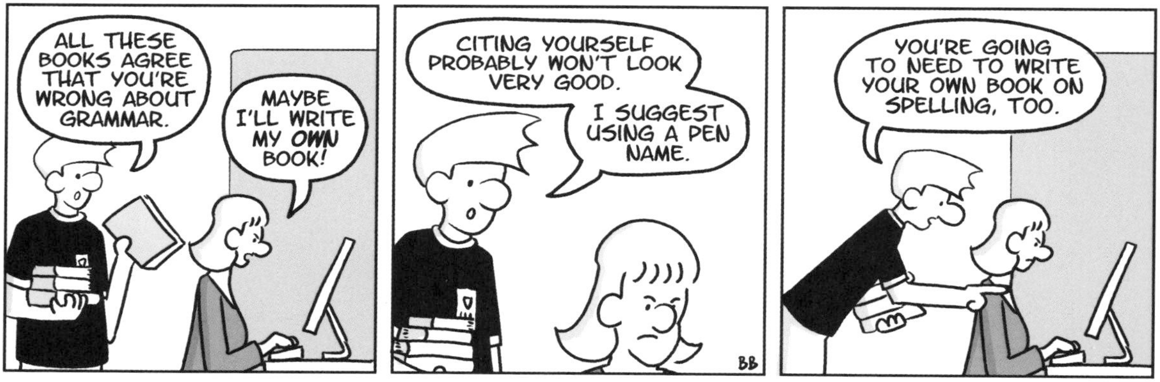
ALL THESE BOOKS AGREE THAT YOU'RE WRONG ABOUT GRAMMAR.
MAYBE I'LL WRITE MY *OWN* BOOK!
CITING YOURSELF PROBABLY WON'T LOOK VERY GOOD.
I SUGGEST USING A PEN NAME.
YOU'RE GOING TO NEED TO WRITE YOUR OWN BOOK ON SPELLING, TOO.
BB

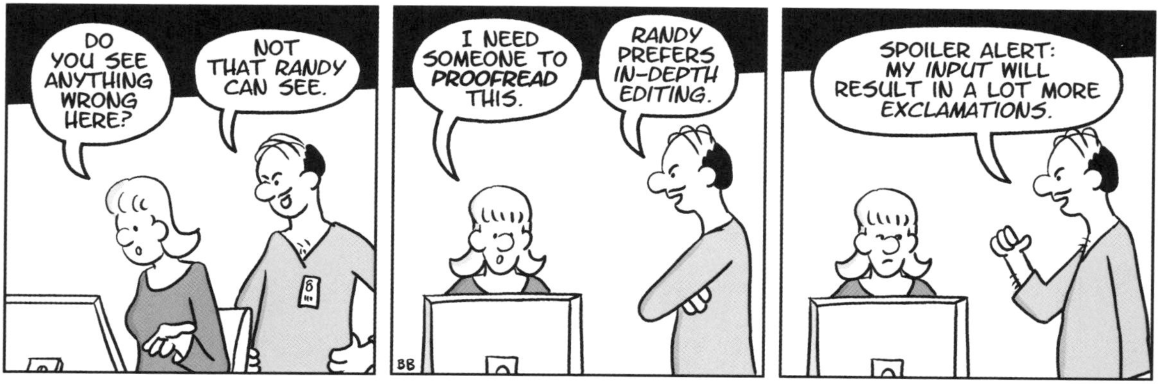
DO YOU SEE ANYTHING WRONG HERE?
NOT THAT RANDY CAN SEE.
I NEED SOMEONE TO *PROOFREAD* THIS.
RANDY PREFERS *IN-DEPTH EDITING.*
SPOILER ALERT: MY *INPUT* WILL RESULT IN A LOT MORE *EXCLAMATIONS*.
BB

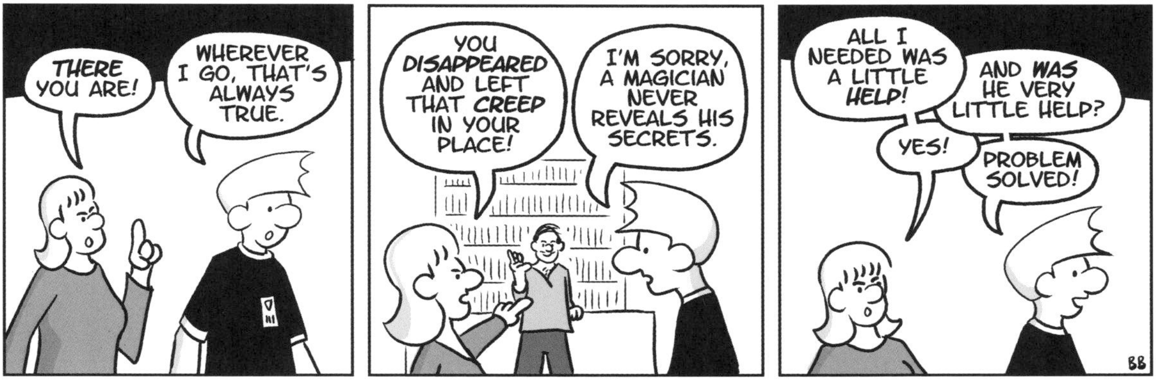
THERE YOU ARE!
WHEREVER I GO, THAT'S ALWAYS TRUE.
YOU DISAPPEARED AND LEFT THAT CREEP IN YOUR PLACE!
I'M SORRY, A MAGICIAN NEVER REVEALS HIS SECRETS.
ALL I NEEDED WAS A LITTLE HELP!
AND WAS HE VERY LITTLE HELP?
YES!
PROBLEM SOLVED!
BB

LIBRARY TIP #100: LAUGHTER IS GOOD FOR THE SOUL

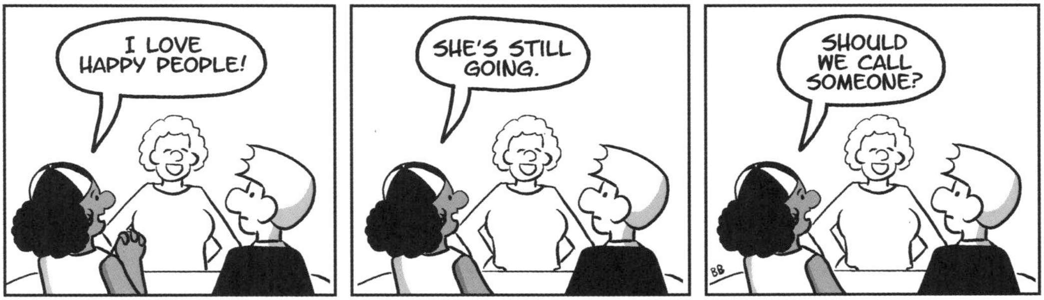
I LOVE HAPPY PEOPLE!
SHE'S STILL GOING.
SHOULD WE CALL SOMEONE?
BB

LIBRARY TIP #101: MOVE ALONG

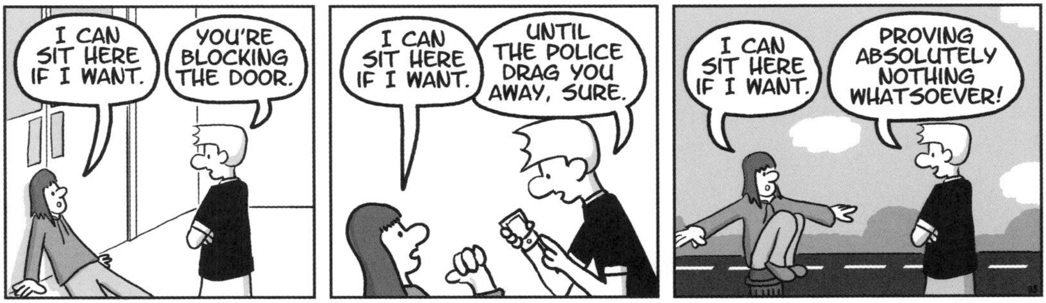
I CAN SIT HERE IF I WANT.
YOU'RE BLOCKING THE DOOR.
I CAN SIT HERE IF I WANT.
UNTIL THE POLICE DRAG YOU AWAY, SURE.
I CAN SIT HERE IF I WANT.
PROVING ABSOLUTELY NOTHING WHATSOEVER!

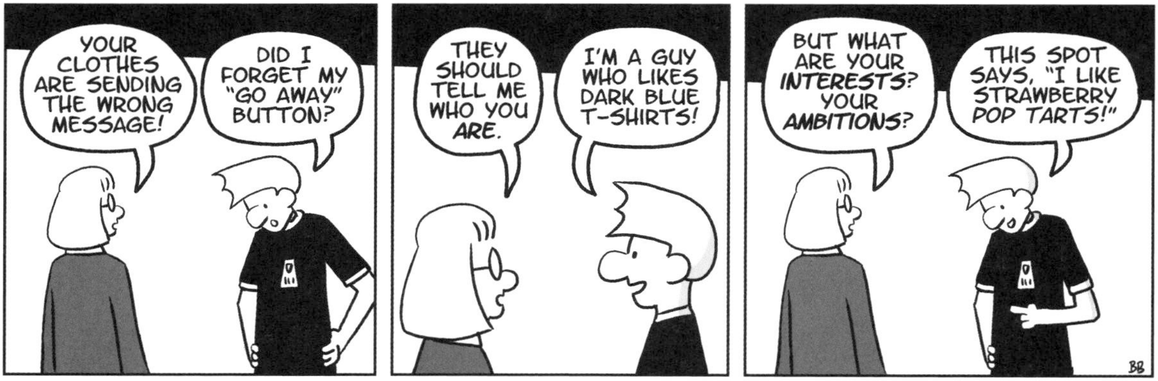
YOUR CLOTHES ARE SENDING THE WRONG MESSAGE!
DID I FORGET MY "GO AWAY" BUTTON?
THEY SHOULD TELL ME WHO YOU *ARE*.
I'M A GUY WHO LIKES DARK BLUE T-SHIRTS!
BUT WHAT ARE YOUR *INTERESTS*? YOUR *AMBITIONS*?
THIS SPOT SAYS, "I LIKE STRAWBERRY POP TARTS!"
BB

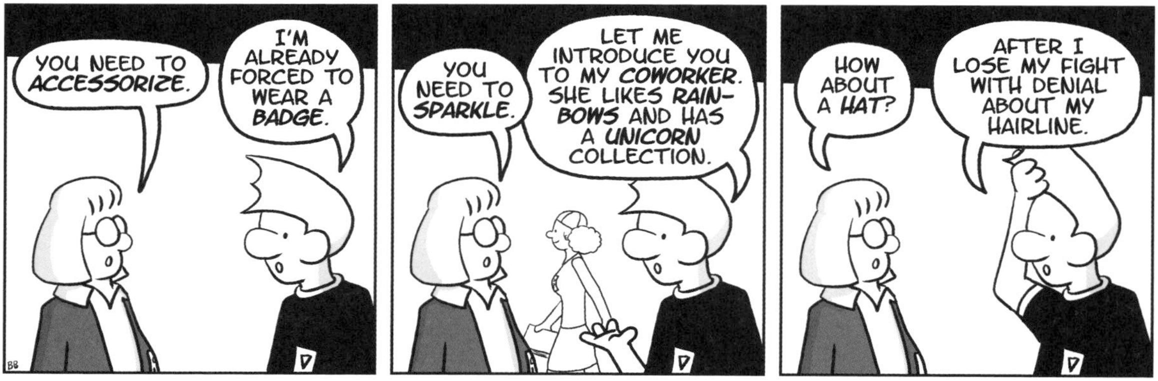
YOU NEED TO *ACCESSORIZE*.
I'M ALREADY FORCED TO WEAR A *BADGE*.
BB
YOU NEED TO *SPARKLE*.
LET ME INTRODUCE YOU TO MY *COWORKER*. SHE LIKES *RAIN-BOWS* AND HAS A *UNICORN* COLLECTION.
HOW ABOUT A *HAT*?
AFTER I LOSE MY FIGHT WITH DENIAL ABOUT MY HAIRLINE.

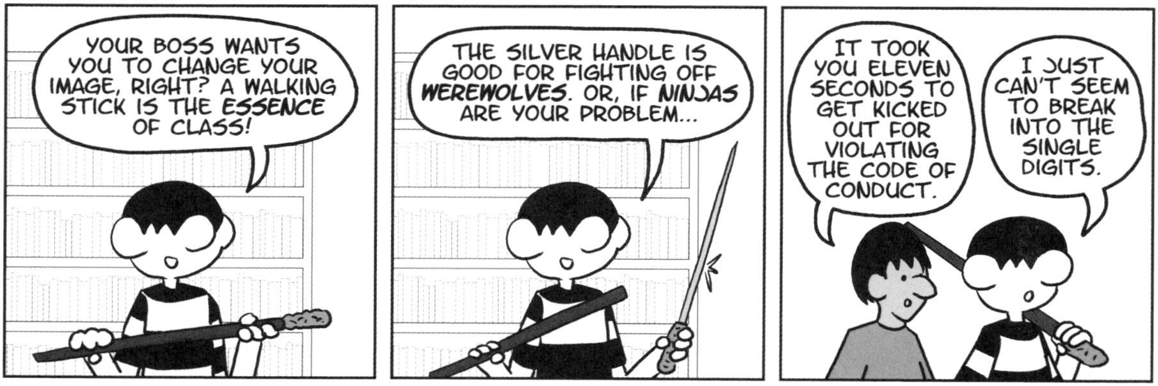
YOUR BOSS WANTS YOU TO CHANGE YOUR IMAGE, RIGHT? A WALKING STICK IS THE *ESSENCE* OF CLASS!
THE SILVER HANDLE IS GOOD FOR FIGHTING OFF *WEREWOLVES*. OR, IF *NINJAS* ARE YOUR PROBLEM...
IT TOOK YOU ELEVEN SECONDS TO GET KICKED OUT FOR VIOLATING THE CODE OF CONDUCT.
I JUST CAN'T SEEM TO BREAK INTO THE SINGLE DIGITS.

Bibliovores

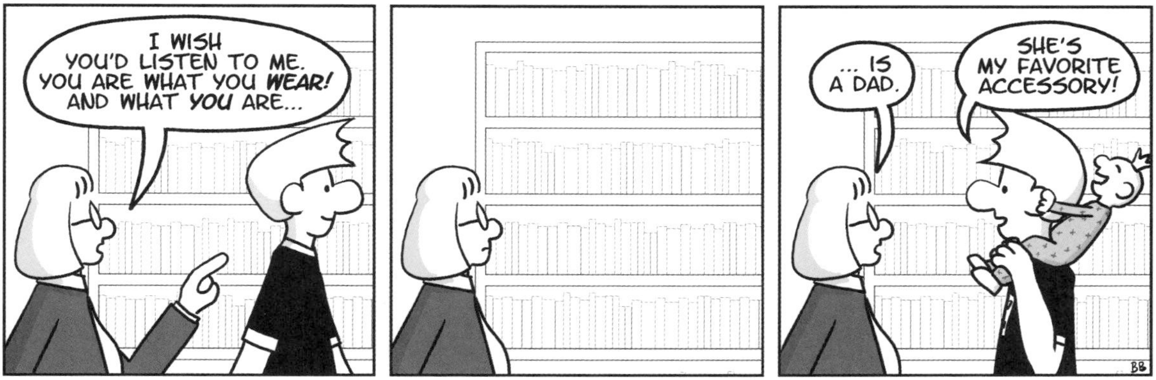

I WISH YOU'D LISTEN TO ME. YOU ARE WHAT YOU WEAR! AND WHAT YOU ARE...
... IS A DAD.
SHE'S MY FAVORITE ACCESSORY!
BB

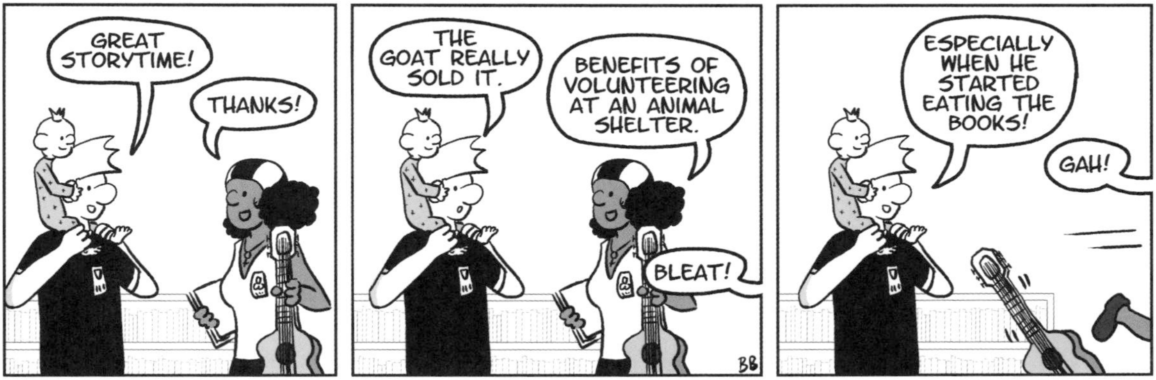

GREAT STORYTIME!
THANKS!
THE GOAT REALLY SOLD IT.
BENEFITS OF VOLUNTEERING AT AN ANIMAL SHELTER.
BLEAT!
BB
ESPECIALLY WHEN HE STARTED EATING THE BOOKS!
GAH!

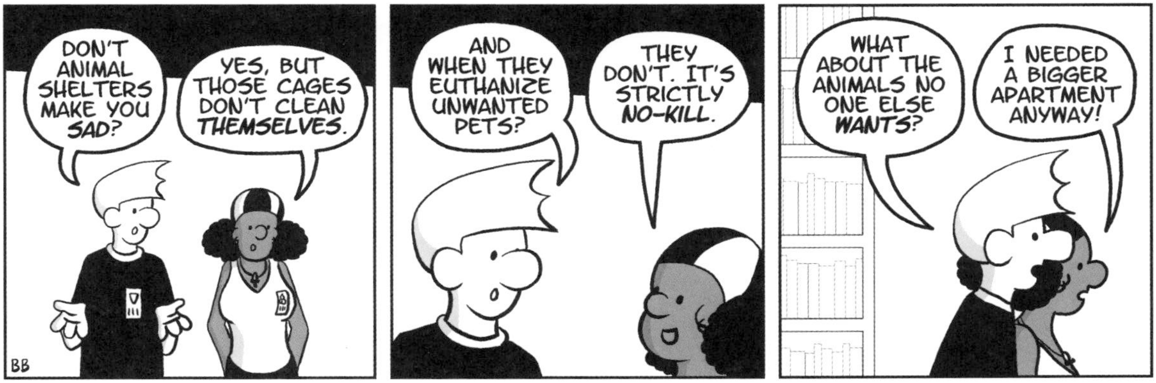

DON'T ANIMAL SHELTERS MAKE YOU SAD?
YES, BUT THOSE CAGES DON'T CLEAN THEMSELVES.
BB
AND WHEN THEY EUTHANIZE UNWANTED PETS?
THEY DON'T. IT'S STRICTLY NO-KILL.
WHAT ABOUT THE ANIMALS NO ONE ELSE WANTS?
I NEEDED A BIGGER APARTMENT ANYWAY!

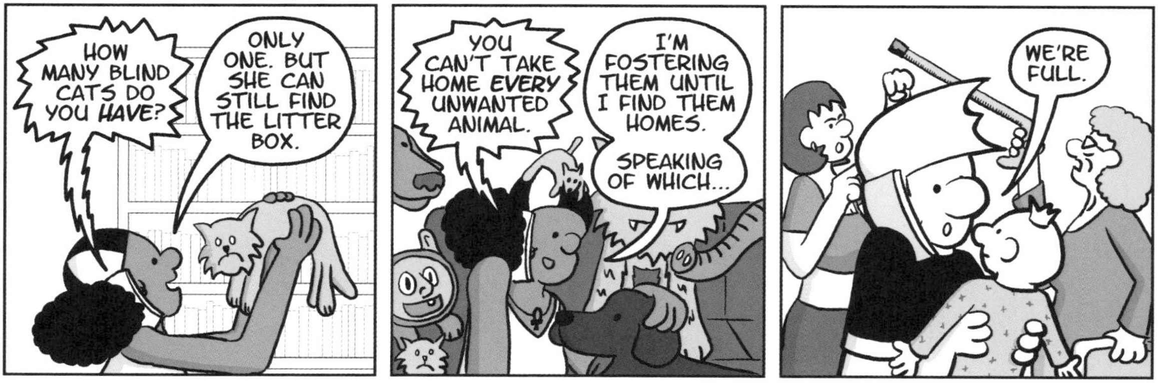
HOW MANY BLIND CATS DO YOU *HAVE*?
ONLY ONE. BUT SHE CAN STILL FIND THE LITTER BOX.
YOU CAN'T TAKE HOME *EVERY* UNWANTED ANIMAL.
I'M FOSTERING THEM UNTIL I FIND THEM HOMES.
SPEAKING OF WHICH...
WE'RE FULL.

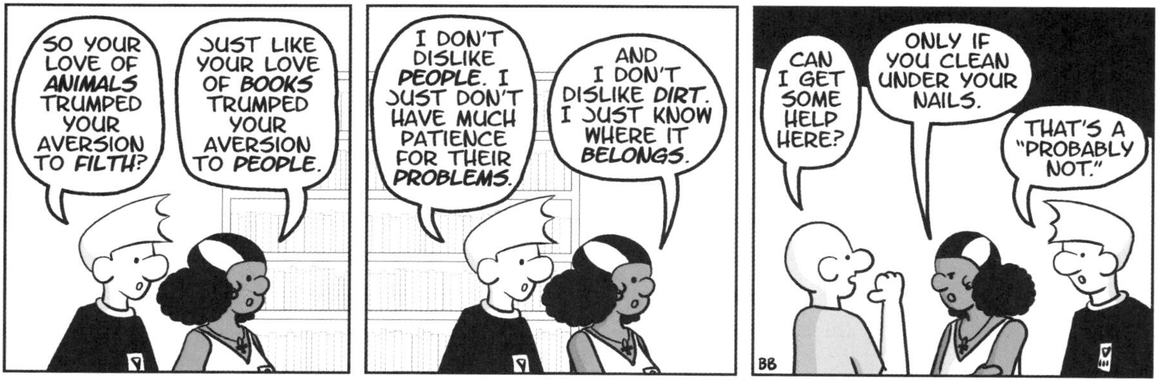
SO YOUR LOVE OF *ANIMALS* TRUMPED YOUR AVERSION TO *FILTH*?
JUST LIKE YOUR LOVE OF *BOOKS* TRUMPED YOUR AVERSION TO *PEOPLE*.
I DON'T DISLIKE *PEOPLE*. I JUST DON'T HAVE MUCH PATIENCE FOR THEIR *PROBLEMS*.
AND I DON'T DISLIKE *DIRT*. I JUST KNOW WHERE IT *BELONGS*.
CAN I GET SOME HELP HERE?
ONLY IF YOU CLEAN UNDER YOUR NAILS.
THAT'S A "PROBABLY NOT."
BB

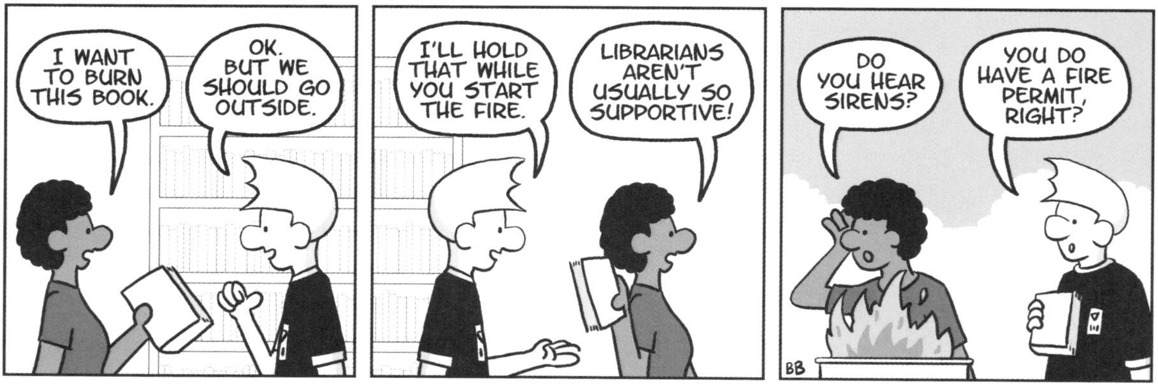
I WANT TO BURN THIS BOOK.
OK. BUT WE SHOULD GO OUTSIDE.
I'LL HOLD THAT WHILE YOU START THE FIRE.
LIBRARIANS AREN'T USUALLY SO SUPPORTIVE!
DO YOU HEAR SIRENS?
YOU DO HAVE A FIRE PERMIT, RIGHT?
BB

Bibliovores

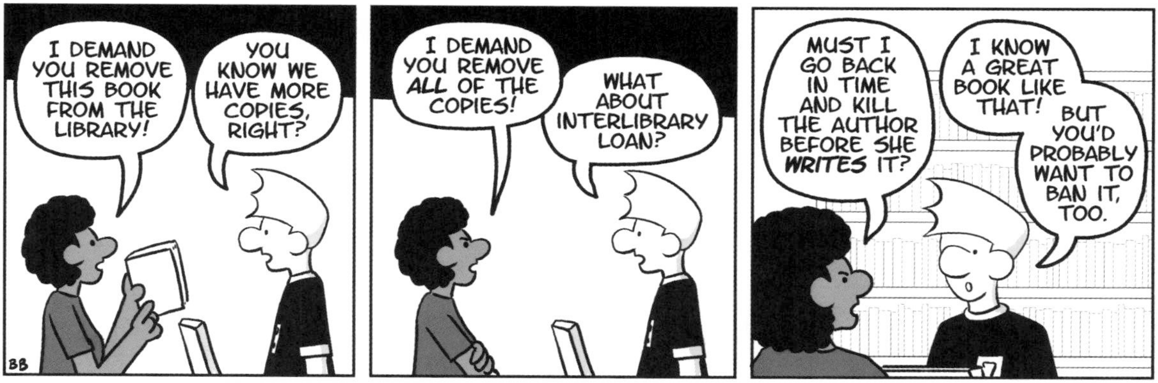

I DEMAND YOU REMOVE THIS BOOK FROM THE LIBRARY!
YOU KNOW WE HAVE MORE COPIES, RIGHT?
I DEMAND YOU REMOVE ALL OF THE COPIES!
WHAT ABOUT INTERLIBRARY LOAN?
MUST I GO BACK IN TIME AND KILL THE AUTHOR BEFORE SHE WRITES IT?
I KNOW A GREAT BOOK LIKE THAT!
BUT YOU'D PROBABLY WANT TO BAN IT, TOO.
BB

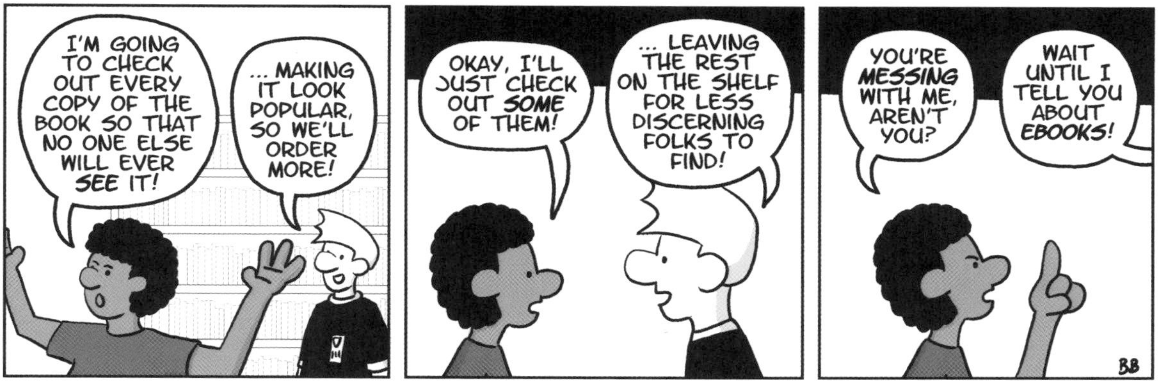

I'M GOING TO CHECK OUT EVERY COPY OF THE BOOK SO THAT NO ONE ELSE WILL EVER SEE IT!
... MAKING IT LOOK POPULAR, SO WE'LL ORDER MORE!
OKAY, I'LL JUST CHECK OUT SOME OF THEM!
... LEAVING THE REST ON THE SHELF FOR LESS DISCERNING FOLKS TO FIND!
YOU'RE MESSING WITH ME, AREN'T YOU?
WAIT UNTIL I TELL YOU ABOUT EBOOKS!
BB

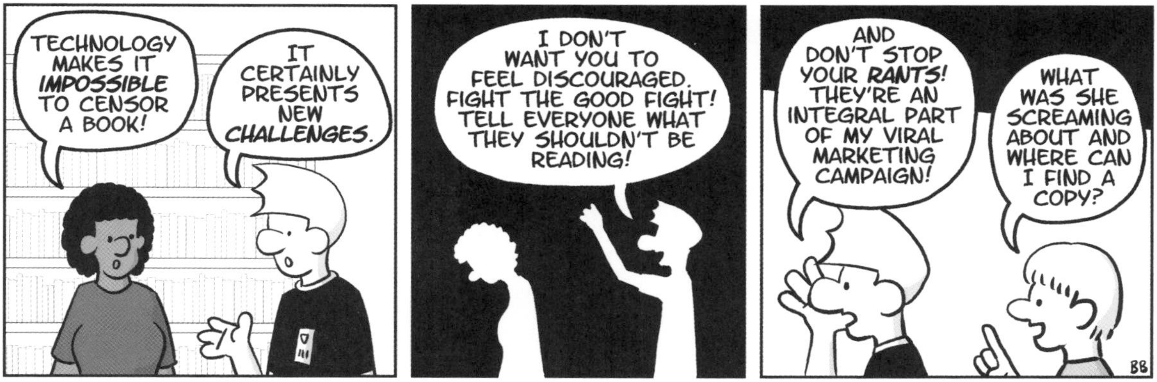

TECHNOLOGY MAKES IT IMPOSSIBLE TO CENSOR A BOOK!
IT CERTAINLY PRESENTS NEW CHALLENGES.
I DON'T WANT YOU TO FEEL DISCOURAGED. FIGHT THE GOOD FIGHT! TELL EVERYONE WHAT THEY SHOULDN'T BE READING!
AND DON'T STOP YOUR RANTS! THEY'RE AN INTEGRAL PART OF MY VIRAL MARKETING CAMPAIGN!
WHAT WAS SHE SCREAMING ABOUT AND WHERE CAN I FIND A COPY?
BB

A BOOK? WHO ARE YOU AND WHAT HAVE YOU DONE WITH MERV?
IT'S A SOURCE FOR THE PAPER I'M WRITING.
LOOKS LIKE YOU COPIED SEVERAL PAGES VERBATIM. IT'S PLAGIARISM UNLESS YOU PUT IT IN YOUR OWN WORDS...
I DID. BY COINCIDENCE THEY ARE EXACTLY THE SAME.
...OR CITE THE SOURCE.
A GOOD MAGICIAN NEVER REVEALS HIS SECRETS.
BB

JUST REWRITE WHAT YOU FOUND.
IT'S ALREADY PERFECT AS IT IS!
MAKE IT SOUND MORE LIKE YOU.
MY TEACHER IS GRADING ON CLARITY.
IS IT "CLEAR" THAT SHE WILL FAIL YOU IF YOU DON'T CHANGE THIS?
FINE, I'LL COPY FROM THE WEB, TOO.
THAT'S MY FINAL OFFER.
BB

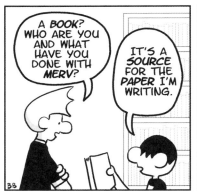

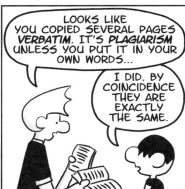

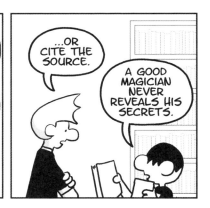

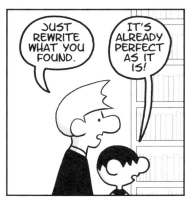

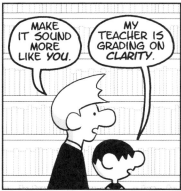

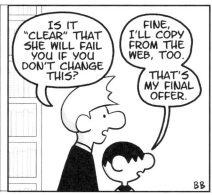

YOU NEED TO PARAPHRASE.
THERE.
YOU ONLY CHANGED ONE VERB.
FINE, HERE'S AN ADJECTIVE.
SATISFIED?
REWRITING IS MORE THAN JUST USING A THESAURUS.
I'M UNINTERESTED.
INDIFFERENT.
APATHETIC.
BB
HERE. HAPPY?
I'M DOING WELL, THANKS. AND YOU?
THE ORIGINAL QUOTE IS COMPLETELY UNRECOGNIZABLE. I'VE RESTATED IT. I'VE REPLACED ALL THE WORDS. NOW IT'S INCOMPREHENSIBLE!
I'D DO BETTER TO WRITE THIS FROM SCRATCH MYSELF!
DON'T FORGET TO CITE YOUR SOURCE.
BB

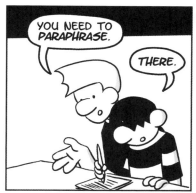

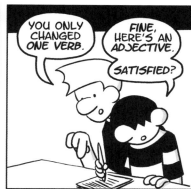

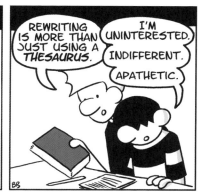

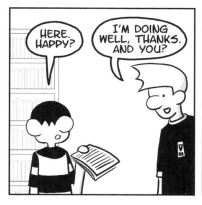

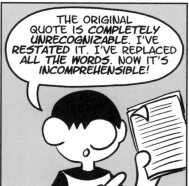

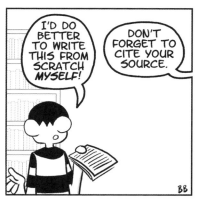

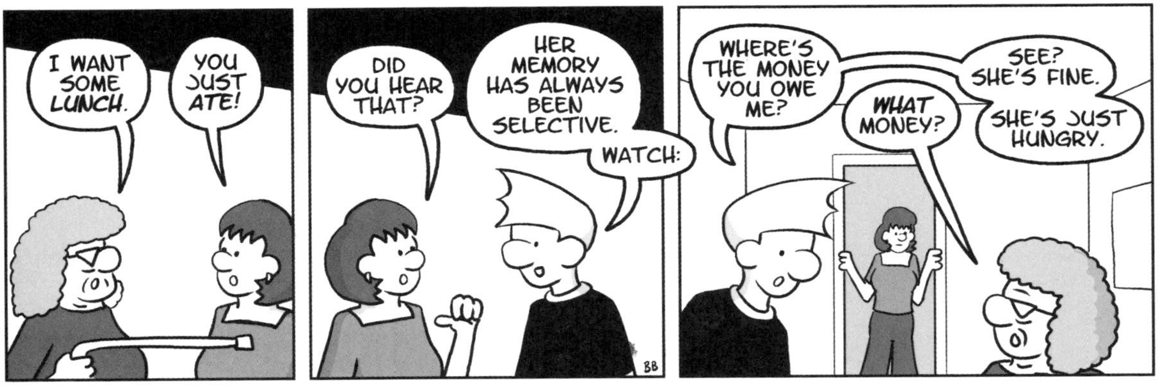
I WANT SOME **LUNCH**.
YOU JUST **ATE**!
DID YOU HEAR THAT?
HER MEMORY HAS ALWAYS BEEN SELECTIVE.
WATCH:
WHERE'S THE MONEY YOU OWE ME?
WHAT MONEY?
SEE? SHE'S FINE.
SHE'S JUST HUNGRY.
BB

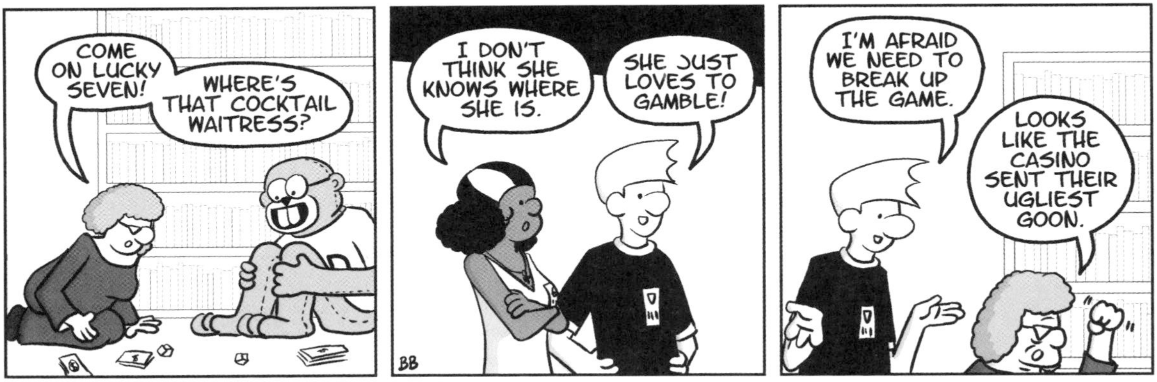
COME ON LUCKY SEVEN!
WHERE'S THAT COCKTAIL WAITRESS?
I DON'T THINK SHE KNOWS WHERE SHE IS.
SHE JUST LOVES TO GAMBLE!
BB
I'M AFRAID WE NEED TO BREAK UP THE GAME.
LOOKS LIKE THE CASINO SENT THEIR UGLIEST GOON.

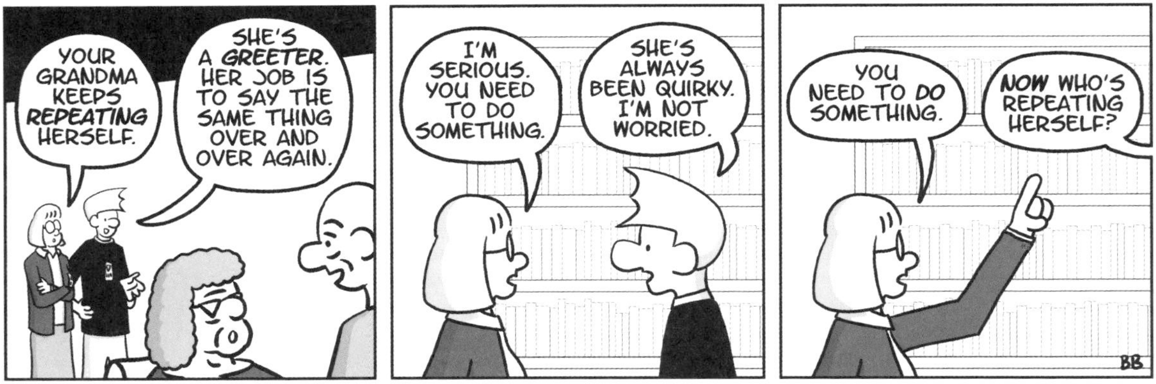
YOUR GRANDMA KEEPS **REPEATING** HERSELF.
SHE'S A **GREETER**. HER JOB IS TO SAY THE SAME THING OVER AND OVER AGAIN.
I'M SERIOUS. YOU NEED TO DO SOMETHING.
SHE'S ALWAYS BEEN QUIRKY. I'M NOT WORRIED.
YOU NEED TO **DO** SOMETHING.
NOW WHO'S REPEATING HERSELF?
BB

Bibliovores

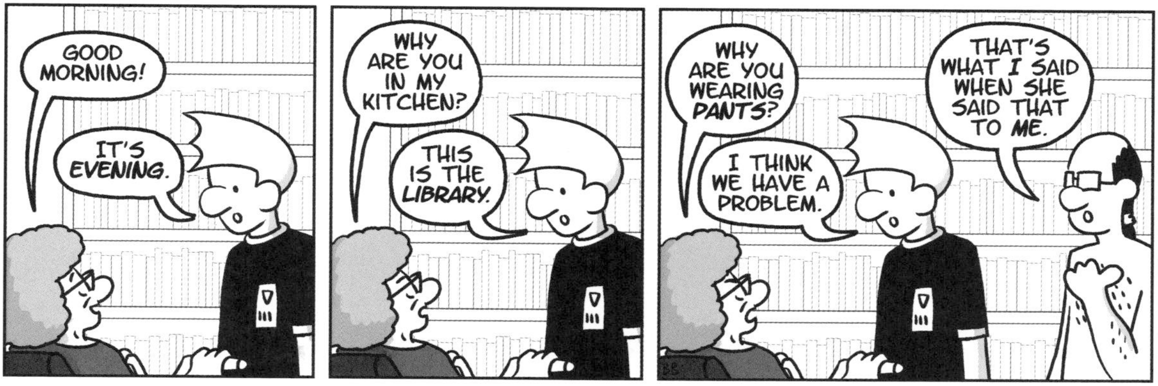
GOOD MORNING!
IT'S *EVENING*.
WHY ARE YOU IN MY KITCHEN?
THIS IS THE *LIBRARY*.
WHY ARE YOU WEARING *PANTS*?
I THINK WE HAVE A PROBLEM.
THAT'S WHAT *I* SAID WHEN SHE SAID THAT TO *ME*.

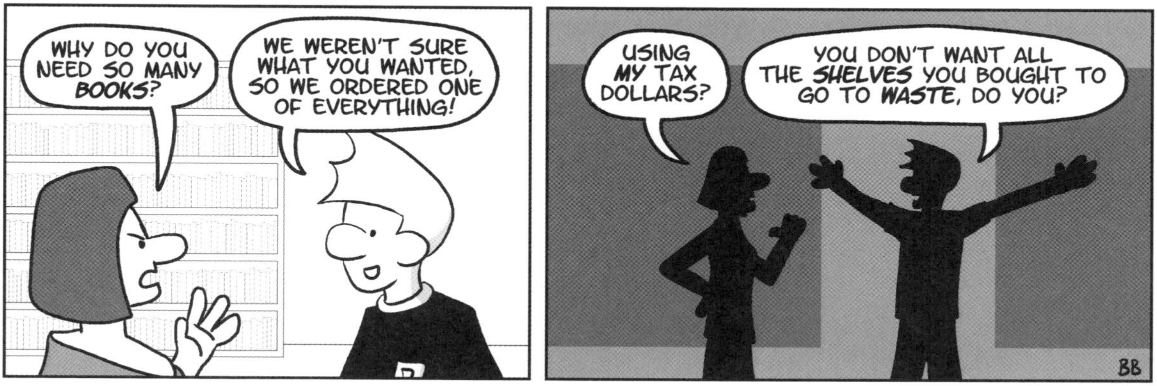
WHY DO YOU NEED SO MANY *BOOKS*?
WE WEREN'T SURE WHAT YOU WANTED, SO WE ORDERED ONE OF EVERYTHING!
USING *MY* TAX DOLLARS?
YOU DON'T WANT ALL THE *SHELVES* YOU BOUGHT TO GO TO *WASTE*, DO YOU?

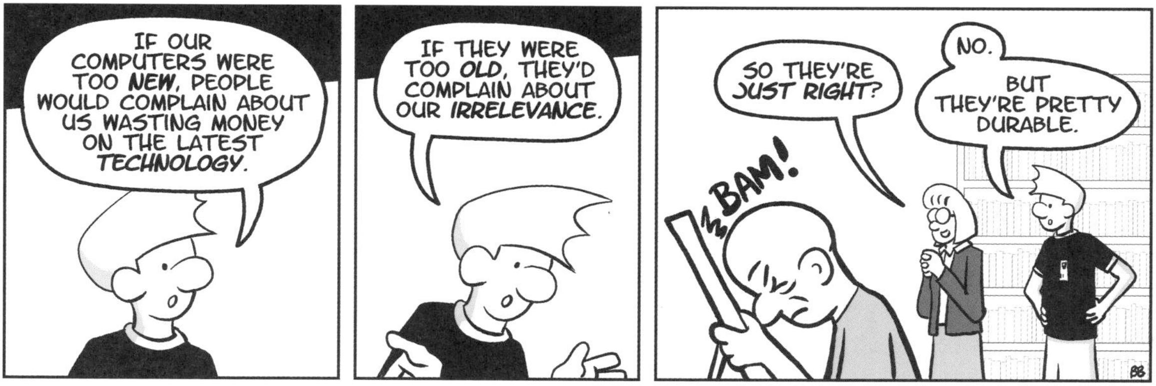
IF OUR COMPUTERS WERE TOO *NEW*, PEOPLE WOULD COMPLAIN ABOUT US WASTING MONEY ON THE LATEST *TECHNOLOGY*.
IF THEY WERE TOO *OLD*, THEY'D COMPLAIN ABOUT OUR *IRRELEVANCE*.
BAM!
SO THEY'RE *JUST RIGHT*?
NO.
BUT THEY'RE PRETTY DURABLE.

LIBRARY TIP #102: SHOOT FOR THE MOON

YOU'RE REALLY TOO SHORT TO BE AN ASTRONAUT.

NOT TO MENTION YOUR GLASSES. YOU'D NEED PERFECT VISION.

YOU MIGHT QUALIFY FOR OTHER CAREERS. LET'S LOOK AT THE ACTUARIAL DATA.

PLEASE REFER CHILDREN'S REFERENCE QUESTIONS TO ME.

LIBRARY TIP #103: DON'T ASK, DON'T SPELL

YOU SPELLED THAT WRONG.

SEE? THE PROGRAM UNDERLINED THE WORD IN RED.

HOW ANNOYING.

YOU CAN DISABLE THAT FEATURE.

IS THERE A WAY TO HIGHLIGHT *OTHER* PEOPLE'S ERRORS? I WOULD ENJOY THAT.

LIBRARY TIP #104: IT'S ALL IN HOW YOU ASK

CAN YOU SHOW ME HOW TO PIRATE A MOVIE?

CERTAINLY NOT.

WILL YOU DEMONSTRATE HOW A SCOFFLAW WOULD GO ABOUT DOWNLOADING VIDEOS ILLEGALLY?

MAIS OUI!

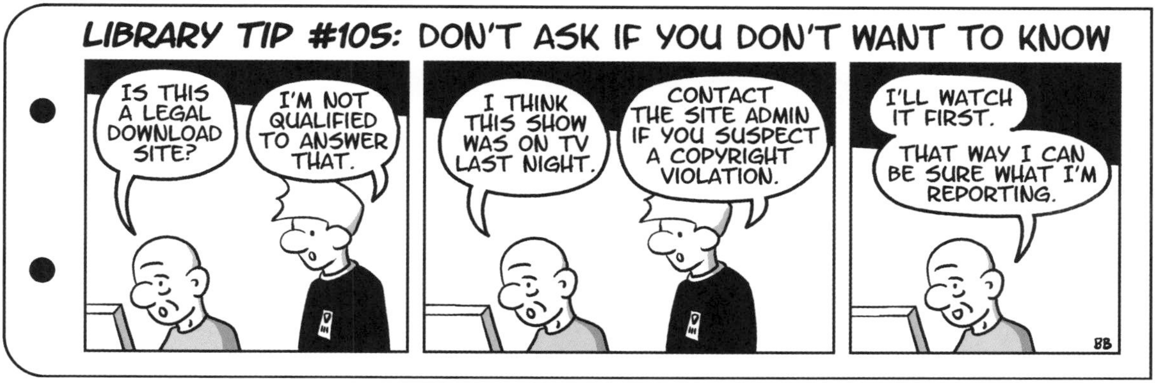
LIBRARY TIP #105: DON'T ASK IF YOU DON'T WANT TO KNOW
IS THIS A LEGAL DOWNLOAD SITE?
I'M NOT QUALIFIED TO ANSWER THAT.
I THINK THIS SHOW WAS ON TV LAST NIGHT.
CONTACT THE SITE ADMIN IF YOU SUSPECT A COPYRIGHT VIOLATION.
I'LL WATCH IT FIRST.
THAT WAY I CAN BE SURE WHAT I'M REPORTING.
BB

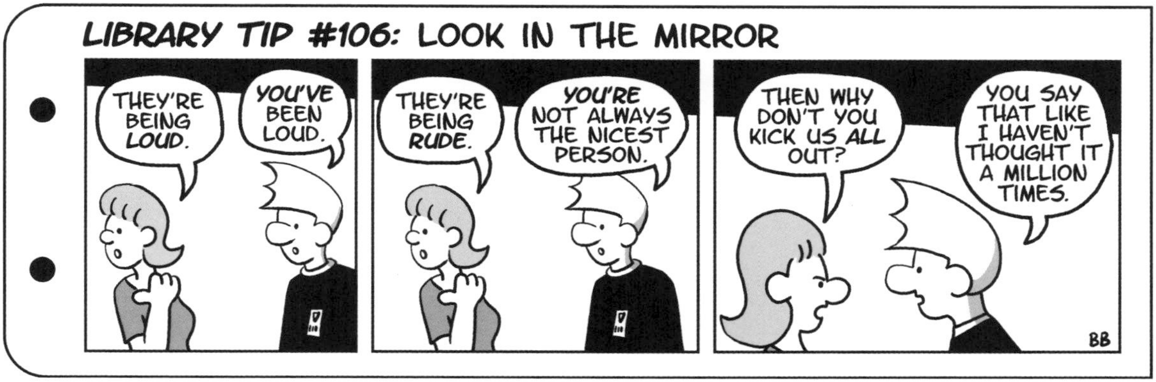
LIBRARY TIP #106: LOOK IN THE MIRROR
THEY'RE BEING *LOUD*.
YOU'VE BEEN LOUD.
THEY'RE BEING *RUDE*.
YOU'RE NOT ALWAYS THE NICEST PERSON.
THEN WHY DON'T YOU KICK US *ALL* OUT?
YOU SAY THAT LIKE I HAVEN'T THOUGHT IT A MILLION TIMES.
BB

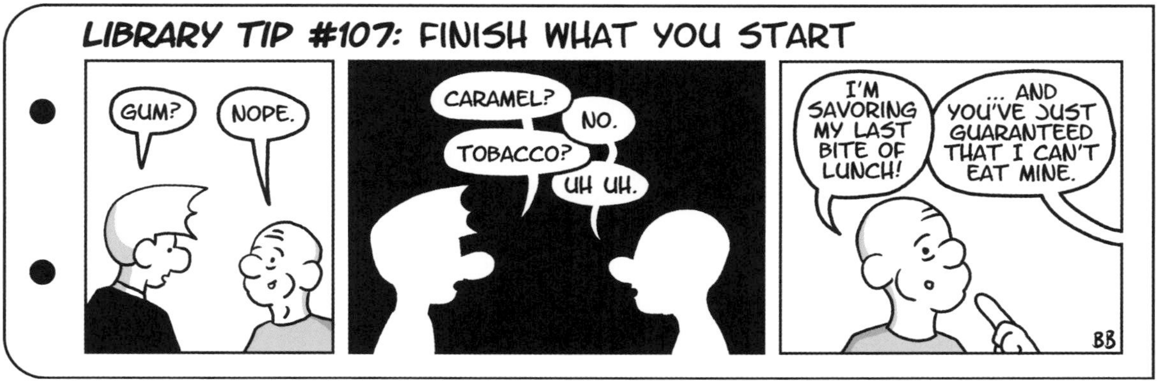
LIBRARY TIP #107: FINISH WHAT YOU START
GUM?
NOPE.
CARAMEL?
NO.
TOBACCO?
UH UH.
I'M SAVORING MY LAST BITE OF LUNCH!
... AND YOU'VE JUST GUARANTEED THAT I CAN'T EAT MINE.
BB

UNSHELVED

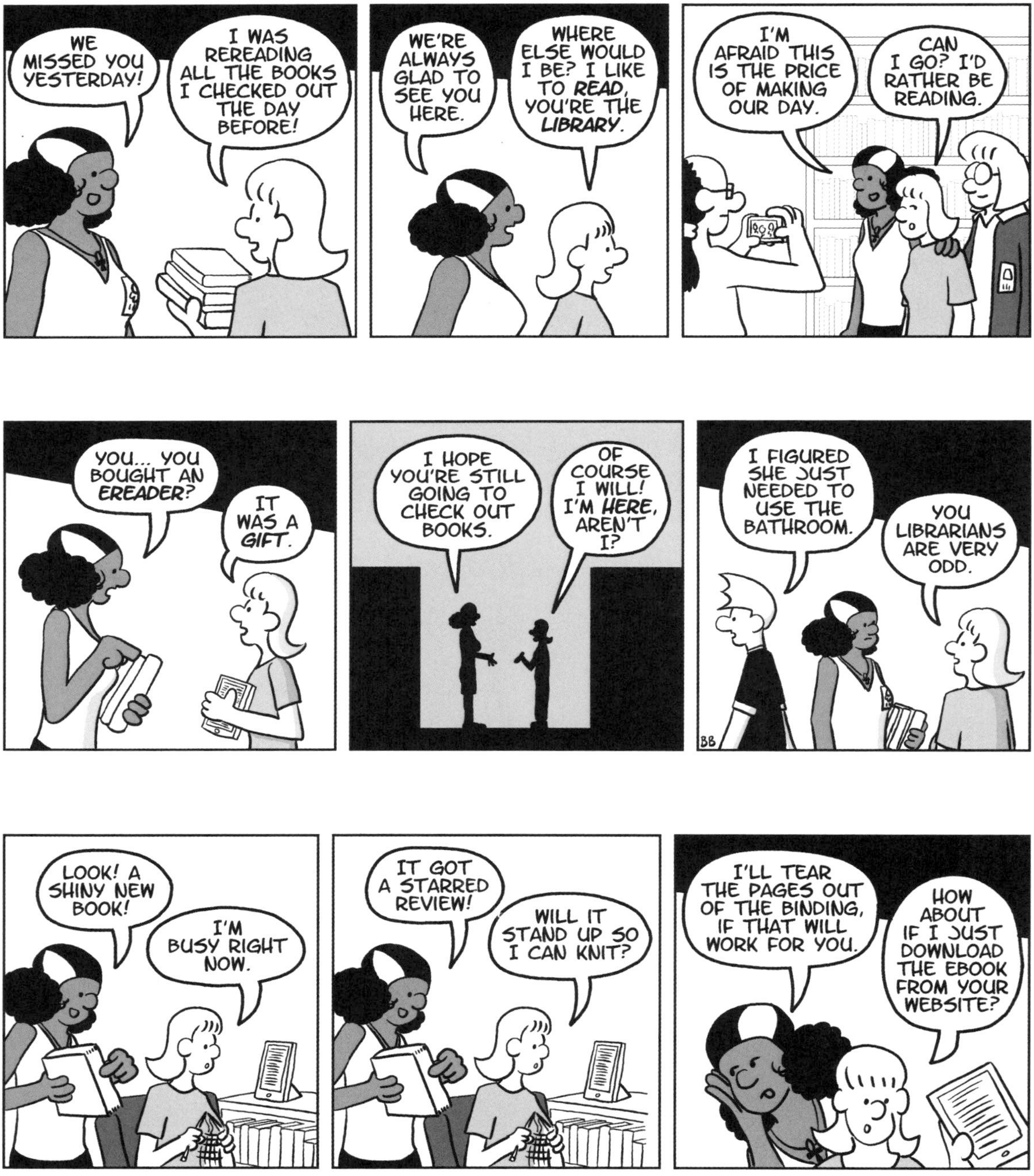
WE MISSED YOU YESTERDAY!
I WAS REREADING ALL THE BOOKS I CHECKED OUT THE DAY BEFORE!
WE'RE ALWAYS GLAD TO SEE YOU HERE.
WHERE ELSE WOULD I BE? I LIKE TO READ, YOU'RE THE LIBRARY.
I'M AFRAID THIS IS THE PRICE OF MAKING OUR DAY.
CAN I GO? I'D RATHER BE READING.
YOU... YOU BOUGHT AN EREADER?
IT WAS A GIFT.
I HOPE YOU'RE STILL GOING TO CHECK OUT BOOKS.
OF COURSE I WILL! I'M HERE, AREN'T I?
I FIGURED SHE JUST NEEDED TO USE THE BATHROOM.
YOU LIBRARIANS ARE VERY ODD.
BB
LOOK! A SHINY NEW BOOK!
I'M BUSY RIGHT NOW.
IT GOT A STARRED REVIEW!
WILL IT STAND UP SO I CAN KNIT?
I'LL TEAR THE PAGES OUT OF THE BINDING, IF THAT WILL WORK FOR YOU.
HOW ABOUT IF I JUST DOWNLOAD THE EBOOK FROM YOUR WEBSITE?

Bibliovores

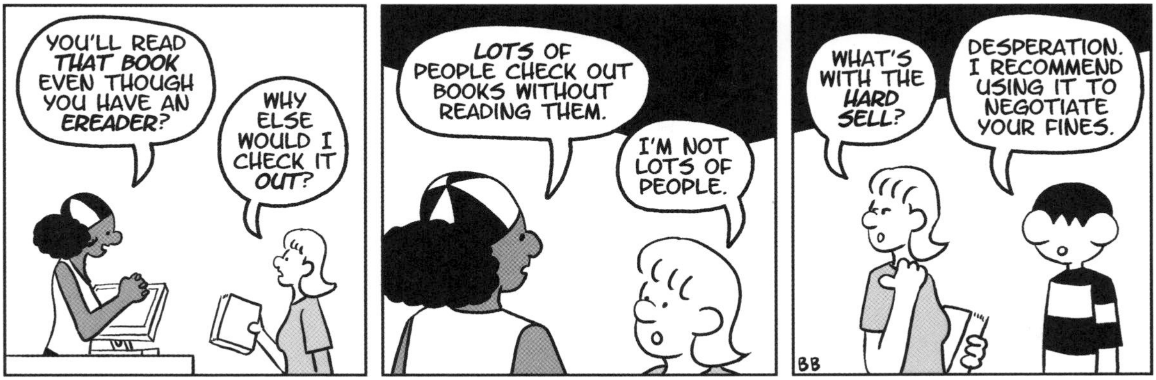
YOU'LL READ THAT BOOK EVEN THOUGH YOU HAVE AN EREADER?
WHY ELSE WOULD I CHECK IT OUT?
LOTS OF PEOPLE CHECK OUT BOOKS WITHOUT READING THEM.
I'M NOT LOTS OF PEOPLE.
WHAT'S WITH THE HARD SELL?
DESPERATION. I RECOMMEND USING IT TO NEGOTIATE YOUR FINES.
BB

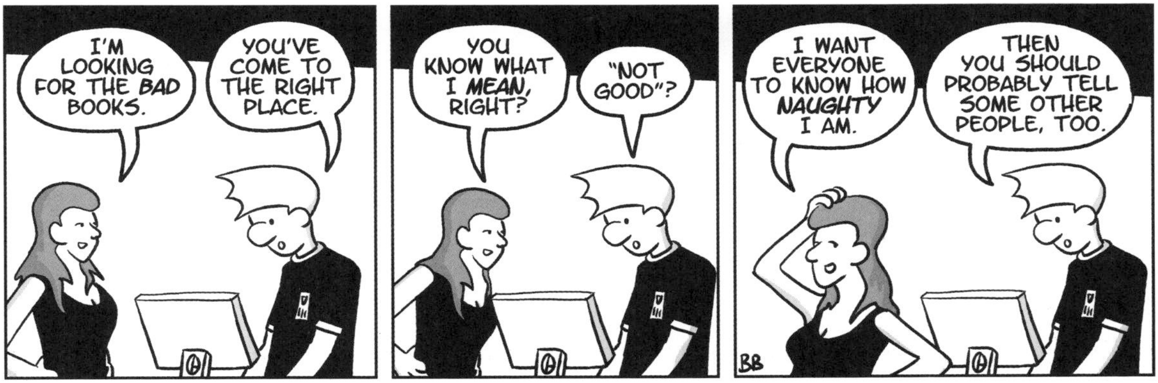
I'M LOOKING FOR THE BAD BOOKS.
YOU'VE COME TO THE RIGHT PLACE.
YOU KNOW WHAT I MEAN, RIGHT?
"NOT GOOD"?
I WANT EVERYONE TO KNOW HOW NAUGHTY I AM.
THEN YOU SHOULD PROBABLY TELL SOME OTHER PEOPLE, TOO.
BB

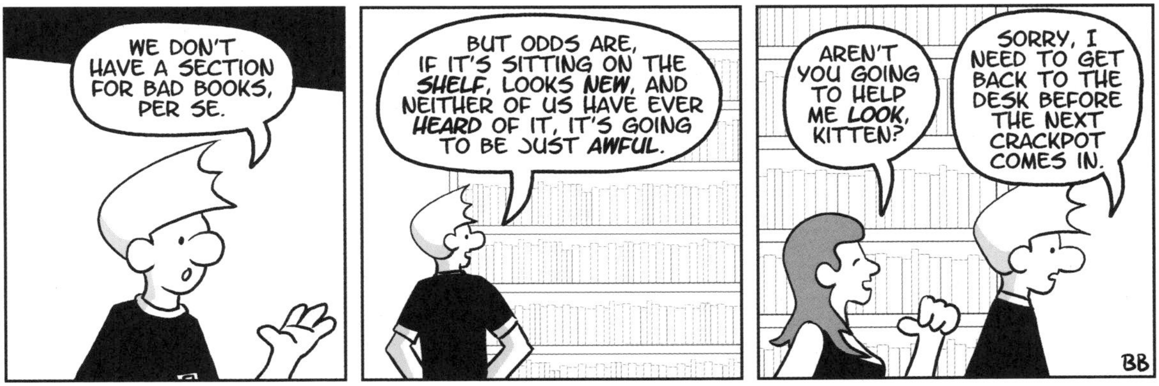
WE DON'T HAVE A SECTION FOR BAD BOOKS, PER SE.
BUT ODDS ARE, IF IT'S SITTING ON THE SHELF, LOOKS NEW, AND NEITHER OF US HAVE EVER HEARD OF IT, IT'S GOING TO BE JUST AWFUL.
AREN'T YOU GOING TO HELP ME LOOK, KITTEN?
SORRY, I NEED TO GET BACK TO THE DESK BEFORE THE NEXT CRACKPOT COMES IN.
BB

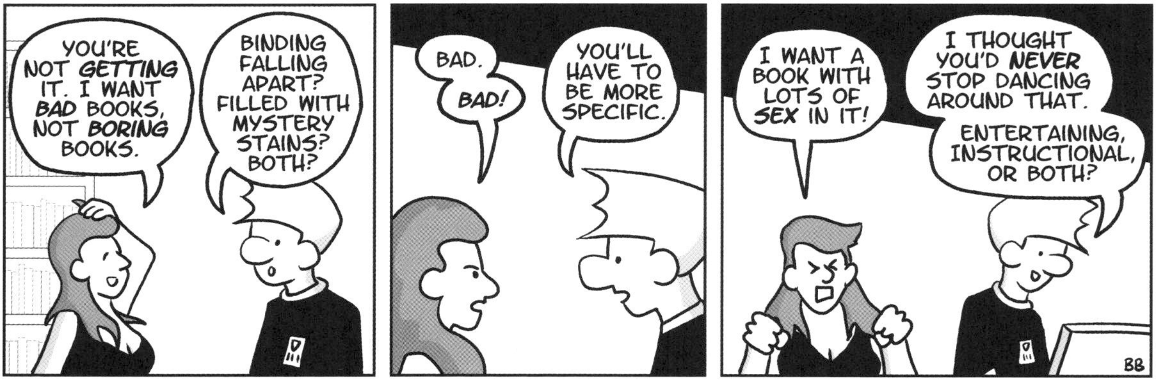
YOU'RE NOT GETTING IT. I WANT BAD BOOKS, NOT BORING BOOKS.
BINDING FALLING APART? FILLED WITH MYSTERY STAINS? BOTH?
BAD.
BAD!
YOU'LL HAVE TO BE MORE SPECIFIC.
I WANT A BOOK WITH LOTS OF SEX IN IT!
I THOUGHT YOU'D NEVER STOP DANCING AROUND THAT.
ENTERTAINING, INSTRUCTIONAL, OR BOTH?
BB

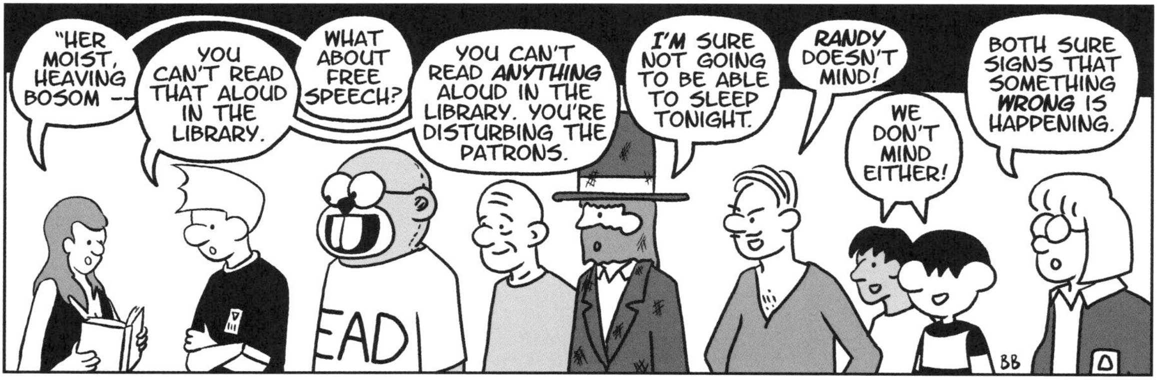
"HER MOIST, HEAVING BOSOM --
YOU CAN'T READ THAT ALOUD IN THE LIBRARY.
WHAT ABOUT FREE SPEECH?
YOU CAN'T READ ANYTHING ALOUD IN THE LIBRARY. YOU'RE DISTURBING THE PATRONS.
I'M SURE NOT GOING TO BE ABLE TO SLEEP TONIGHT.
RANDY DOESN'T MIND!
WE DON'T MIND EITHER!
BOTH SURE SIGNS THAT SOMETHING WRONG IS HAPPENING.
EAD
BB

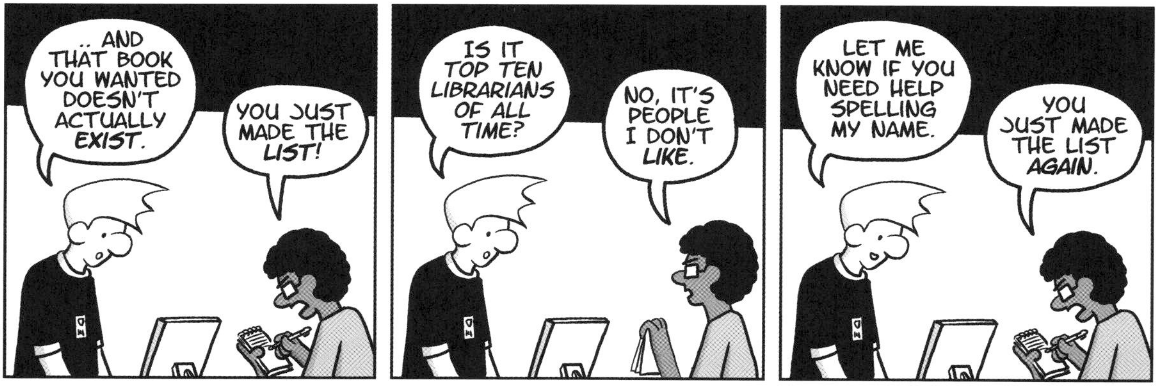
.. AND THAT BOOK YOU WANTED DOESN'T ACTUALLY EXIST.
YOU JUST MADE THE LIST!
IS IT TOP TEN LIBRARIANS OF ALL TIME?
NO, IT'S PEOPLE I DON'T LIKE.
LET ME KNOW IF YOU NEED HELP SPELLING MY NAME.
YOU JUST MADE THE LIST AGAIN.

Bibliovores

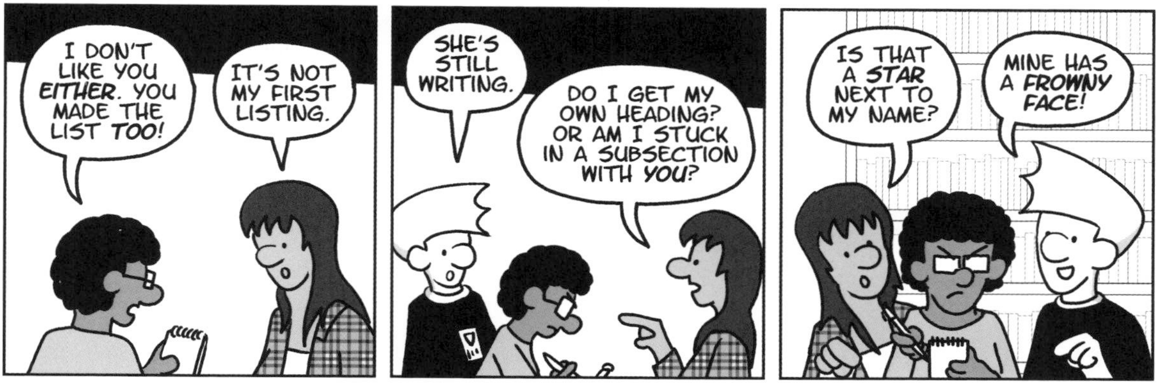
I DON'T LIKE YOU EITHER. YOU MADE THE LIST TOO!
IT'S NOT MY FIRST LISTING.
SHE'S STILL WRITING.
DO I GET MY OWN HEADING? OR AM I STUCK IN A SUBSECTION WITH YOU?
IS THAT A STAR NEXT TO MY NAME?
MINE HAS A FROWNY FACE!

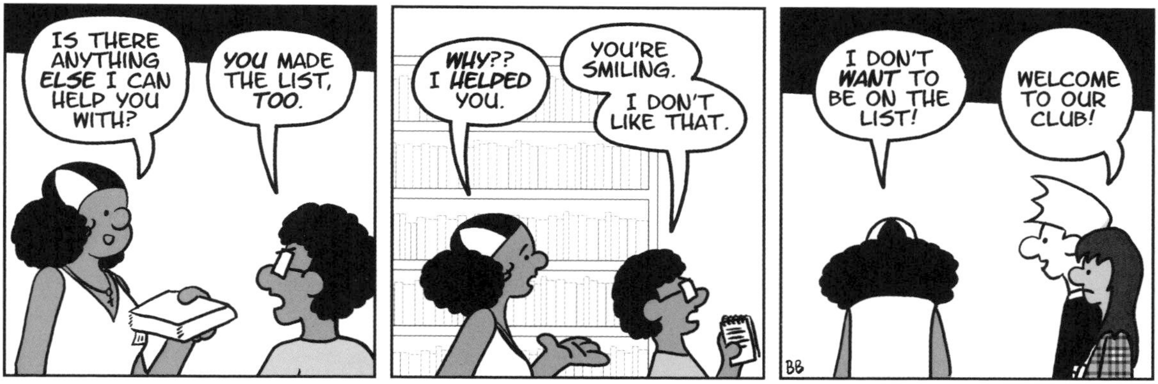
IS THERE ANYTHING ELSE I CAN HELP YOU WITH?
YOU MADE THE LIST, TOO.
WHY?? I HELPED YOU.
YOU'RE SMILING.
I DON'T LIKE THAT.
I DON'T WANT TO BE ON THE LIST!
WELCOME TO OUR CLUB!
BB

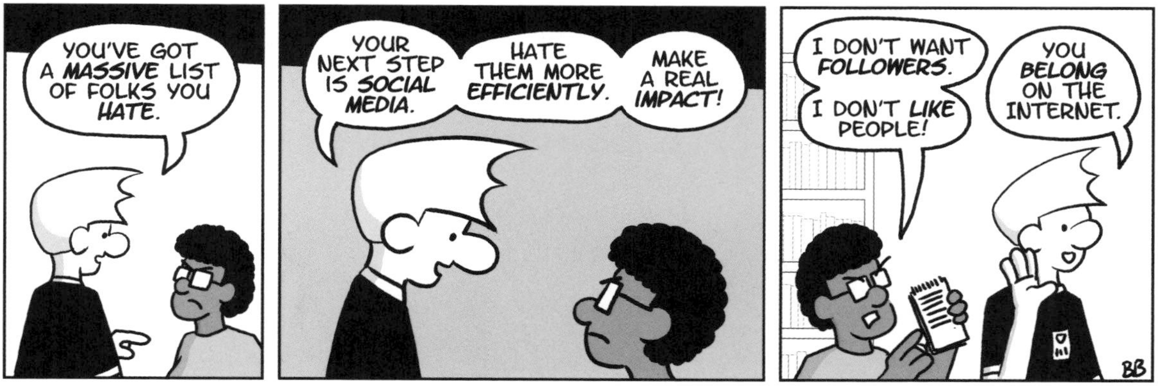
YOU'VE GOT A MASSIVE LIST OF FOLKS YOU HATE.
YOUR NEXT STEP IS SOCIAL MEDIA.
HATE THEM MORE EFFICIENTLY.
MAKE A REAL IMPACT!
I DON'T WANT FOLLOWERS.
I DON'T LIKE PEOPLE!
YOU BELONG ON THE INTERNET.
BB

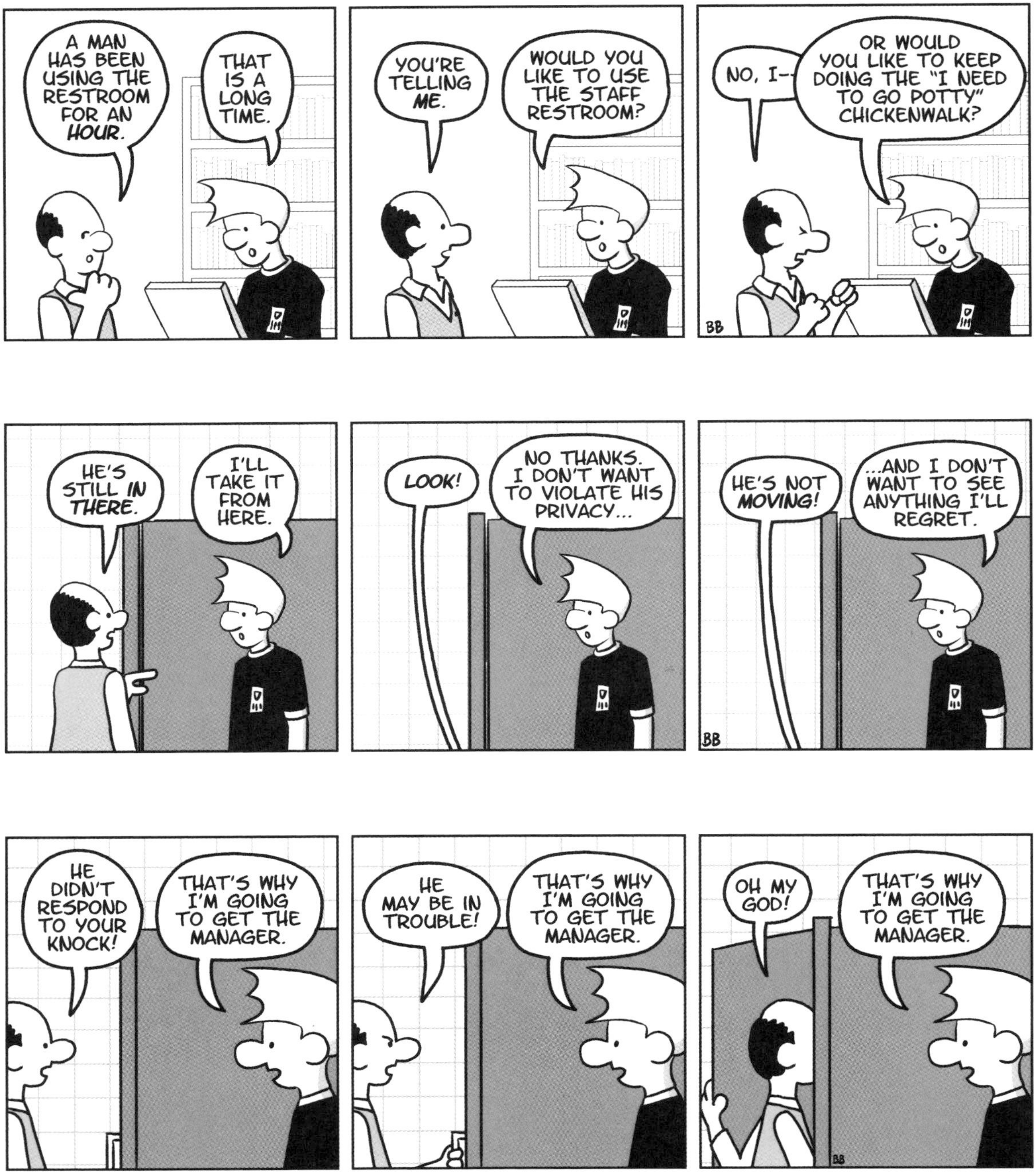
A MAN HAS BEEN USING THE RESTROOM FOR AN *HOUR*.
THAT IS A LONG TIME.
YOU'RE TELLING *ME*.
WOULD YOU LIKE TO USE THE STAFF RESTROOM?
NO, I--
OR WOULD YOU LIKE TO KEEP DOING THE "I NEED TO GO POTTY" CHICKENWALK?
BB
HE'S STILL *IN THERE*.
I'LL TAKE IT FROM HERE.
LOOK!
NO THANKS. I DON'T WANT TO VIOLATE HIS PRIVACY...
HE'S NOT *MOVING!*
...AND I DON'T WANT TO SEE ANYTHING I'LL REGRET.
BB
HE DIDN'T RESPOND TO YOUR KNOCK!
THAT'S WHY I'M GOING TO GET THE MANAGER.
HE MAY BE IN TROUBLE!
THAT'S WHY I'M GOING TO GET THE MANAGER.
OH MY GOD!
THAT'S WHY I'M GOING TO GET THE MANAGER.
BB

Bibliovores

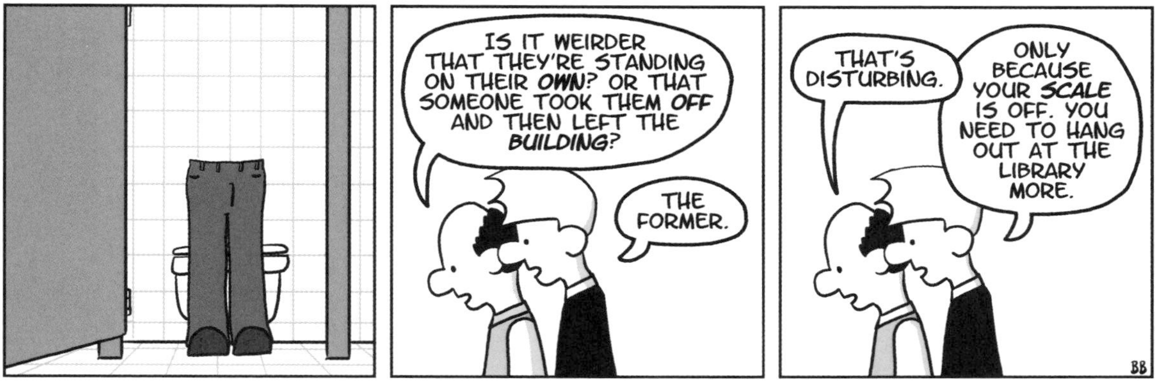
IS IT WEIRDER THAT THEY'RE STANDING ON THEIR *OWN*? OR THAT SOMEONE TOOK THEM *OFF* AND THEN LEFT THE *BUILDING*?
THE FORMER.
THAT'S DISTURBING.
ONLY BECAUSE YOUR *SCALE* IS OFF. YOU NEED TO HANG OUT AT THE LIBRARY MORE.
BB

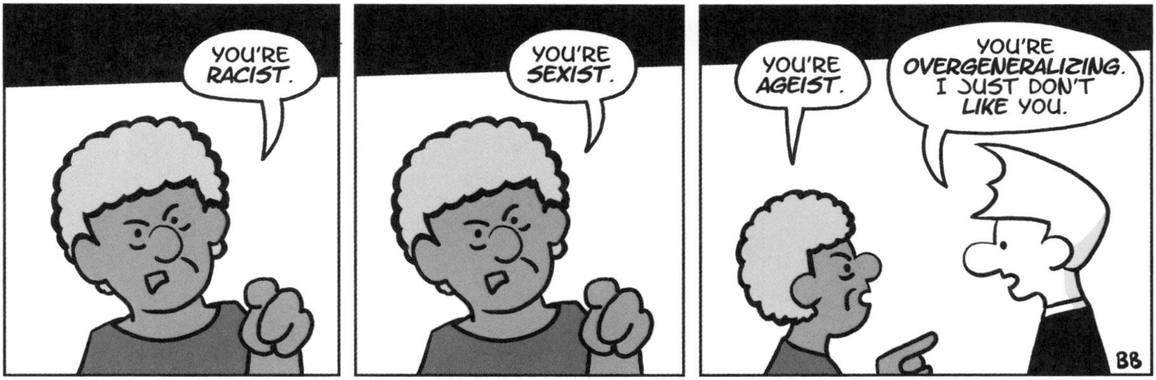
YOU'RE *RACIST*.
YOU'RE *SEXIST*.
YOU'RE *AGEIST*.
YOU'RE *OVERGENERALIZING*. I JUST DON'T *LIKE* YOU.
BB

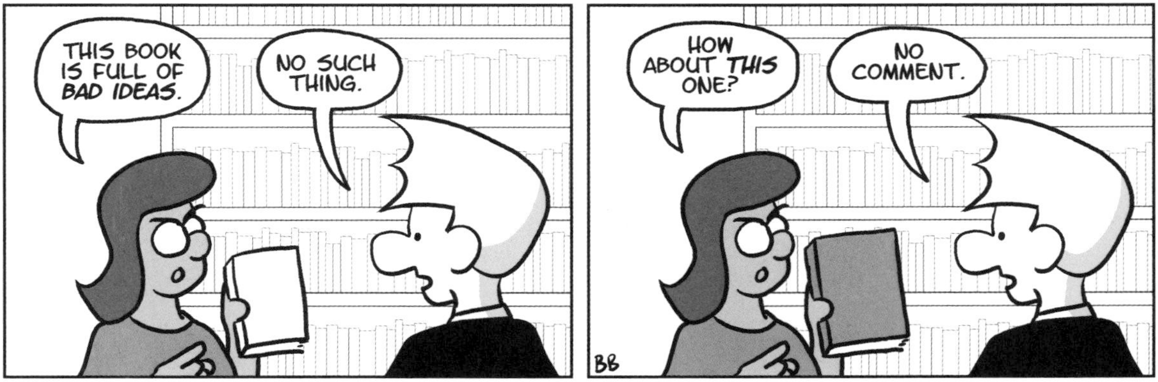
THIS BOOK IS FULL OF *BAD IDEAS*.
NO SUCH THING.
BB
HOW ABOUT *THIS* ONE?
NO COMMENT.

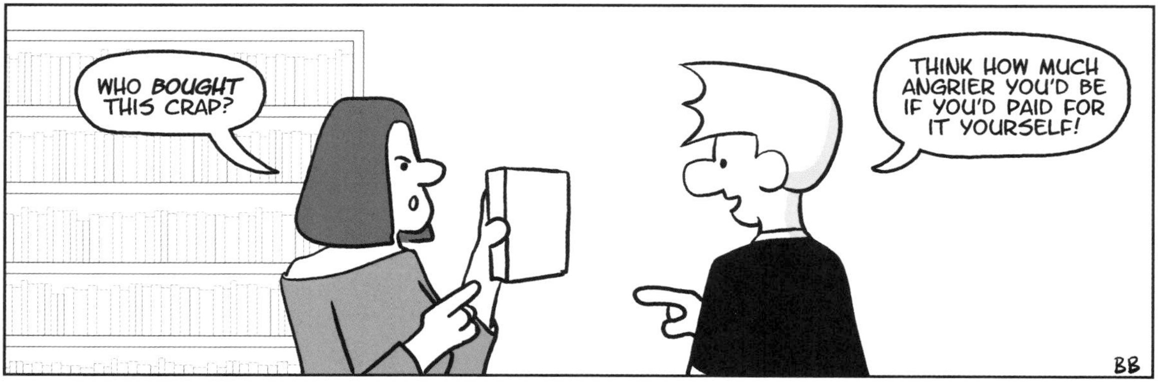
WHO BOUGHT THIS CRAP?
THINK HOW MUCH ANGRIER YOU'D BE IF YOU'D PAID FOR IT YOURSELF!
BB

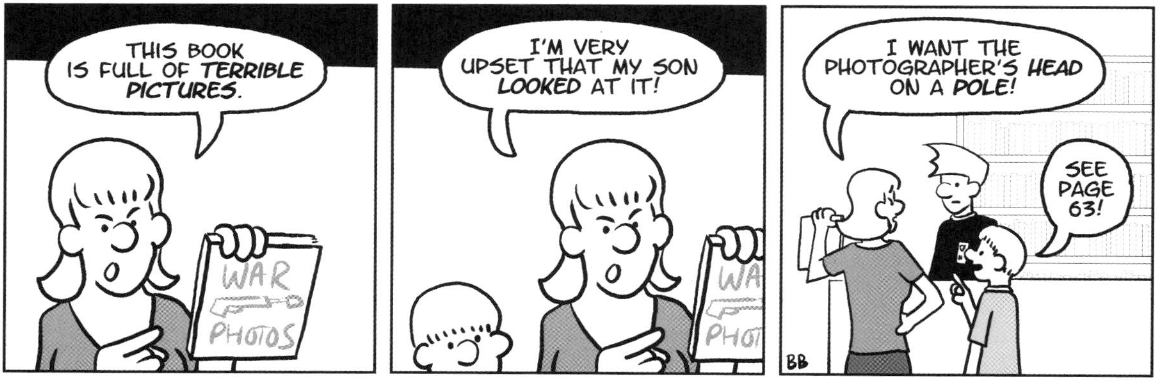
THIS BOOK IS FULL OF TERRIBLE PICTURES.
WAR PHOTOS
I'M VERY UPSET THAT MY SON LOOKED AT IT!
I WANT THE PHOTOGRAPHER'S HEAD ON A POLE!
SEE PAGE 63!
BB

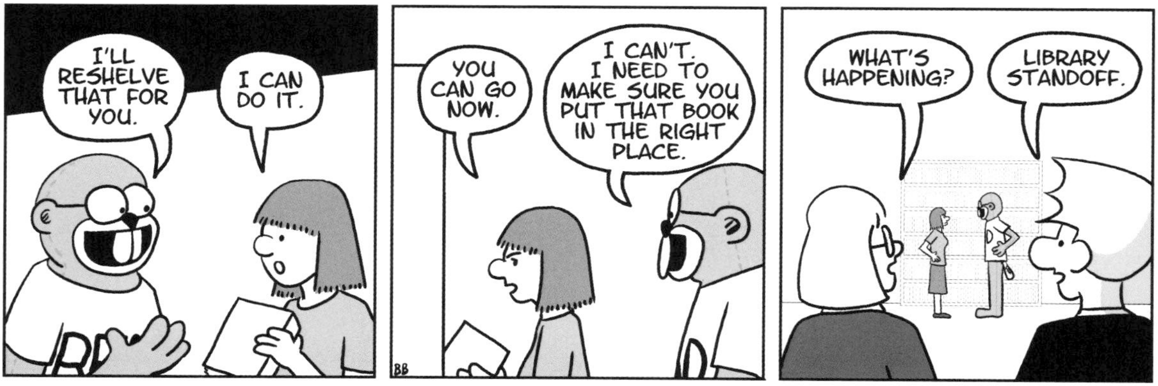
I'LL RESHELVE THAT FOR YOU.
I CAN DO IT.
YOU CAN GO NOW.
I CAN'T. I NEED TO MAKE SURE YOU PUT THAT BOOK IN THE RIGHT PLACE.
BB
WHAT'S HAPPENING?
LIBRARY STANDOFF.

Bibliovores

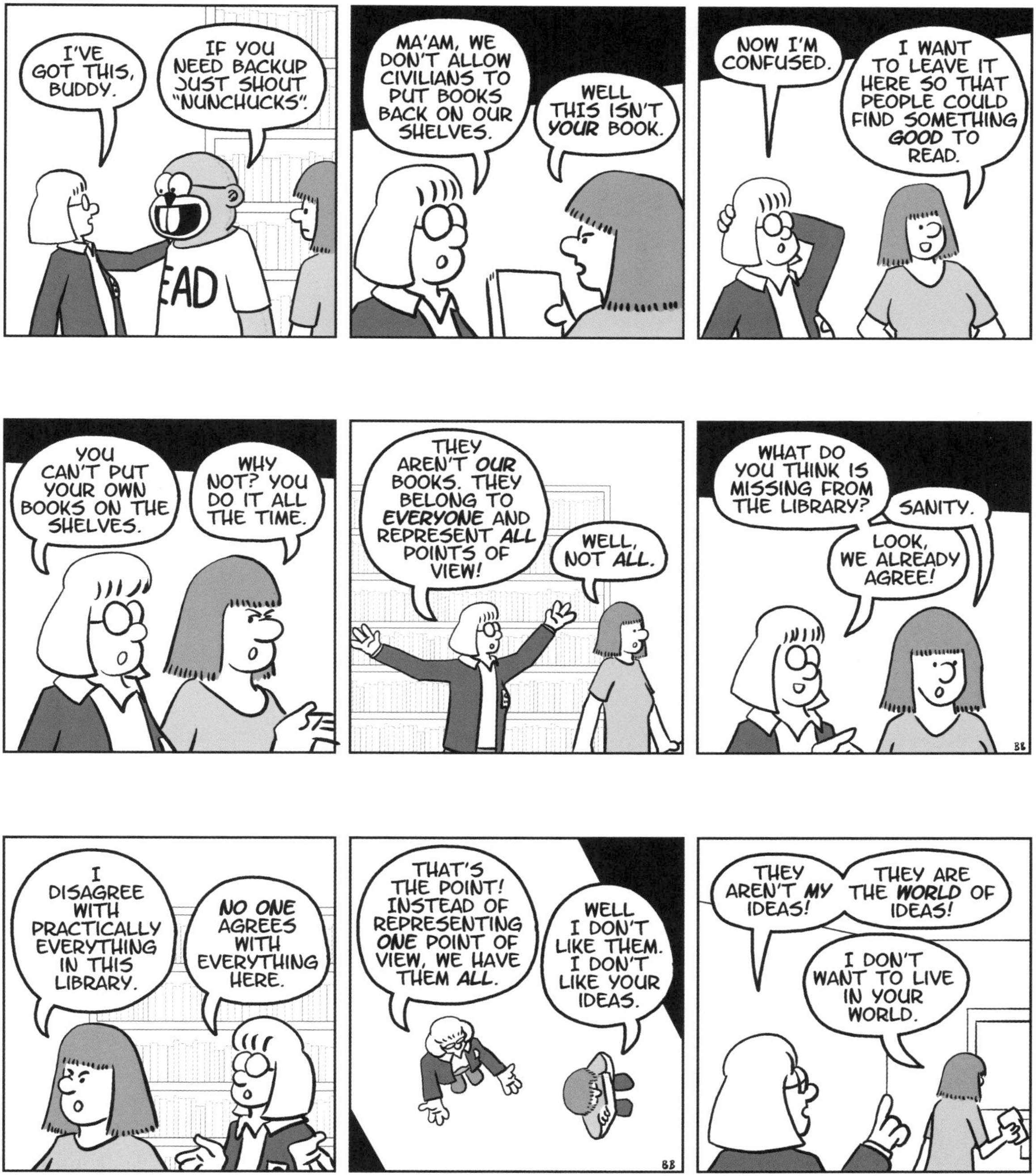

I'VE GOT THIS, BUDDY.
IF YOU NEED BACKUP JUST SHOUT "NUNCHUCKS".
EAD
MA'AM, WE DON'T ALLOW CIVILIANS TO PUT BOOKS BACK ON OUR SHELVES.
WELL THIS ISN'T *YOUR* BOOK.
NOW I'M CONFUSED.
I WANT TO LEAVE IT HERE SO THAT PEOPLE COULD FIND SOMETHING *GOOD* TO READ.
YOU CAN'T PUT YOUR OWN BOOKS ON THE SHELVES.
WHY NOT? YOU DO IT ALL THE TIME.
THEY AREN'T *OUR* BOOKS. THEY BELONG TO *EVERYONE* AND REPRESENT *ALL* POINTS OF VIEW!
WELL, NOT *ALL*.
WHAT DO YOU THINK IS MISSING FROM THE LIBRARY?
SANITY.
LOOK, WE ALREADY AGREE!
BB
I DISAGREE WITH PRACTICALLY EVERYTHING IN THIS LIBRARY.
NO ONE AGREES WITH EVERYTHING HERE.
THAT'S THE POINT! INSTEAD OF REPRESENTING *ONE* POINT OF VIEW, WE HAVE THEM *ALL*.
WELL I DON'T LIKE THEM. I DON'T LIKE YOUR IDEAS.
BB
THEY AREN'T *MY* IDEAS!
THEY ARE THE *WORLD* OF IDEAS!
I DON'T WANT TO LIVE IN YOUR WORLD.

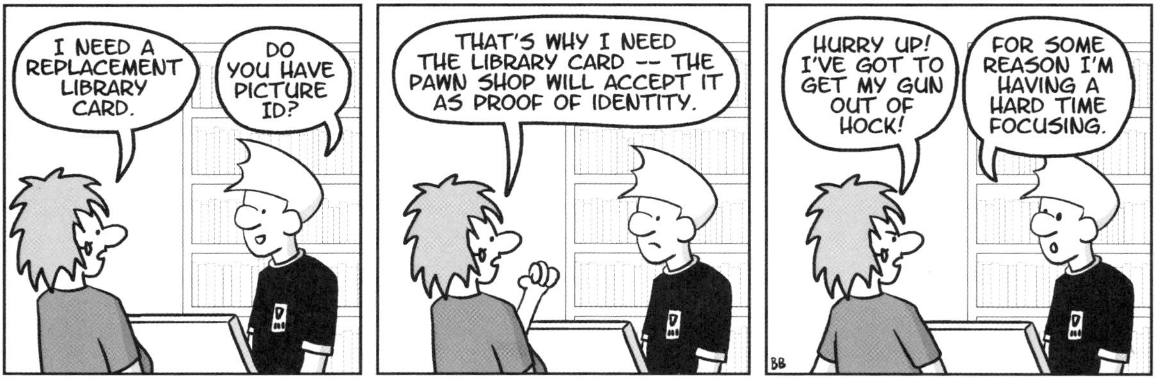
I NEED A REPLACEMENT LIBRARY CARD.
DO YOU HAVE PICTURE ID?
THAT'S WHY I NEED THE LIBRARY CARD -- THE PAWN SHOP WILL ACCEPT IT AS PROOF OF IDENTITY.
HURRY UP! I'VE GOT TO GET MY GUN OUT OF HOCK!
FOR SOME REASON I'M HAVING A HARD TIME FOCUSING.
BB

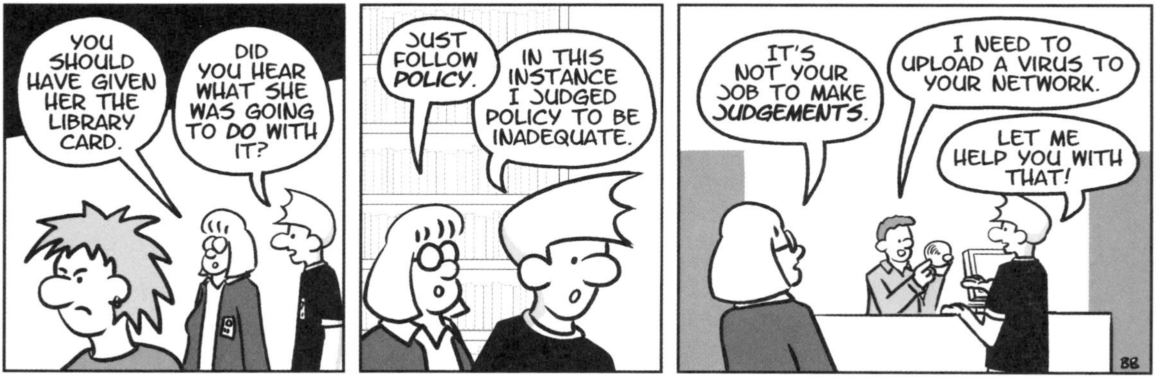
YOU SHOULD HAVE GIVEN HER THE LIBRARY CARD.
DID YOU HEAR WHAT SHE WAS GOING TO *DO* WITH IT?
JUST FOLLOW ***POLICY***.
IN THIS INSTANCE I JUDGED POLICY TO BE INADEQUATE.
IT'S NOT YOUR JOB TO MAKE ***JUDGEMENTS***.
I NEED TO UPLOAD A VIRUS TO YOUR NETWORK.
LET ME HELP YOU WITH THAT!
BB

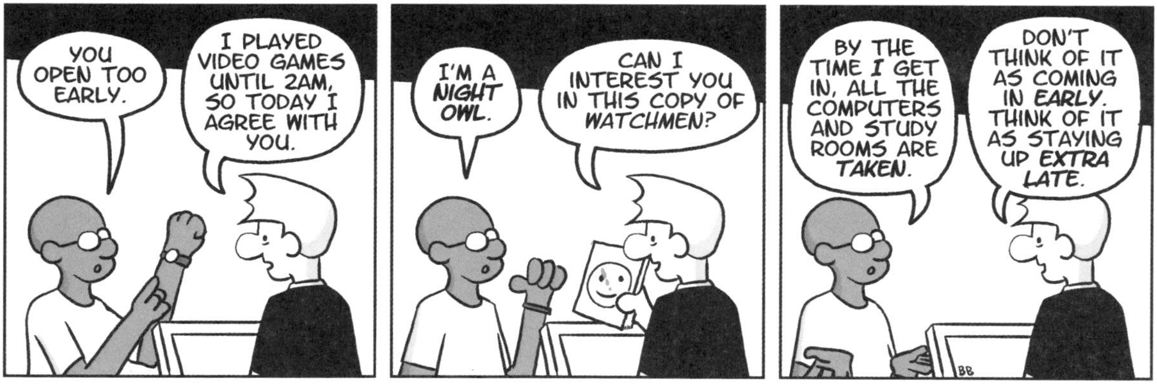
YOU OPEN TOO EARLY.
I PLAYED VIDEO GAMES UNTIL 2AM, SO TODAY I AGREE WITH YOU.
I'M A ***NIGHT OWL***.
CAN I INTEREST YOU IN THIS COPY OF *WATCHMEN*?
BY THE TIME *I* GET IN, ALL THE COMPUTERS AND STUDY ROOMS ARE ***TAKEN***.
DON'T THINK OF IT AS COMING IN ***EARLY***. THINK OF IT AS STAYING UP ***EXTRA LATE***.
BB

Bibliovores

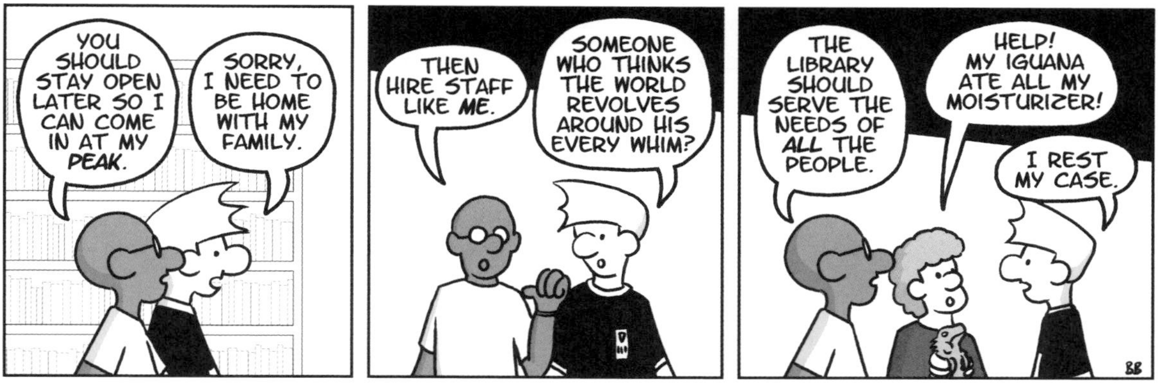
YOU SHOULD STAY OPEN LATER SO I CAN COME IN AT MY *PEAK*.
SORRY, I NEED TO BE HOME WITH MY FAMILY.
THEN HIRE STAFF LIKE *ME*.
SOMEONE WHO THINKS THE WORLD REVOLVES AROUND HIS EVERY WHIM?
THE LIBRARY SHOULD SERVE THE NEEDS OF *ALL* THE PEOPLE.
HELP! MY IGUANA ATE ALL MY MOISTURIZER!
I REST MY CASE.
BB

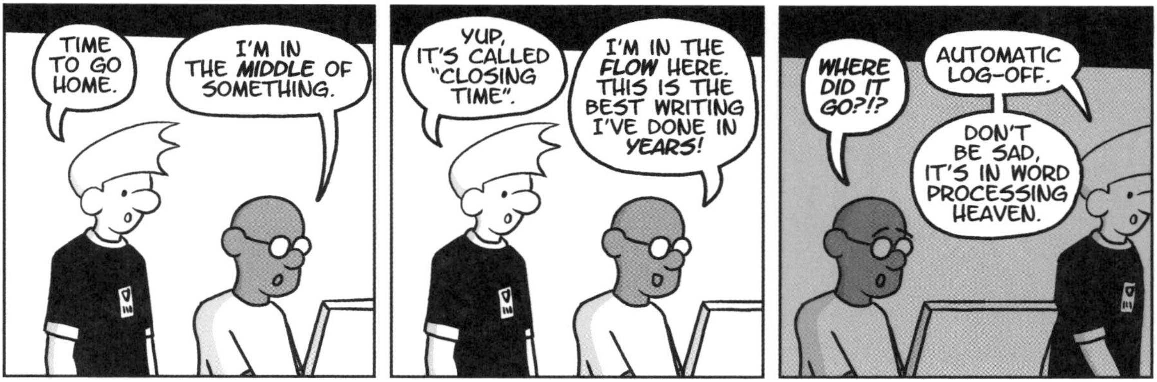
TIME TO GO HOME.
I'M IN THE *MIDDLE* OF SOMETHING.
YUP, IT'S CALLED "CLOSING TIME".
I'M IN THE *FLOW* HERE. THIS IS THE BEST WRITING I'VE DONE IN *YEARS*!
WHERE DID IT GO?!?
AUTOMATIC LOG-OFF.
DON'T BE SAD, IT'S IN WORD PROCESSING HEAVEN.

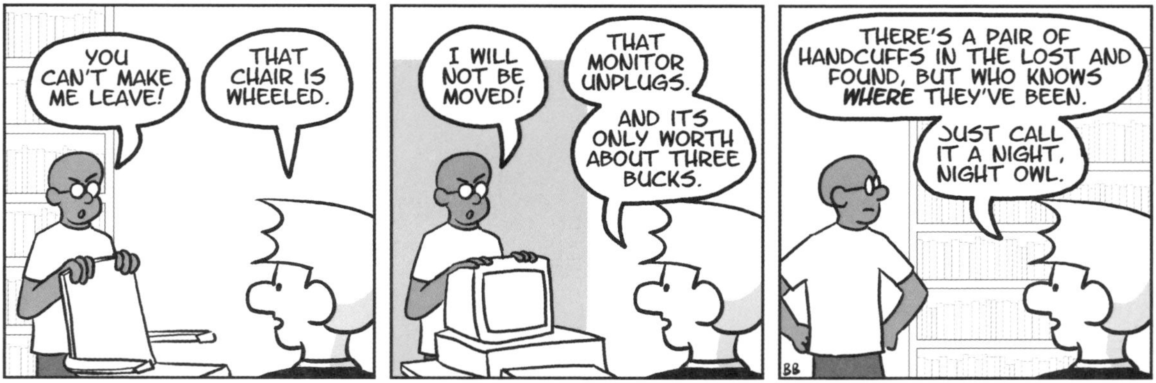
YOU CAN'T MAKE ME LEAVE!
THAT CHAIR IS WHEELED.
I WILL NOT BE MOVED!
THAT MONITOR UNPLUGS.
AND ITS ONLY WORTH ABOUT THREE BUCKS.
THERE'S A PAIR OF HANDCUFFS IN THE LOST AND FOUND, BUT WHO KNOWS *WHERE* THEY'VE BEEN.
JUST CALL IT A NIGHT, NIGHT OWL.
BB

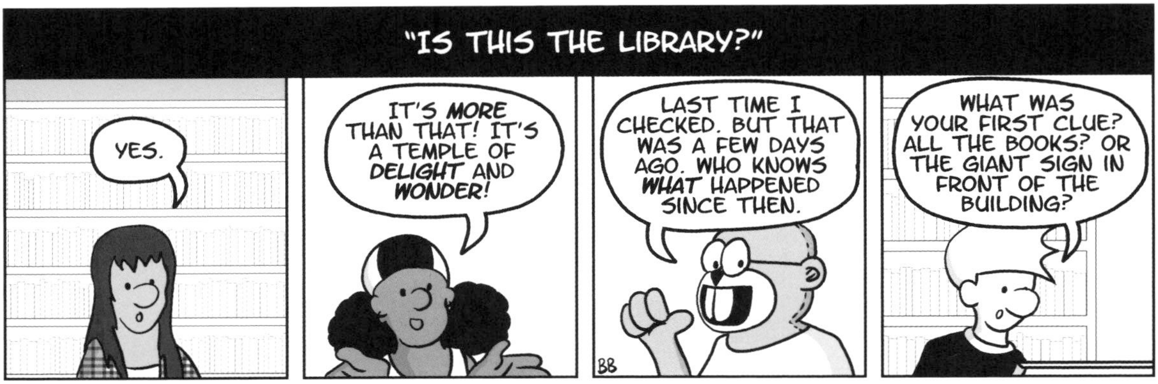
"IS THIS THE LIBRARY?"
YES.
IT'S MORE THAN THAT! IT'S A TEMPLE OF DELIGHT AND WONDER!
LAST TIME I CHECKED. BUT THAT WAS A FEW DAYS AGO. WHO KNOWS WHAT HAPPENED SINCE THEN.
BB
WHAT WAS YOUR FIRST CLUE? ALL THE BOOKS? OR THE GIANT SIGN IN FRONT OF THE BUILDING?

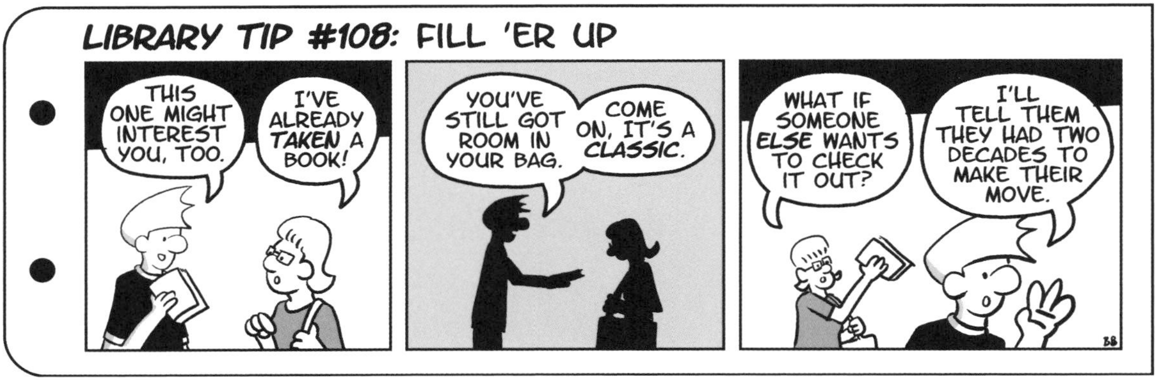
LIBRARY TIP #108: FILL 'ER UP
THIS ONE MIGHT INTEREST YOU, TOO.
I'VE ALREADY TAKEN A BOOK!
YOU'VE STILL GOT ROOM IN YOUR BAG.
COME ON, IT'S A CLASSIC.
WHAT IF SOMEONE ELSE WANTS TO CHECK IT OUT?
I'LL TELL THEM THEY HAD TWO DECADES TO MAKE THEIR MOVE.
BB

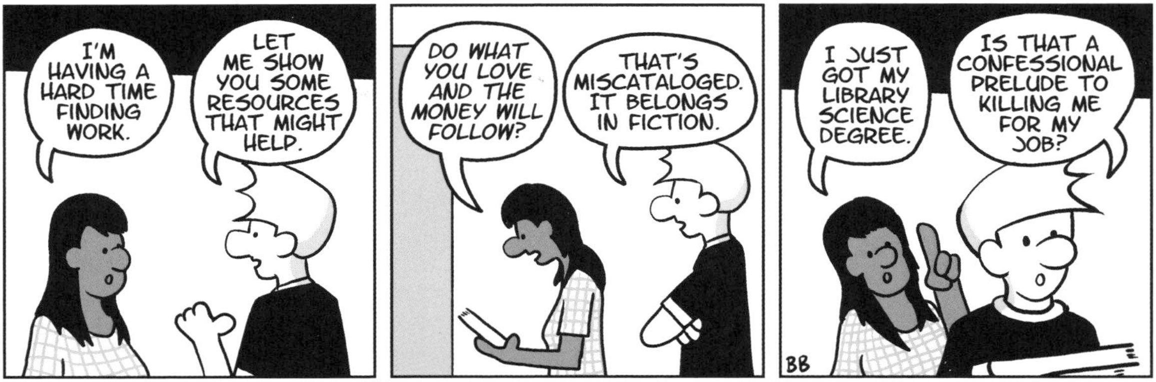
I'M HAVING A HARD TIME FINDING WORK.
LET ME SHOW YOU SOME RESOURCES THAT MIGHT HELP.
DO WHAT YOU LOVE AND THE MONEY WILL FOLLOW?
THAT'S MISCATALOGED. IT BELONGS IN FICTION.
I JUST GOT MY LIBRARY SCIENCE DEGREE.
IS THAT A CONFESSIONAL PRELUDE TO KILLING ME FOR MY JOB?
BB

Bibliovores

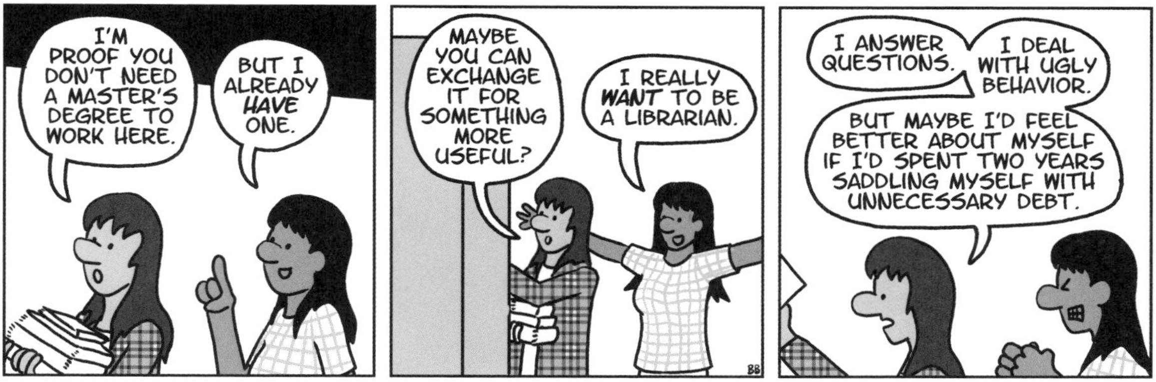
I'M PROOF YOU DON'T NEED A MASTER'S DEGREE TO WORK HERE.
BUT I ALREADY *HAVE* ONE.
MAYBE YOU CAN EXCHANGE IT FOR SOMETHING MORE USEFUL?
I REALLY *WANT* TO BE A LIBRARIAN.
I ANSWER QUESTIONS.
I DEAL WITH UGLY BEHAVIOR.
BUT MAYBE I'D FEEL BETTER ABOUT MYSELF IF I'D SPENT TWO YEARS SADDLING MYSELF WITH UNNECESSARY DEBT.
BB

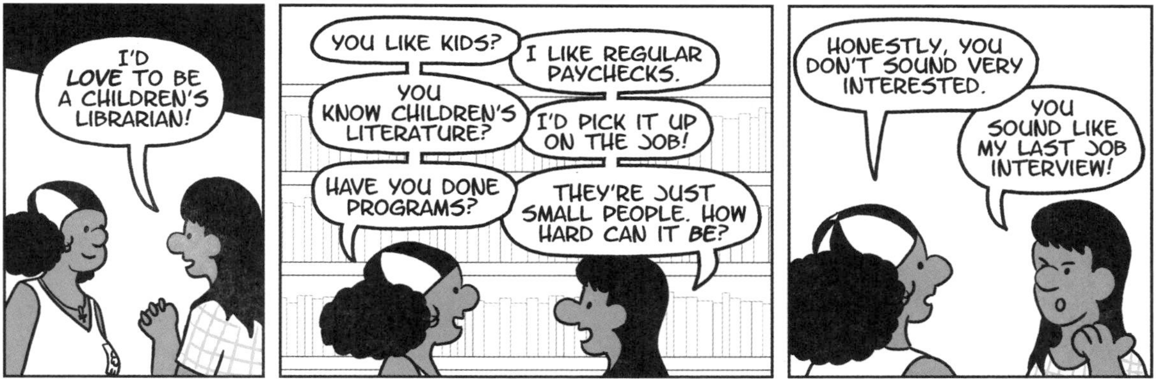
I'D *LOVE* TO BE A CHILDREN'S LIBRARIAN!
YOU LIKE KIDS?
I LIKE REGULAR PAYCHECKS.
YOU KNOW CHILDREN'S LITERATURE?
I'D PICK IT UP ON THE JOB!
HAVE YOU DONE PROGRAMS?
THEY'RE JUST SMALL PEOPLE. HOW HARD CAN IT *BE*?
HONESTLY, YOU DON'T SOUND VERY INTERESTED.
YOU SOUND LIKE MY LAST JOB INTERVIEW!

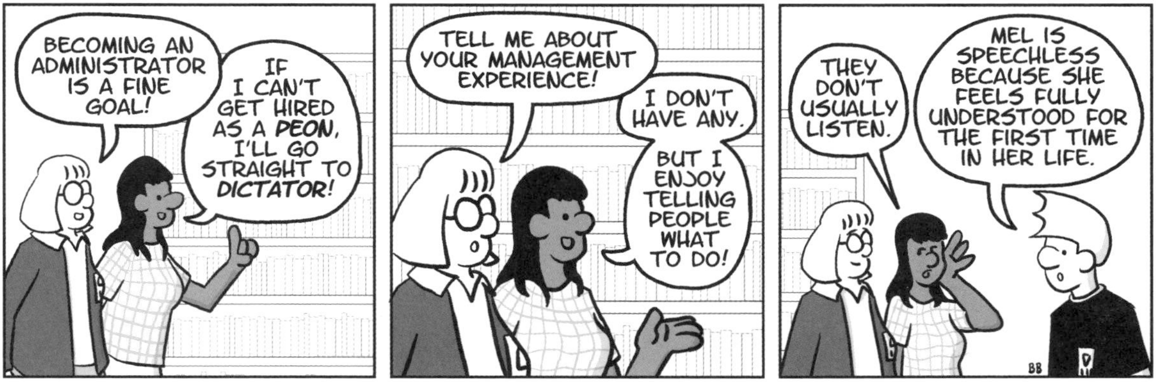
BECOMING AN ADMINISTRATOR IS A FINE GOAL!
IF I CAN'T GET HIRED AS A *PEON*, I'LL GO STRAIGHT TO *DICTATOR*!
TELL ME ABOUT YOUR MANAGEMENT EXPERIENCE!
I DON'T HAVE ANY.
BUT I ENJOY TELLING PEOPLE WHAT TO DO!
THEY DON'T USUALLY LISTEN.
MEL IS SPEECHLESS BECAUSE SHE FEELS FULLY UNDERSTOOD FOR THE FIRST TIME IN HER LIFE.
BB

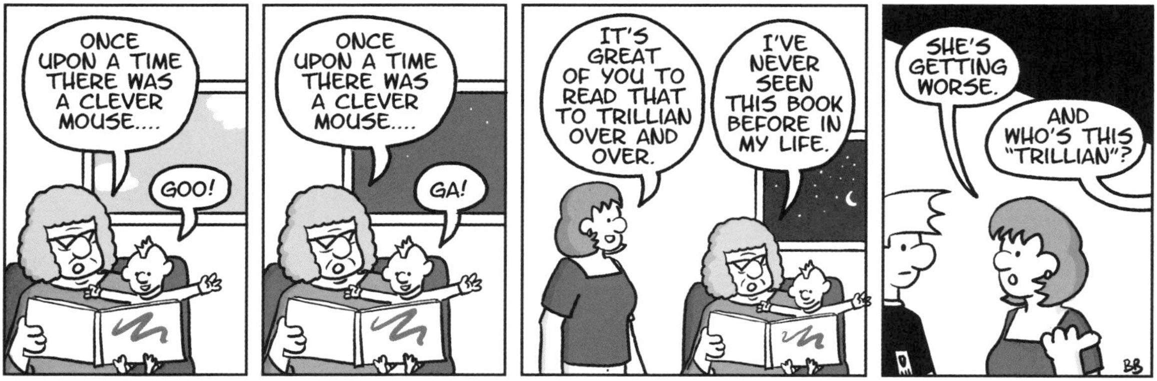
ONCE UPON A TIME THERE WAS A CLEVER MOUSE....
GOO!
ONCE UPON A TIME THERE WAS A CLEVER MOUSE....
GA!
IT'S GREAT OF YOU TO READ THAT TO TRILLIAN OVER AND OVER.
I'VE NEVER SEEN THIS BOOK BEFORE IN MY LIFE.
SHE'S GETTING WORSE.
AND WHO'S THIS "TRILLIAN"?
BB

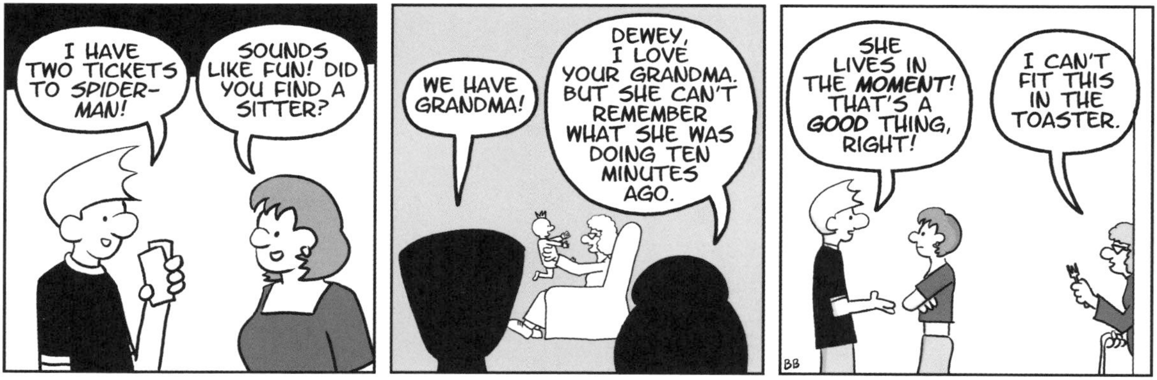
I HAVE TWO TICKETS TO *SPIDER-MAN*!
SOUNDS LIKE FUN! DID YOU FIND A SITTER?
WE HAVE GRANDMA!
DEWEY, I LOVE YOUR GRANDMA. BUT SHE CAN'T REMEMBER WHAT SHE WAS DOING TEN MINUTES AGO.
SHE LIVES IN THE ***MOMENT***! THAT'S A ***GOOD*** THING, RIGHT!
I CAN'T FIT THIS IN THE TOASTER.
BB

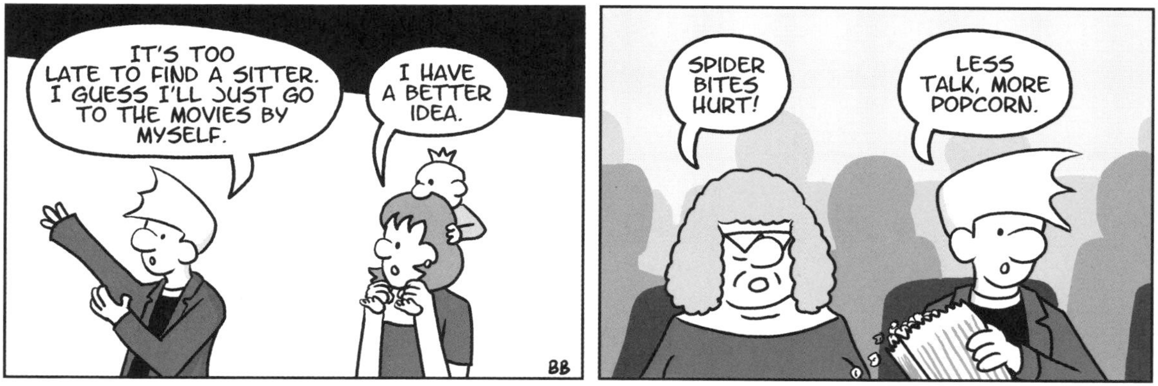
IT'S TOO LATE TO FIND A SITTER. I GUESS I'LL JUST GO TO THE MOVIES BY MYSELF.
I HAVE A BETTER IDEA.
BB
SPIDER BITES HURT!
LESS TALK, MORE POPCORN.

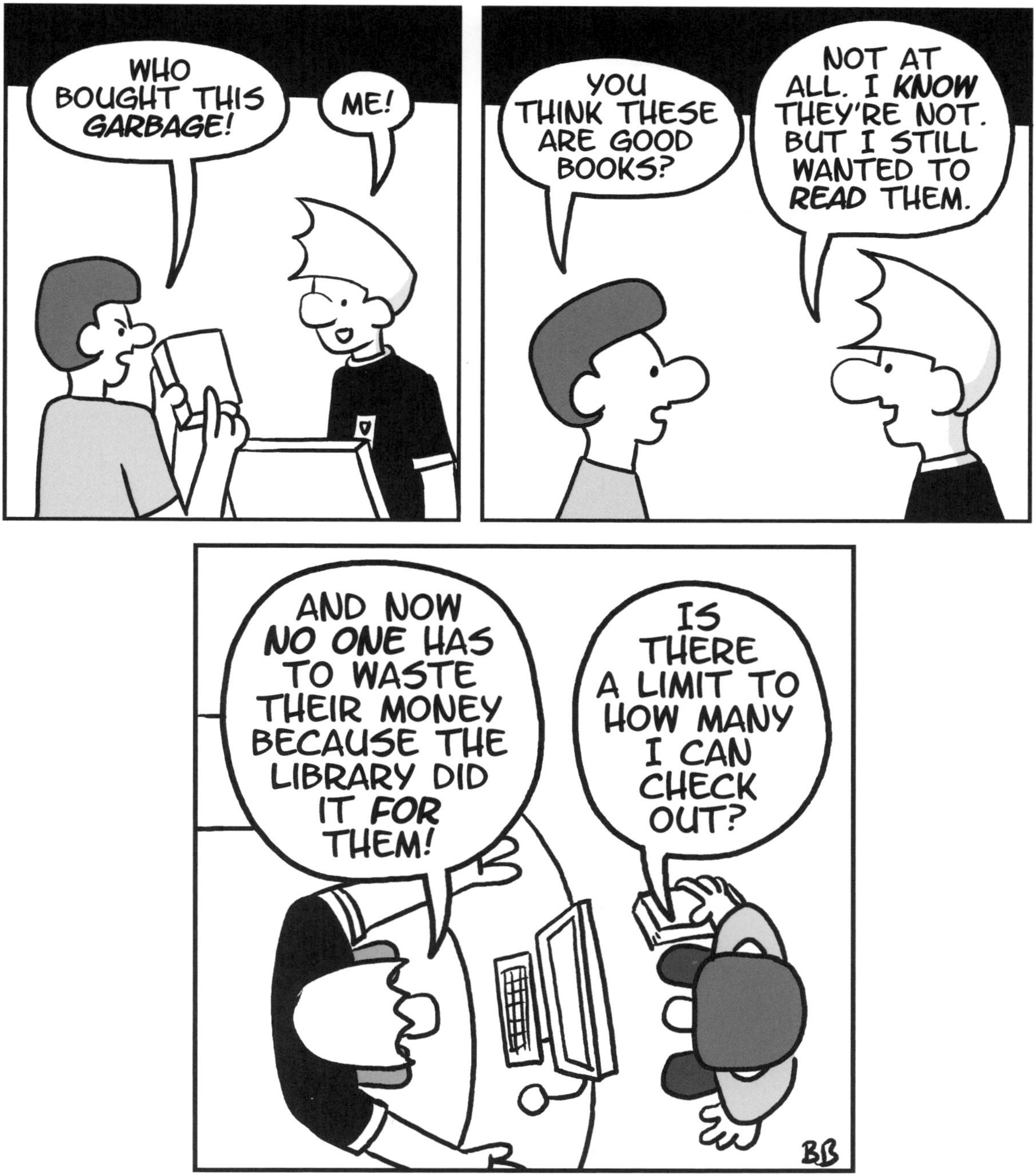
WHO BOUGHT THIS GARBAGE!
ME!
YOU THINK THESE ARE GOOD BOOKS?
NOT AT ALL. I KNOW THEY'RE NOT. BUT I STILL WANTED TO READ THEM.
AND NOW NO ONE HAS TO WASTE THEIR MONEY BECAUSE THE LIBRARY DID IT FOR THEM!
IS THERE A LIMIT TO HOW MANY I CAN CHECK OUT?
BB

UNSHELVED

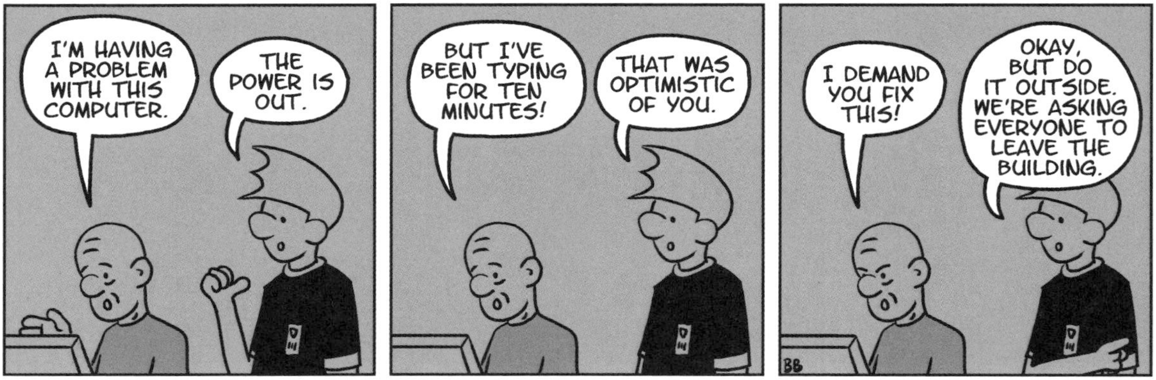

I'M HAVING A PROBLEM WITH THIS COMPUTER.
THE POWER IS OUT.
BUT I'VE BEEN TYPING FOR TEN MINUTES!
THAT WAS OPTIMISTIC OF YOU.
I DEMAND YOU FIX THIS!
OKAY, BUT DO IT OUTSIDE. WE'RE ASKING EVERYONE TO LEAVE THE BUILDING.
BB

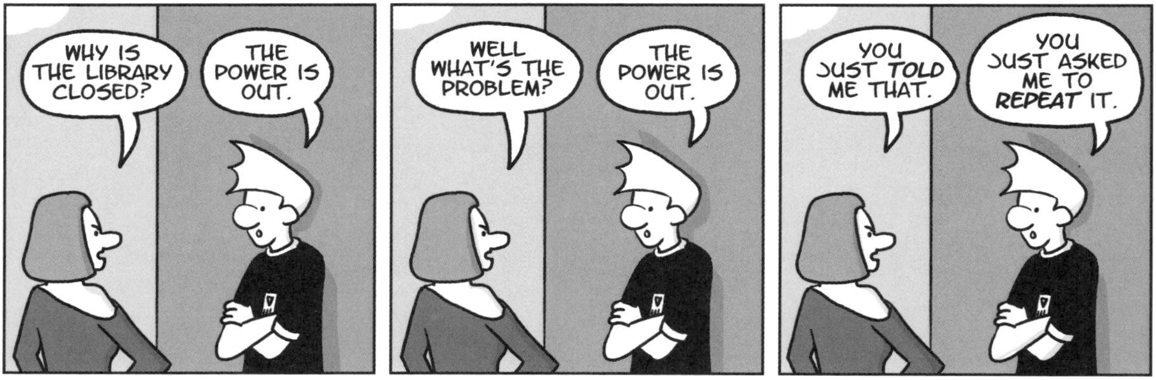

WHY IS THE LIBRARY CLOSED?
THE POWER IS OUT.
WELL WHAT'S THE PROBLEM?
THE POWER IS OUT.
YOU JUST **TOLD** ME THAT.
YOU JUST ASKED ME TO **REPEAT** IT.

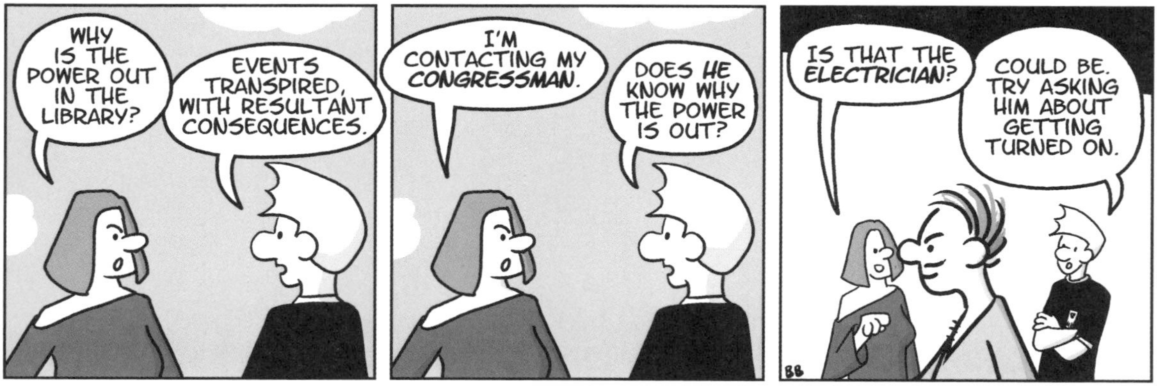

WHY IS THE POWER OUT IN THE LIBRARY?
EVENTS TRANSPIRED, WITH RESULTANT CONSEQUENCES.
I'M CONTACTING MY **CONGRESSMAN**.
DOES **HE** KNOW WHY THE POWER IS OUT?
IS THAT THE **ELECTRICIAN**?
COULD BE. TRY ASKING HIM ABOUT GETTING TURNED ON.
BB

Bibliovores

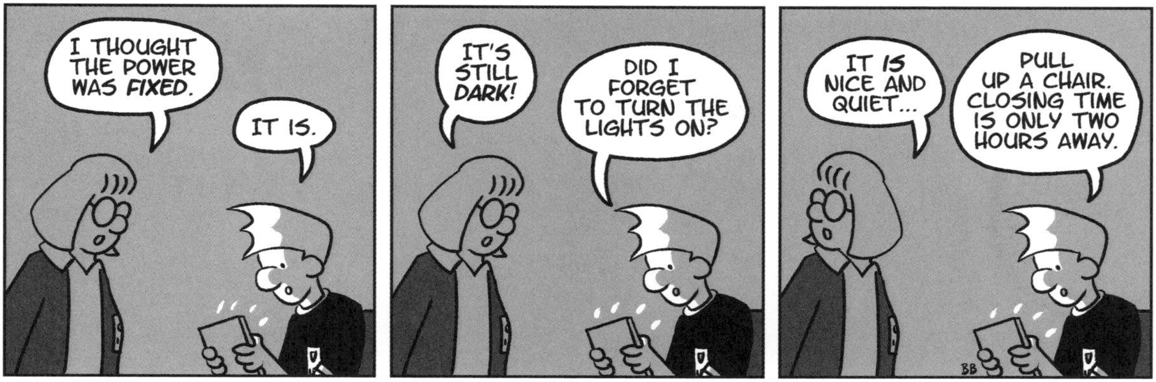
I THOUGHT THE POWER WAS FIXED.
IT IS.
IT'S STILL DARK!
DID I FORGET TO TURN THE LIGHTS ON?
IT IS NICE AND QUIET...
PULL UP A CHAIR. CLOSING TIME IS ONLY TWO HOURS AWAY.
BB

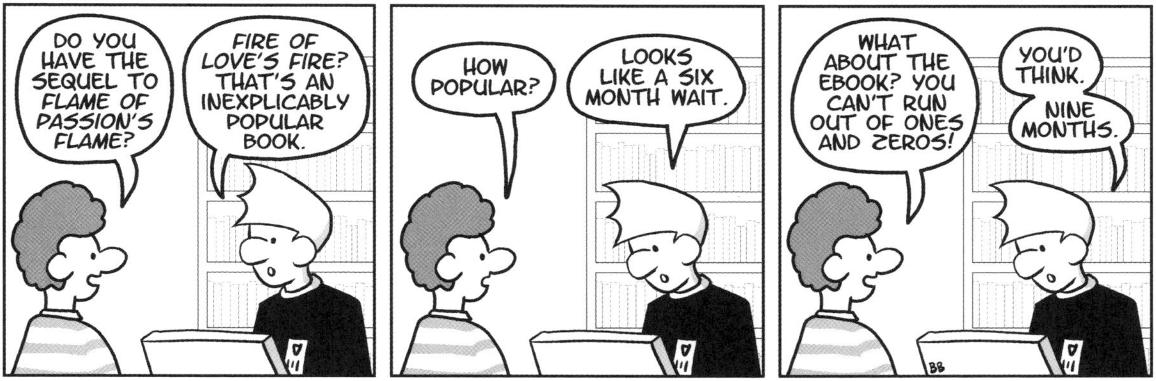
DO YOU HAVE THE SEQUEL TO FLAME OF PASSION'S FLAME?
FIRE OF LOVE'S FIRE? THAT'S AN INEXPLICABLY POPULAR BOOK.
HOW POPULAR?
LOOKS LIKE A SIX MONTH WAIT.
WHAT ABOUT THE EBOOK? YOU CAN'T RUN OUT OF ONES AND ZEROS!
YOU'D THINK.
NINE MONTHS.
BB

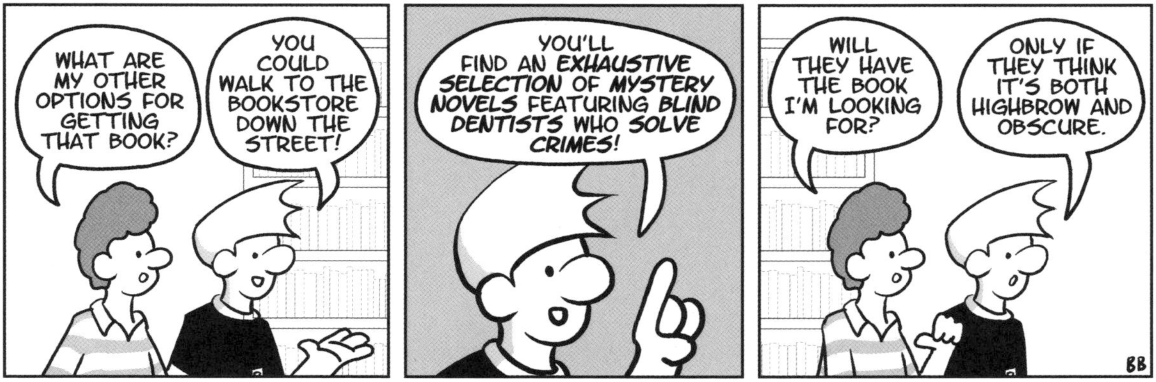
WHAT ARE MY OTHER OPTIONS FOR GETTING THAT BOOK?
YOU COULD WALK TO THE BOOKSTORE DOWN THE STREET!
YOU'LL FIND AN EXHAUSTIVE SELECTION OF MYSTERY NOVELS FEATURING BLIND DENTISTS WHO SOLVE CRIMES!
WILL THEY HAVE THE BOOK I'M LOOKING FOR?
ONLY IF THEY THINK IT'S BOTH HIGHBROW AND OBSCURE.
BB

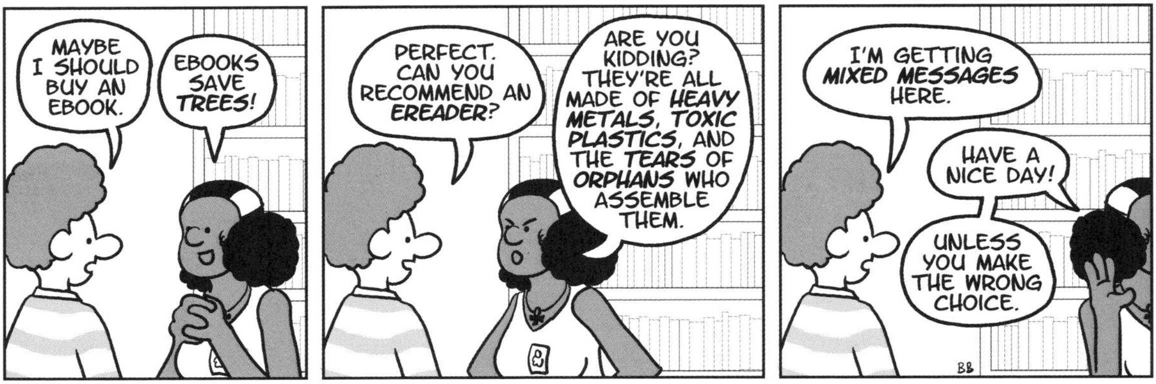
MAYBE I SHOULD BUY AN EBOOK.
EBOOKS SAVE TREES!
PERFECT. CAN YOU RECOMMEND AN EREADER?
ARE YOU KIDDING? THEY'RE ALL MADE OF HEAVY METALS, TOXIC PLASTICS, AND THE TEARS OF ORPHANS WHO ASSEMBLE THEM.
I'M GETTING MIXED MESSAGES HERE.
HAVE A NICE DAY!
UNLESS YOU MAKE THE WRONG CHOICE.
BB

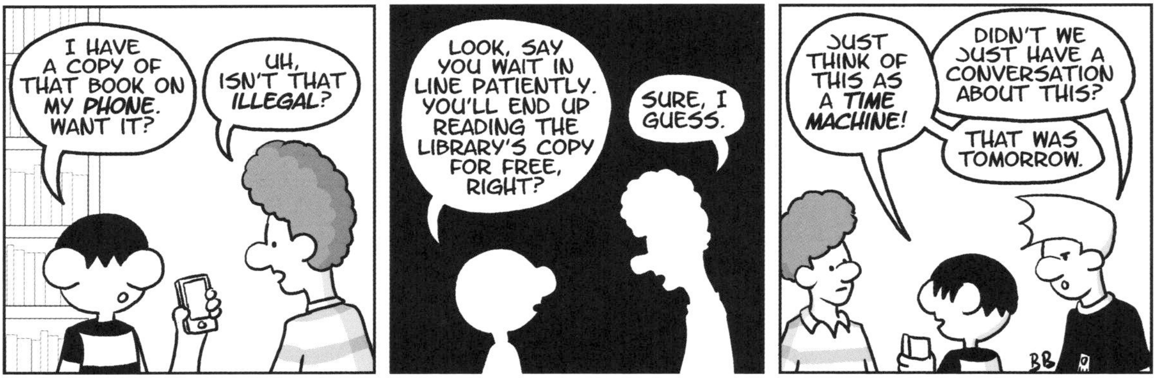
I HAVE A COPY OF THAT BOOK ON MY PHONE. WANT IT?
UH, ISN'T THAT ILLEGAL?
LOOK, SAY YOU WAIT IN LINE PATIENTLY. YOU'LL END UP READING THE LIBRARY'S COPY FOR FREE, RIGHT?
SURE, I GUESS.
JUST THINK OF THIS AS A TIME MACHINE!
DIDN'T WE JUST HAVE A CONVERSATION ABOUT THIS?
THAT WAS TOMORROW.
BB

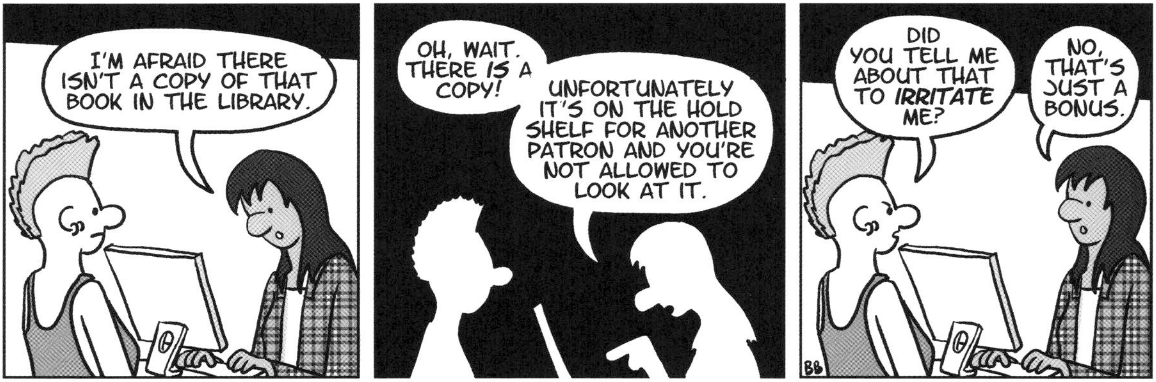
I'M AFRAID THERE ISN'T A COPY OF THAT BOOK IN THE LIBRARY.
OH, WAIT. THERE IS A COPY!
UNFORTUNATELY IT'S ON THE HOLD SHELF FOR ANOTHER PATRON AND YOU'RE NOT ALLOWED TO LOOK AT IT.
DID YOU TELL ME ABOUT THAT TO IRRITATE ME?
NO, THAT'S JUST A BONUS.
BB

Bibliovores

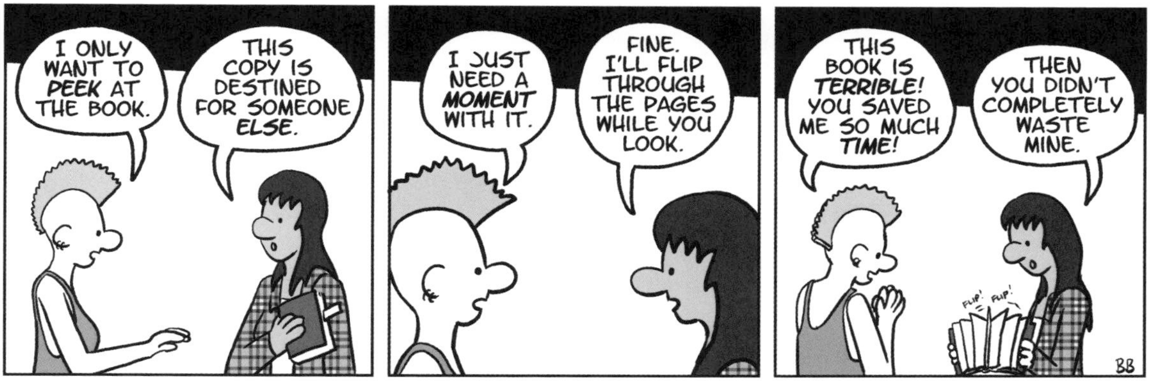
I ONLY WANT TO PEEK AT THE BOOK.
THIS COPY IS DESTINED FOR SOMEONE ELSE.
I JUST NEED A MOMENT WITH IT.
FINE. I'LL FLIP THROUGH THE PAGES WHILE YOU LOOK.
THIS BOOK IS TERRIBLE! YOU SAVED ME SO MUCH TIME!
THEN YOU DIDN'T COMPLETELY WASTE MINE.
FLIP! FLIP!
BB

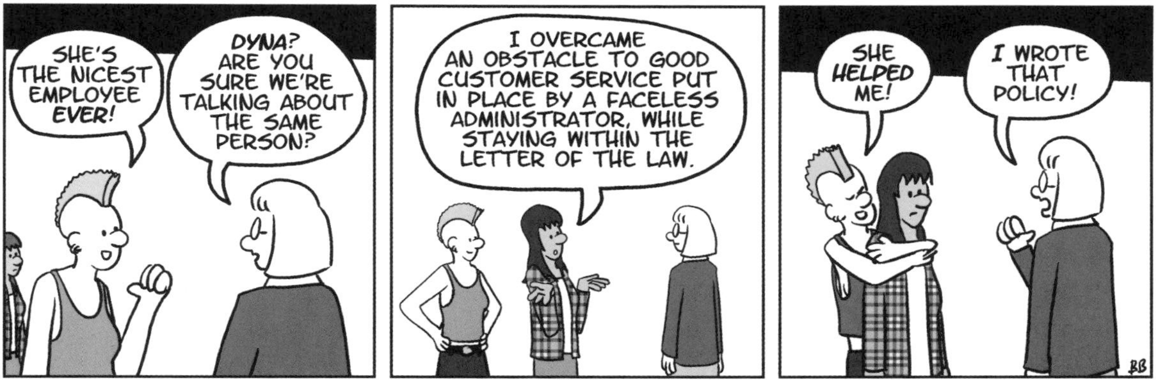
SHE'S THE NICEST EMPLOYEE EVER!
DYNA? ARE YOU SURE WE'RE TALKING ABOUT THE SAME PERSON?
I OVERCAME AN OBSTACLE TO GOOD CUSTOMER SERVICE PUT IN PLACE BY A FACELESS ADMINISTRATOR, WHILE STAYING WITHIN THE LETTER OF THE LAW.
SHE HELPED ME!
I WROTE THAT POLICY!
BB

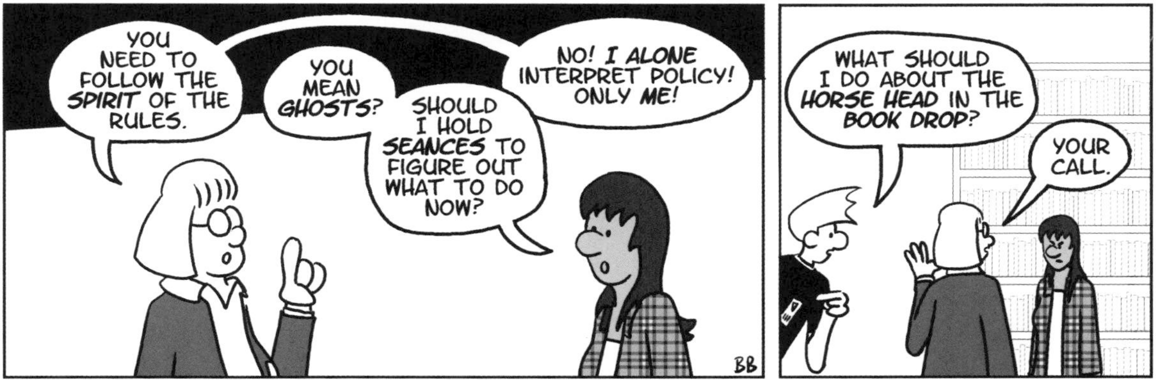
YOU NEED TO FOLLOW THE SPIRIT OF THE RULES.
YOU MEAN GHOSTS?
SHOULD I HOLD SEANCES TO FIGURE OUT WHAT TO DO NOW?
NO! I ALONE INTERPRET POLICY! ONLY ME!
BB
WHAT SHOULD I DO ABOUT THE HORSE HEAD IN THE BOOK DROP?
YOUR CALL.

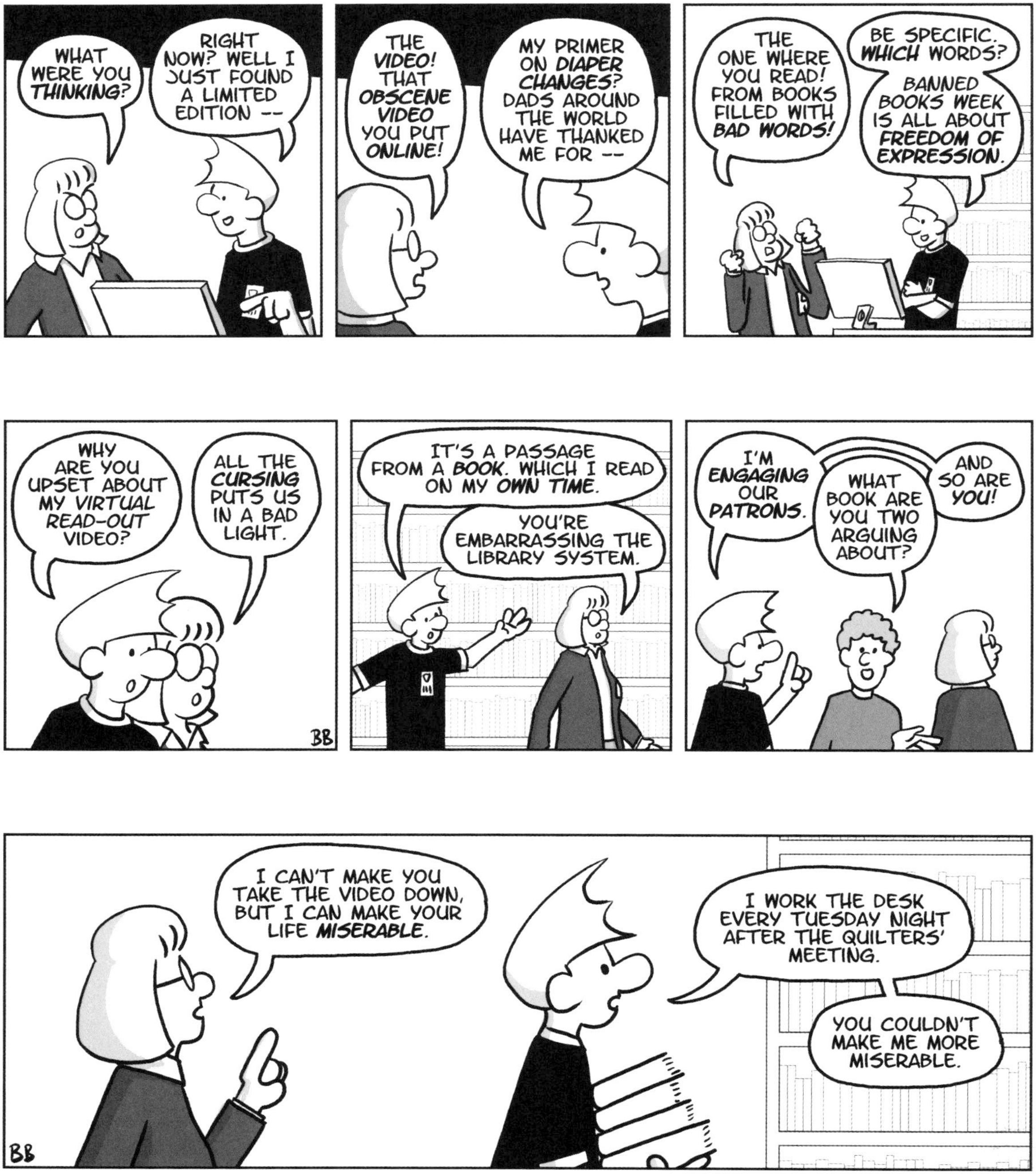
WHAT WERE YOU THINKING?
RIGHT NOW? WELL I JUST FOUND A LIMITED EDITION --
THE VIDEO! THAT OBSCENE VIDEO YOU PUT ONLINE!
MY PRIMER ON DIAPER CHANGES? DADS AROUND THE WORLD HAVE THANKED ME FOR --
THE ONE WHERE YOU READ! FROM BOOKS FILLED WITH BAD WORDS!
BE SPECIFIC. WHICH WORDS?
BANNED BOOKS WEEK IS ALL ABOUT FREEDOM OF EXPRESSION.
WHY ARE YOU UPSET ABOUT MY VIRTUAL READ-OUT VIDEO?
ALL THE CURSING PUTS US IN A BAD LIGHT.
BB
IT'S A PASSAGE FROM A BOOK. WHICH I READ ON MY OWN TIME.
YOU'RE EMBARRASSING THE LIBRARY SYSTEM.
I'M ENGAGING OUR PATRONS.
WHAT BOOK ARE YOU TWO ARGUING ABOUT?
AND SO ARE YOU!
I CAN'T MAKE YOU TAKE THE VIDEO DOWN, BUT I CAN MAKE YOUR LIFE MISERABLE.
I WORK THE DESK EVERY TUESDAY NIGHT AFTER THE QUILTERS' MEETING.
YOU COULDN'T MAKE ME MORE MISERABLE.
BB

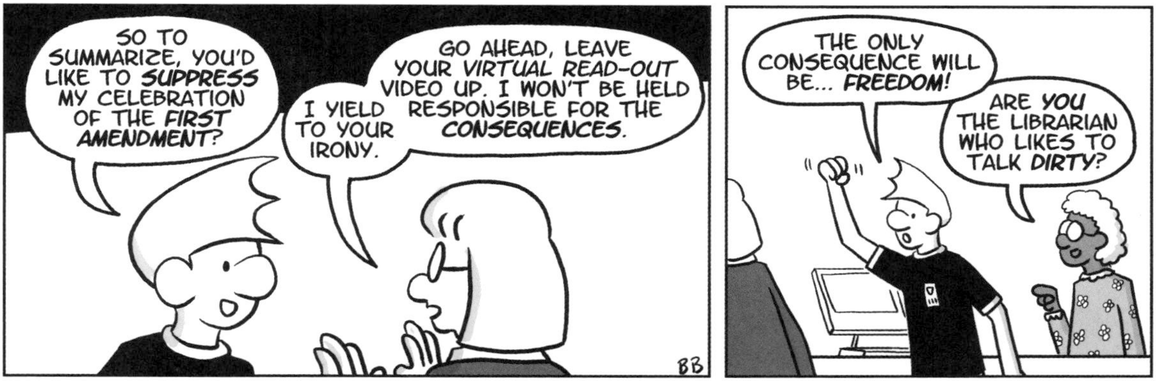
SO TO SUMMARIZE, YOU'D LIKE TO SUPPRESS MY CELEBRATION OF THE FIRST AMENDMENT?
I YIELD TO YOUR IRONY.
GO AHEAD, LEAVE YOUR VIRTUAL READ-OUT VIDEO UP. I WON'T BE HELD RESPONSIBLE FOR THE CONSEQUENCES.
BB
THE ONLY CONSEQUENCE WILL BE... FREEDOM!
ARE YOU THE LIBRARIAN WHO LIKES TO TALK DIRTY?

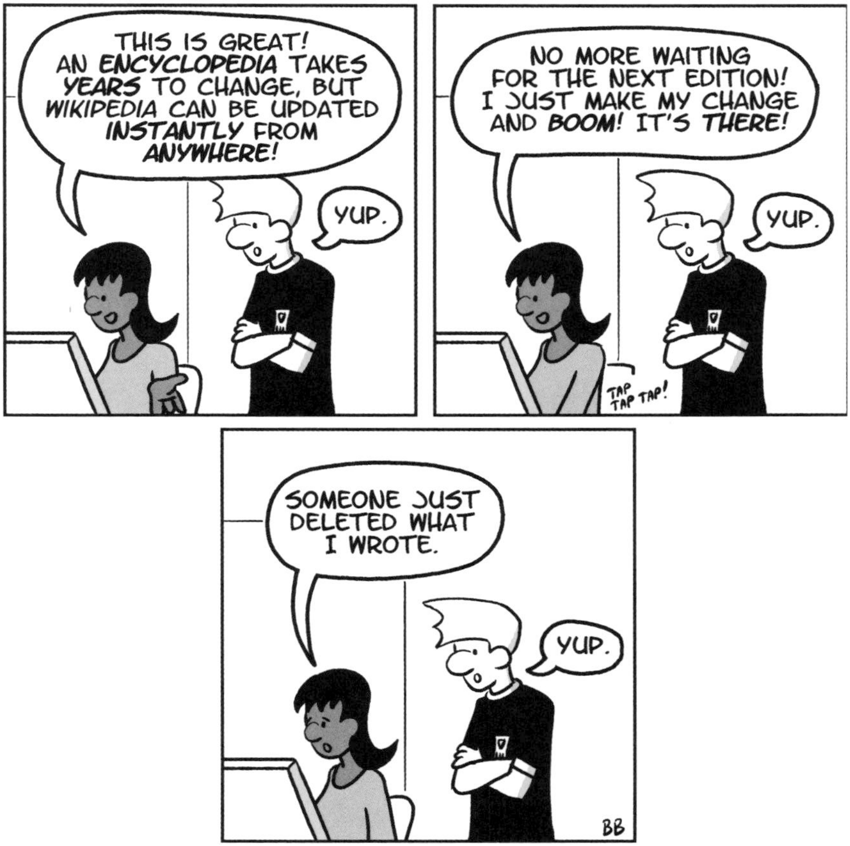
THIS IS GREAT! AN ENCYCLOPEDIA TAKES YEARS TO CHANGE, BUT WIKIPEDIA CAN BE UPDATED INSTANTLY FROM ANYWHERE!
YUP.
NO MORE WAITING FOR THE NEXT EDITION! I JUST MAKE MY CHANGE AND BOOM! IT'S THERE!
YUP.
TAP TAP TAP!
SOMEONE JUST DELETED WHAT I WROTE.
YUP.
BB

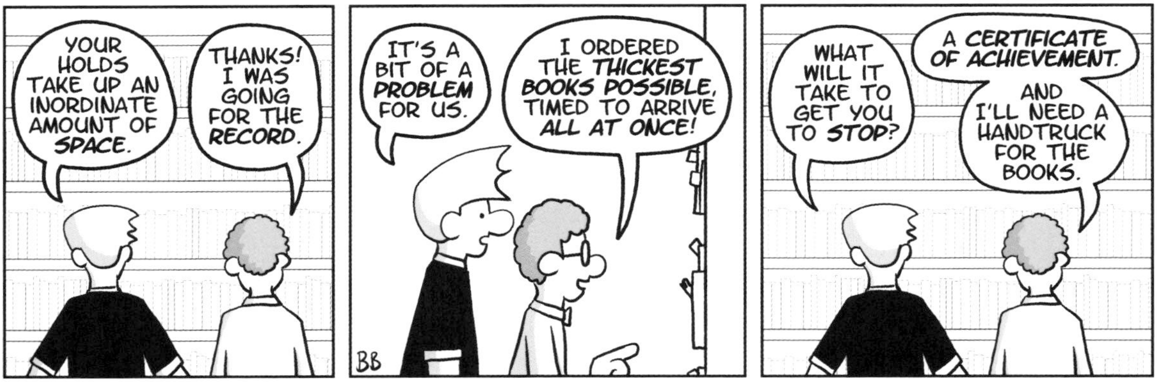
YOUR HOLDS TAKE UP AN INORDINATE AMOUNT OF SPACE.
THANKS! I WAS GOING FOR THE RECORD.
IT'S A BIT OF A PROBLEM FOR US.
I ORDERED THE THICKEST BOOKS POSSIBLE, TIMED TO ARRIVE ALL AT ONCE!
BB
WHAT WILL IT TAKE TO GET YOU TO STOP?
A CERTIFICATE OF ACHIEVEMENT.
AND I'LL NEED A HANDTRUCK FOR THE BOOKS.

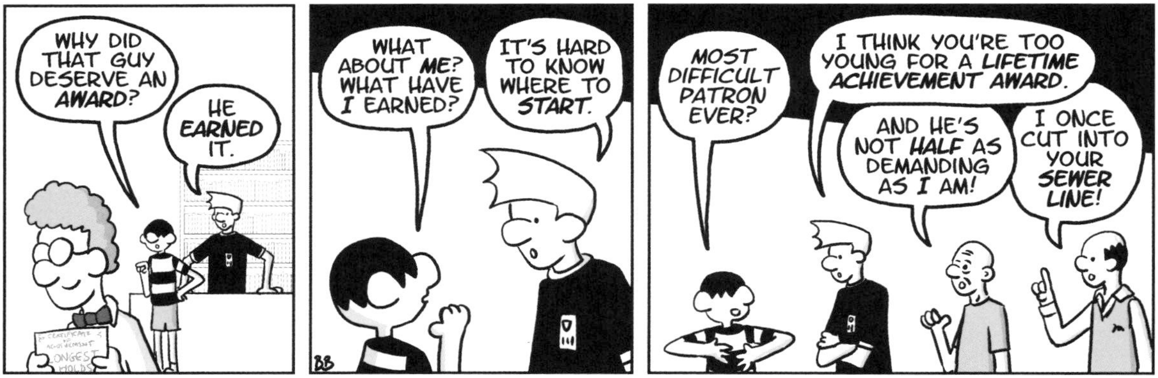
WHY DID THAT GUY DESERVE AN AWARD?
HE EARNED IT.
WHAT ABOUT ME? WHAT HAVE I EARNED?
IT'S HARD TO KNOW WHERE TO START.
BB
MOST DIFFICULT PATRON EVER?
I THINK YOU'RE TOO YOUNG FOR A LIFETIME ACHIEVEMENT AWARD.
AND HE'S NOT HALF AS DEMANDING AS I AM!
I ONCE CUT INTO YOUR SEWER LINE!

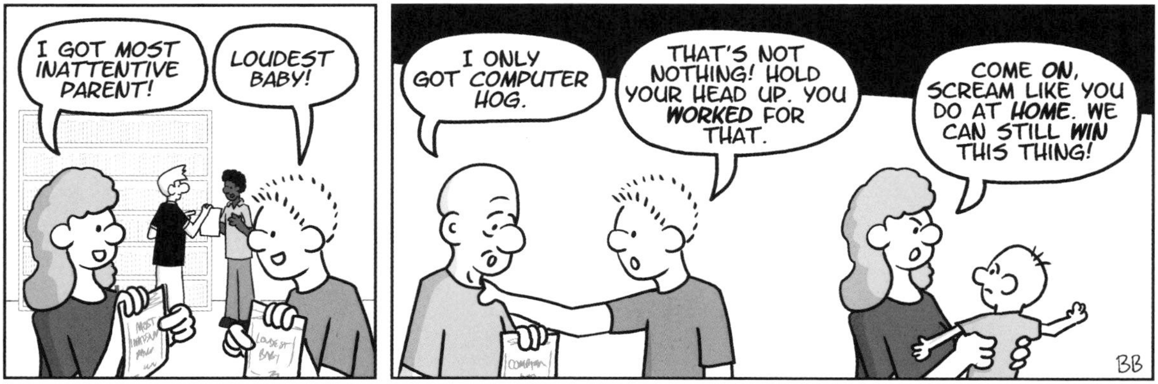
I GOT MOST INATTENTIVE PARENT!
LOUDEST BABY!
I ONLY GOT COMPUTER HOG.
THAT'S NOT NOTHING! HOLD YOUR HEAD UP. YOU WORKED FOR THAT.
COME ON, SCREAM LIKE YOU DO AT HOME. WE CAN STILL WIN THIS THING!
BB

Bibliovores

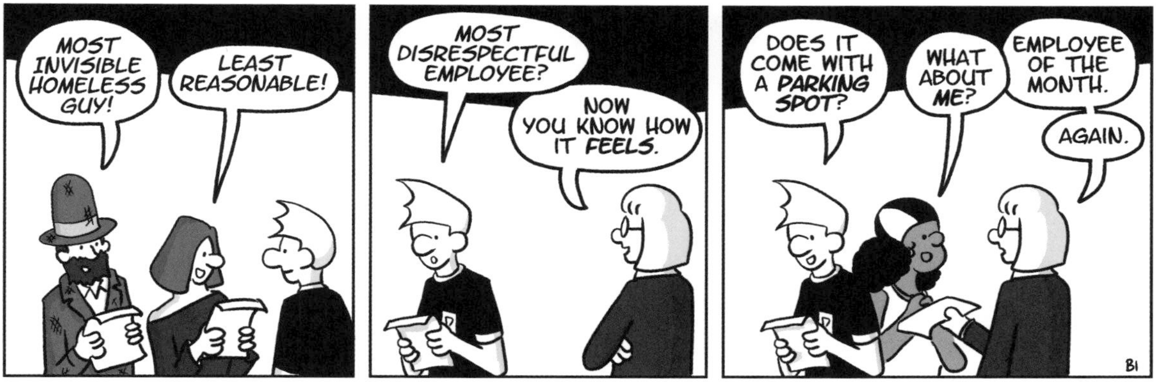
MOST INVISIBLE HOMELESS GUY!
LEAST REASONABLE!
MOST DISRESPECTFUL EMPLOYEE?
NOW YOU KNOW HOW IT FEELS.
DOES IT COME WITH A PARKING SPOT?
WHAT ABOUT ME?
EMPLOYEE OF THE MONTH.
AGAIN.

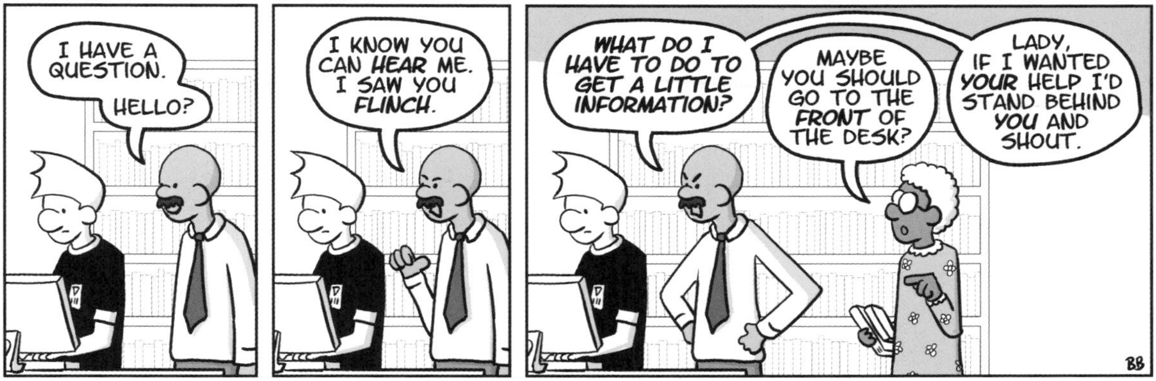
I HAVE A QUESTION.
HELLO?
I KNOW YOU CAN HEAR ME. I SAW YOU FLINCH.
WHAT DO I HAVE TO DO TO GET A LITTLE INFORMATION?
MAYBE YOU SHOULD GO TO THE FRONT OF THE DESK?
LADY, IF I WANTED YOUR HELP I'D STAND BEHIND YOU AND SHOUT.
BB

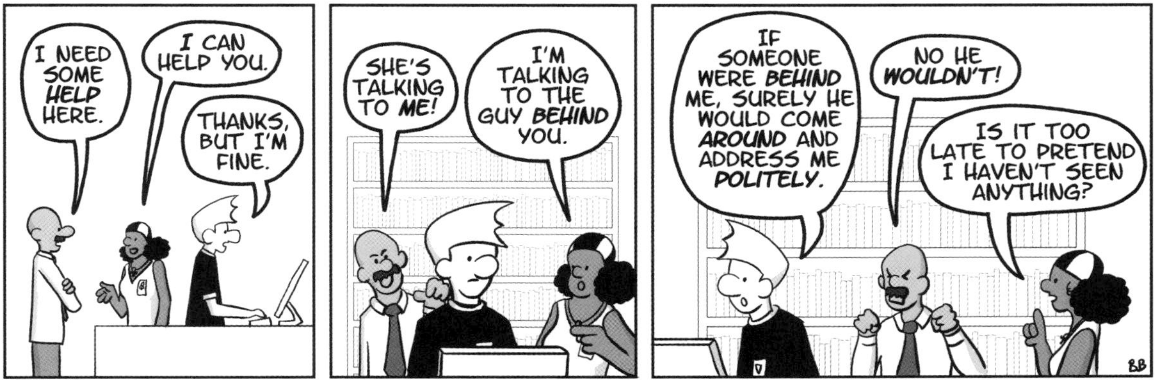
I NEED SOME HELP HERE.
I CAN HELP YOU.
THANKS, BUT I'M FINE.
SHE'S TALKING TO ME!
I'M TALKING TO THE GUY BEHIND YOU.
IF SOMEONE WERE BEHIND ME, SURELY HE WOULD COME AROUND AND ADDRESS ME POLITELY.
NO HE WOULDN'T!
IS IT TOO LATE TO PRETEND I HAVEN'T SEEN ANYTHING?
BB

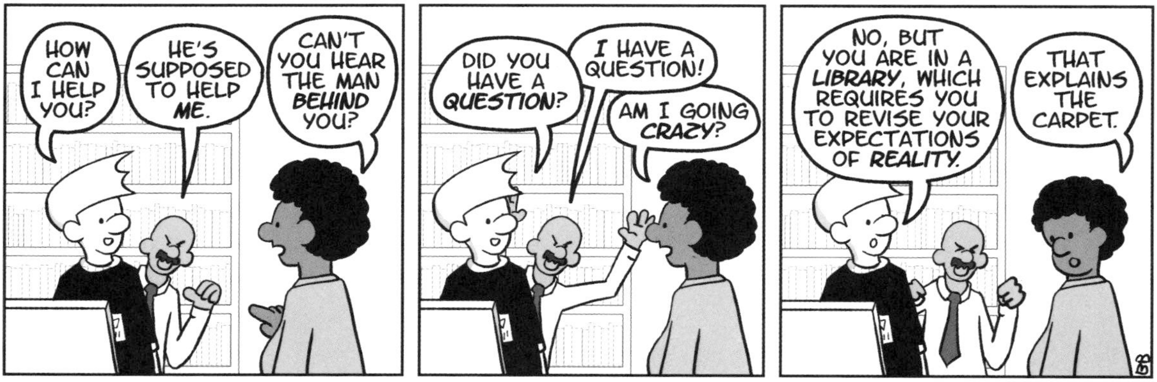
HOW CAN I HELP YOU?
HE'S SUPPOSED TO HELP ME.
CAN'T YOU HEAR THE MAN BEHIND YOU?
DID YOU HAVE A QUESTION?
I HAVE A QUESTION!
AM I GOING CRAZY?
NO, BUT YOU ARE IN A LIBRARY, WHICH REQUIRES YOU TO REVISE YOUR EXPECTATIONS OF REALITY.
THAT EXPLAINS THE CARPET.

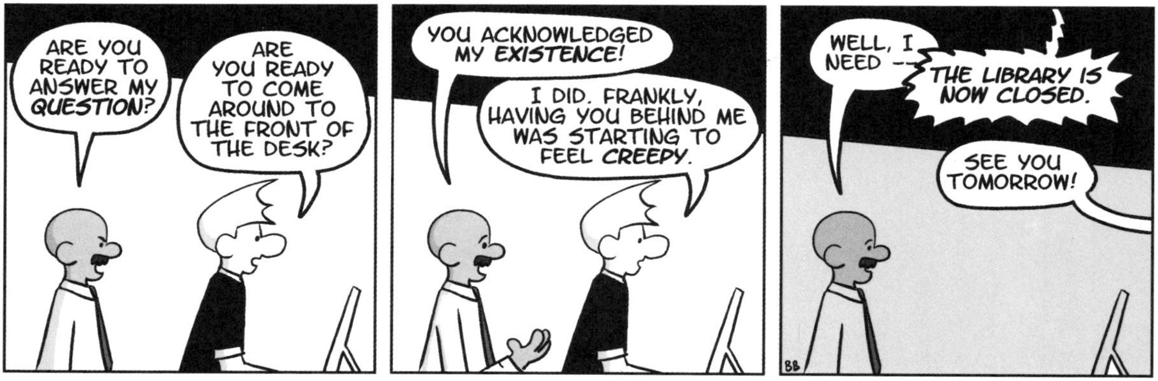
ARE YOU READY TO ANSWER MY QUESTION?
ARE YOU READY TO COME AROUND TO THE FRONT OF THE DESK?
YOU ACKNOWLEDGED MY EXISTENCE!
I DID. FRANKLY, HAVING YOU BEHIND ME WAS STARTING TO FEEL CREEPY.
WELL, I NEED --
THE LIBRARY IS NOW CLOSED.
SEE YOU TOMORROW!
BB

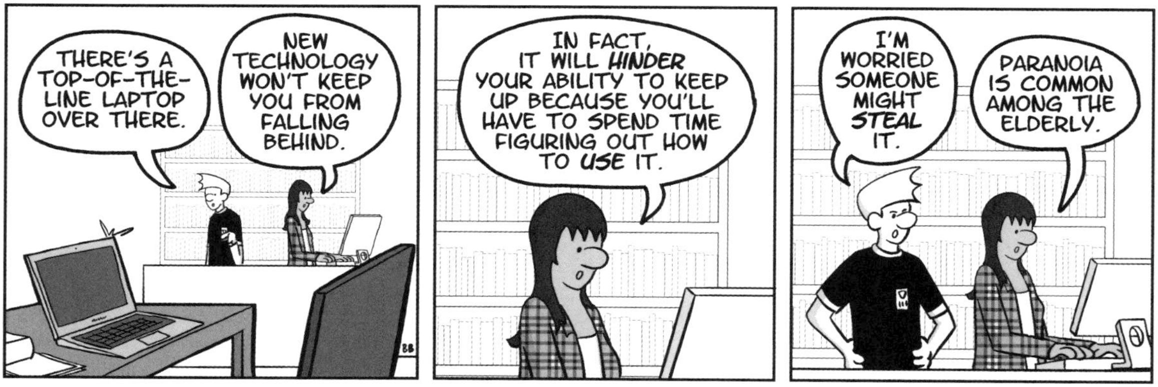
THERE'S A TOP-OF-THE-LINE LAPTOP OVER THERE.
NEW TECHNOLOGY WON'T KEEP YOU FROM FALLING BEHIND.
BB
IN FACT, IT WILL HINDER YOUR ABILITY TO KEEP UP BECAUSE YOU'LL HAVE TO SPEND TIME FIGURING OUT HOW TO USE IT.
I'M WORRIED SOMEONE MIGHT STEAL IT.
PARANOIA IS COMMON AMONG THE ELDERLY.

Bibliovores

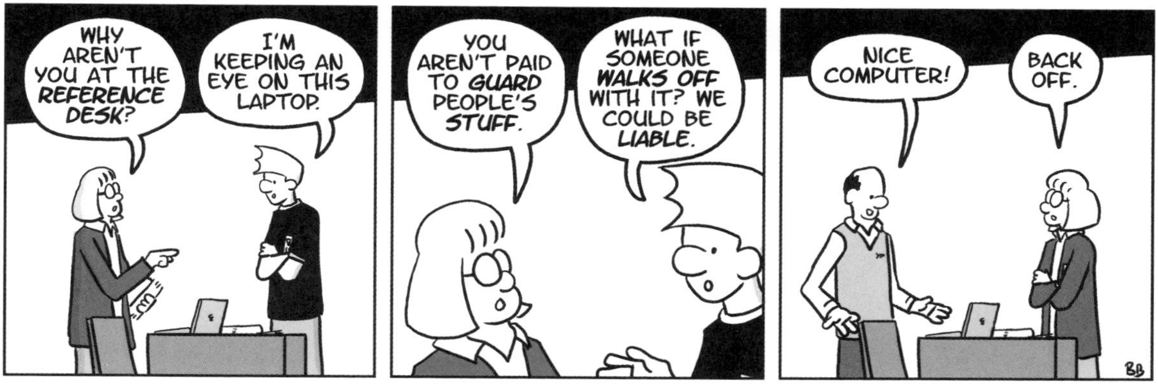
WHY AREN'T YOU AT THE REFERENCE DESK?
I'M KEEPING AN EYE ON THIS LAPTOP.
YOU AREN'T PAID TO GUARD PEOPLE'S STUFF.
WHAT IF SOMEONE WALKS OFF WITH IT? WE COULD BE LIABLE.
NICE COMPUTER!
BACK OFF.
BB

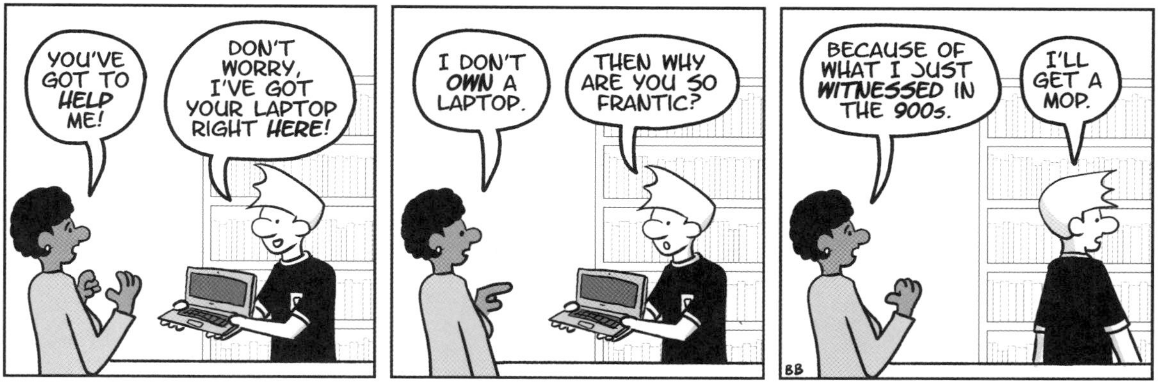
YOU'VE GOT TO HELP ME!
DON'T WORRY, I'VE GOT YOUR LAPTOP RIGHT HERE!
I DON'T OWN A LAPTOP.
THEN WHY ARE YOU SO FRANTIC?
BECAUSE OF WHAT I JUST WITNESSED IN THE 900s.
I'LL GET A MOP.
BB

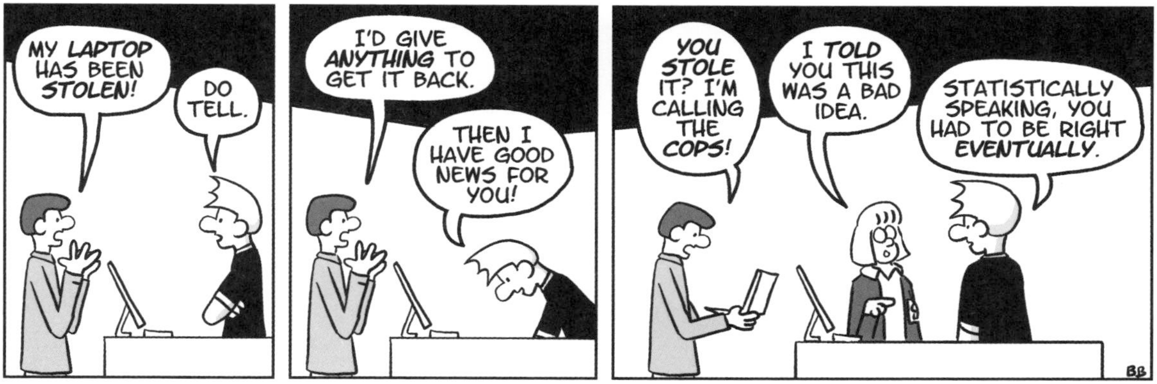
MY LAPTOP HAS BEEN STOLEN!
DO TELL.
I'D GIVE ANYTHING TO GET IT BACK.
THEN I HAVE GOOD NEWS FOR YOU!
YOU STOLE IT? I'M CALLING THE COPS!
I TOLD YOU THIS WAS A BAD IDEA.
STATISTICALLY SPEAKING, YOU HAD TO BE RIGHT EVENTUALLY.
BB

I DON'T LIKE THE ANSWER YOU GAVE ME.
IT IS NONETHELESS CORRECT.
HOW DO YOU KNOW?
IT'S UTTERLY UNAMBIGUOUS. ALL EXPERTS AGREE.
WELL I DON'T.
IF YOU'RE SUCH AN EXPERT, WHY ARE YOU ASKING ME?
BB

WELL?
THAT'S THE SAME QUESTION YOU JUST ASKED ME.
NOT EXACTLY THE SAME. I REPHRASED IT.
IF YOU'D LIKE I COULD REPHRASE MY ANSWER.
NO! I WANT A TOTALLY DIFFERENT ANSWER!
THEN YOU'LL HAVE TO ASK A TOTALLY DIFFERENT QUESTION.
BB

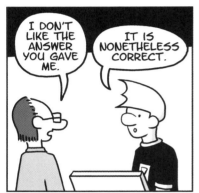

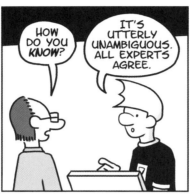

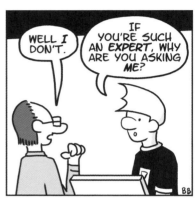

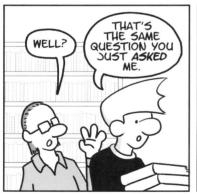

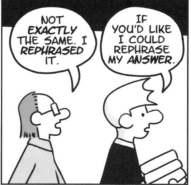

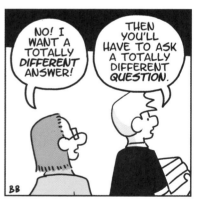

I WANT YOU TO HELP ME FIND EVIDENCE THAT SUPPORTS MY OPINION.
"CRACKPOT WEBSITES"?
TAP TAP
I'VE ALREADY SEEN THOSE.
MAYBE IT'S TIME TO START YOUR OWN.
TAP TAP

I'M NOT LEAVING UNTIL I GET THE TRUTH!
YOU COULDN'T HANDLE THE TRUTH.
THAT'S NOT TRUE.
I REST MY CASE.

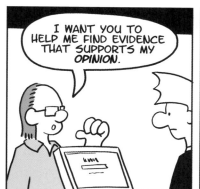

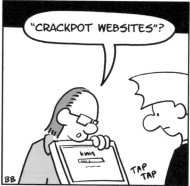

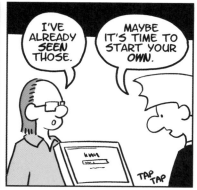

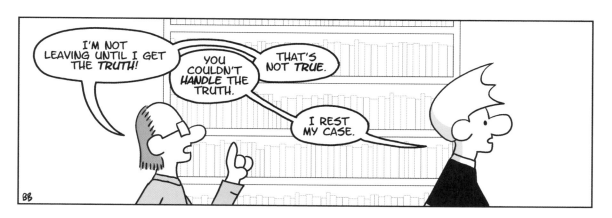

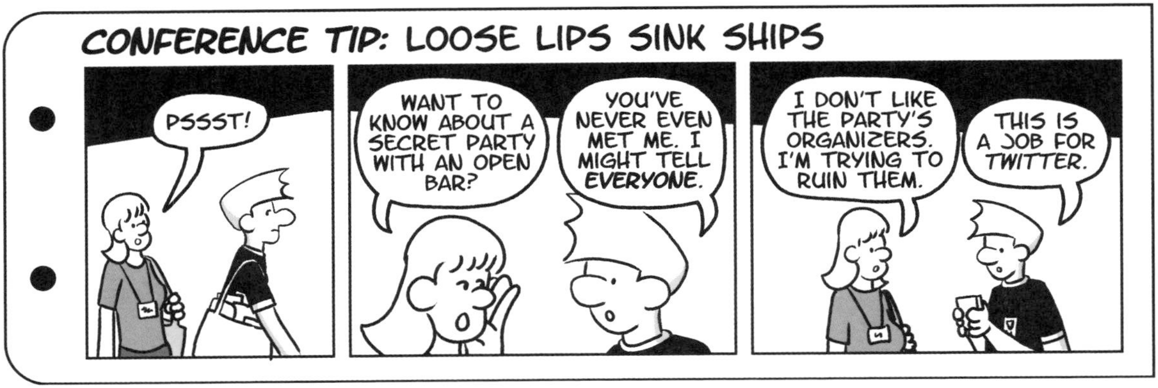
CONFERENCE TIP: LOOSE LIPS SINK SHIPS
PSSST!
WANT TO KNOW ABOUT A SECRET PARTY WITH AN OPEN BAR?
YOU'VE NEVER EVEN MET ME. I MIGHT TELL EVERYONE.
I DON'T LIKE THE PARTY'S ORGANIZERS. I'M TRYING TO RUIN THEM.
THIS IS A JOB FOR TWITTER.

Every year we provide helpful advice to attendees of the ALA conference.

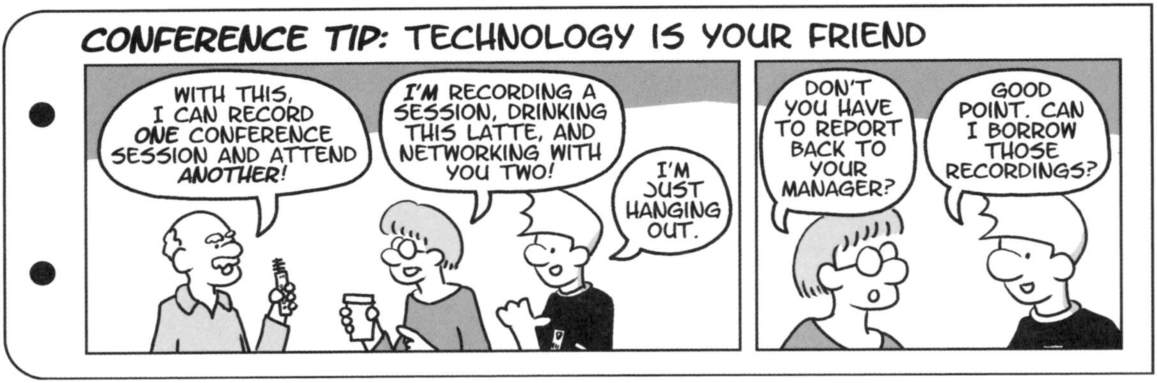
CONFERENCE TIP: TECHNOLOGY IS YOUR FRIEND
WITH THIS, I CAN RECORD ONE CONFERENCE SESSION AND ATTEND ANOTHER!
I'M RECORDING A SESSION, DRINKING THIS LATTE, AND NETWORKING WITH YOU TWO!
I'M JUST HANGING OUT.
DON'T YOU HAVE TO REPORT BACK TO YOUR MANAGER?
GOOD POINT. CAN I BORROW THOSE RECORDINGS?

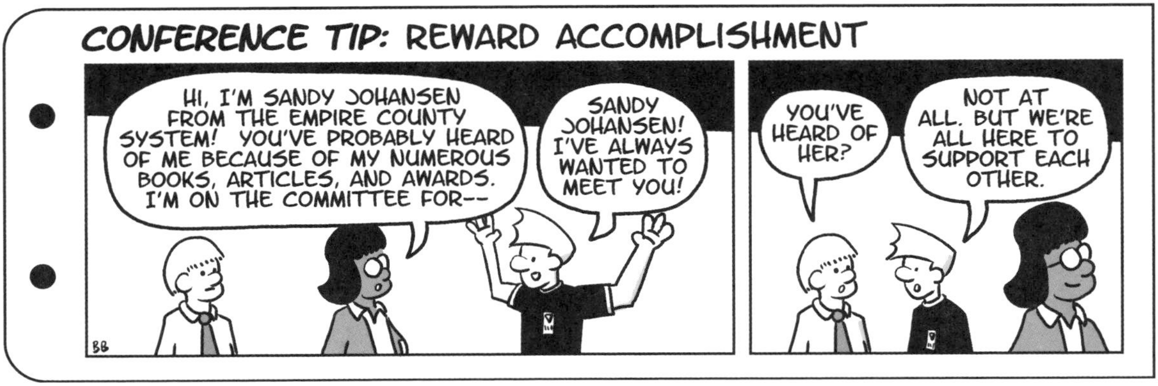
CONFERENCE TIP: REWARD ACCOMPLISHMENT
HI, I'M SANDY JOHANSEN FROM THE EMPIRE COUNTY SYSTEM! YOU'VE PROBABLY HEARD OF ME BECAUSE OF MY NUMEROUS BOOKS, ARTICLES, AND AWARDS. I'M ON THE COMMITTEE FOR--
SANDY JOHANSEN! I'VE ALWAYS WANTED TO MEET YOU!
YOU'VE HEARD OF HER?
NOT AT ALL. BUT WE'RE ALL HERE TO SUPPORT EACH OTHER.

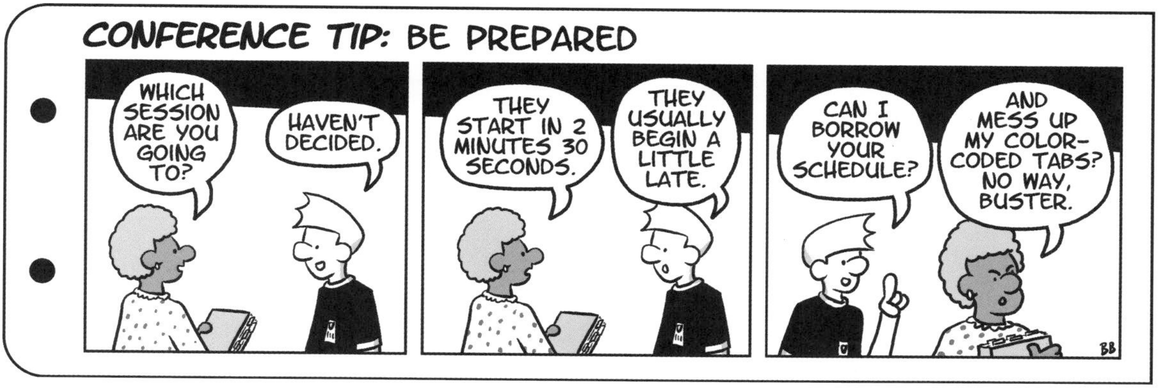
CONFERENCE TIP: BE PREPARED
WHICH SESSION ARE YOU GOING TO?
HAVEN'T DECIDED.
THEY START IN 2 MINUTES 30 SECONDS.
THEY USUALLY BEGIN A LITTLE LATE.
CAN I BORROW YOUR SCHEDULE?
AND MESS UP MY COLOR-CODED TABS? NO WAY, BUSTER.
BB

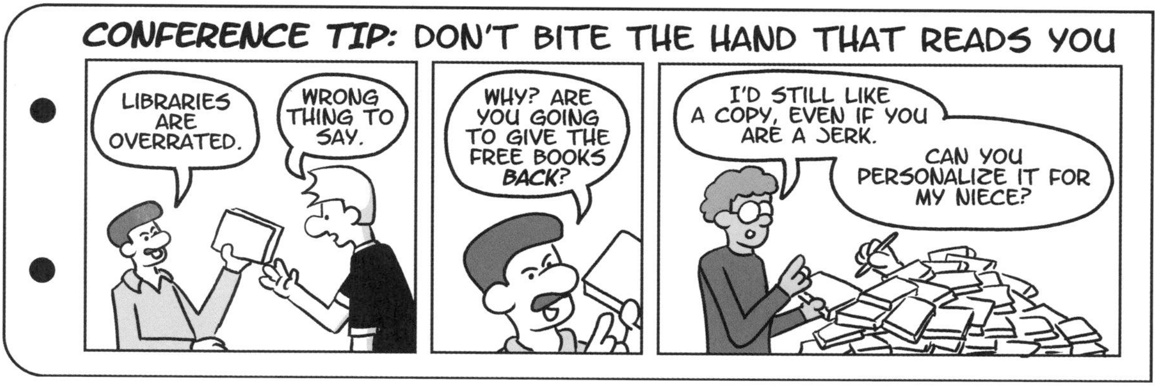
CONFERENCE TIP: DON'T BITE THE HAND THAT READS YOU
LIBRARIES ARE OVERRATED.
WRONG THING TO SAY.
WHY? ARE YOU GOING TO GIVE THE FREE BOOKS BACK?
I'D STILL LIKE A COPY, EVEN IF YOU ARE A JERK.
CAN YOU PERSONALIZE IT FOR MY NIECE?

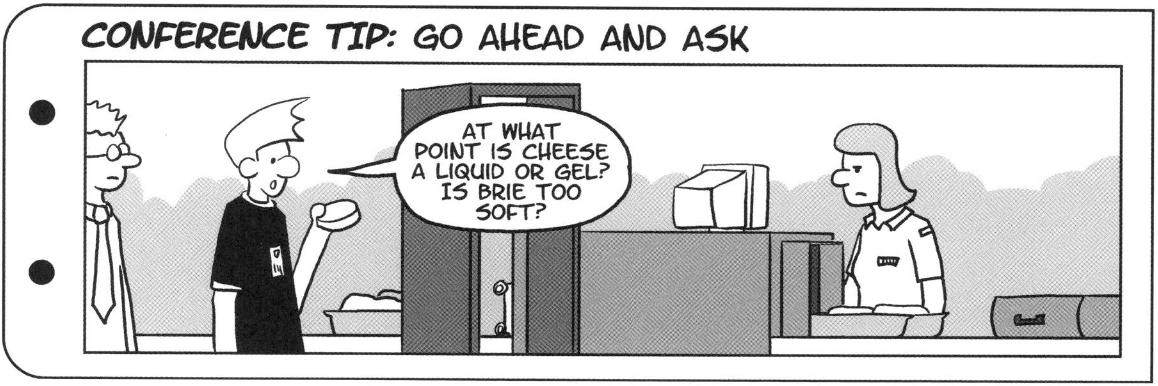
CONFERENCE TIP: GO AHEAD AND ASK
AT WHAT POINT IS CHEESE A LIQUID OR GEL? IS BRIE TOO SOFT?

CONFERENCE TIP: THERE ARE OTHER FISH IN THE SEA

YOU LOOK REALLY UPSET.
THEY RAN OUT OF THE GALLEY I WANTED!
WAIT, THAT'S IT! YOU GOT ONE!
THIS THING? I WAS JUST ABOUT TO THROW IT AWAY.
SO I CAN HAVE IT?
ARE YOU KIDDING? IF YOU WANT IT THAT BADLY IT MUST BE GREAT!

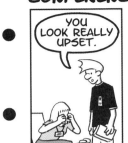

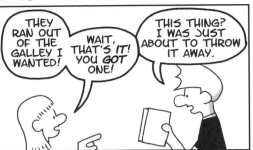

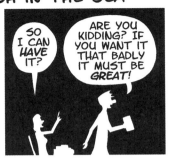

CONFERENCE TIP: NEVER SAY NEVER

YOU GIVING THESE AWAY?
NO. NOT AT ALL. UNDER NO CIRCUMSTANCES WHATSOEVER
WHAT IF I TOLD YOU I COME FROM AN ENORMOUS LIBRARY SYSTEM WITH VIRTUALLY UNLIMITED FUNDS?
DO YOU?
NO. BUT NOW WE'RE NEGOTIATING.
BB

CONFERENCE TIP: GIVE UP YOUR SEAT

IS THIS SEAT TAKEN?
YES.
EXPECTING A FRIEND?
OPEN YOUR EYES. MY BAG IS THERE.
I THINK IT WOULD PREFER THE FLOOR.
IT'S A BAG. I DOUBT IT CARES EITHER WAY.
BB

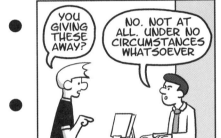

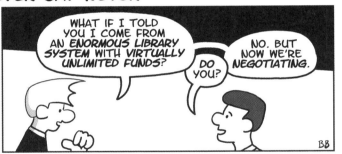

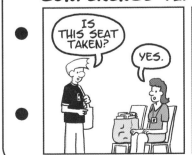

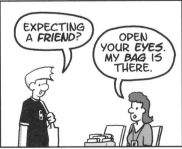

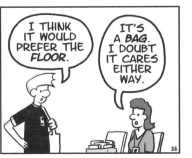

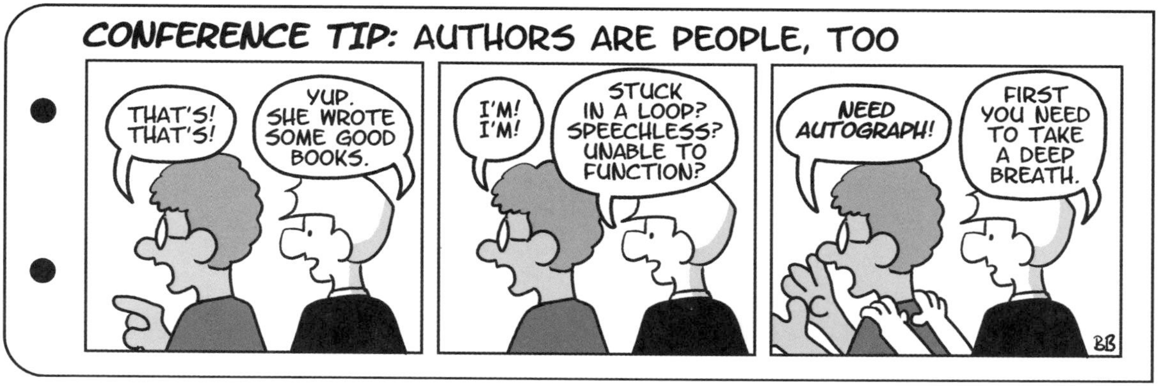
CONFERENCE TIP: AUTHORS ARE PEOPLE, TOO
THAT'S! THAT'S!
YUP. SHE WROTE SOME GOOD BOOKS.
I'M! I'M!
STUCK IN A LOOP? SPEECHLESS? UNABLE TO FUNCTION?
NEED AUTOGRAPH!
FIRST YOU NEED TO TAKE A DEEP BREATH.
BB

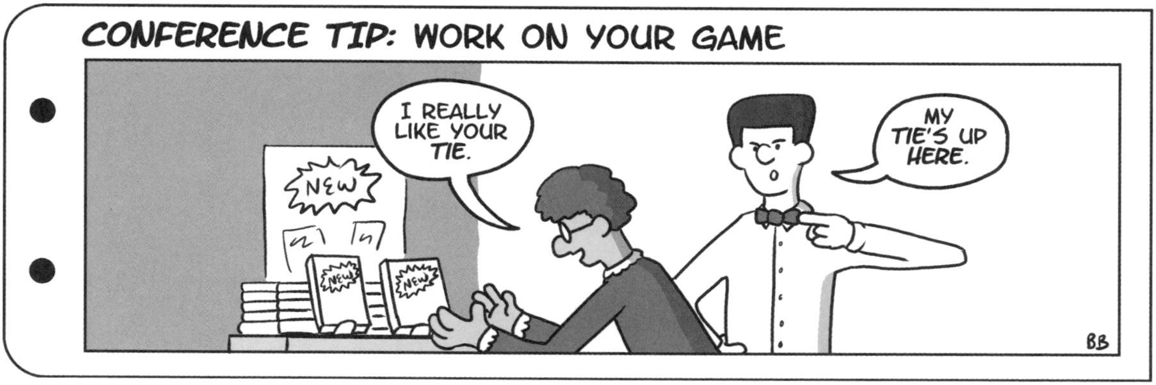
CONFERENCE TIP: WORK ON YOUR GAME
NEW
I REALLY LIKE YOUR TIE.
MY TIE'S UP HERE.
BB

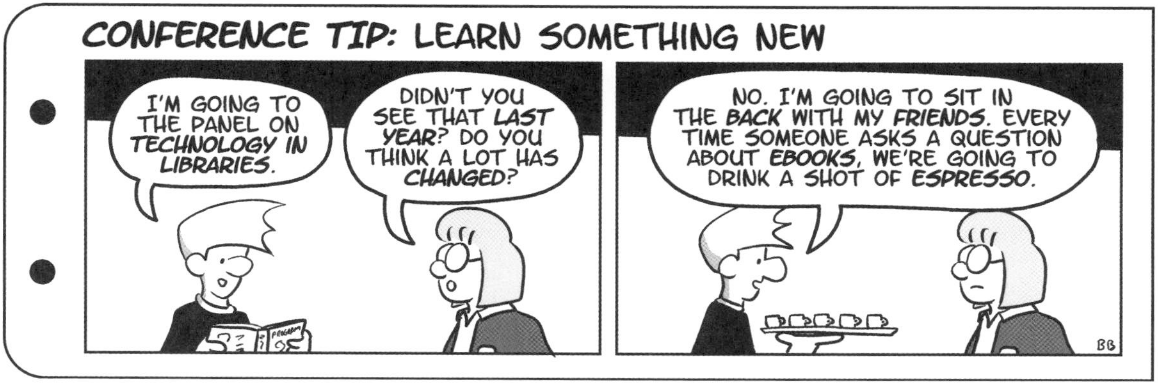
CONFERENCE TIP: LEARN SOMETHING NEW
I'M GOING TO THE PANEL ON TECHNOLOGY IN LIBRARIES.
DIDN'T YOU SEE THAT LAST YEAR? DO YOU THINK A LOT HAS CHANGED?
NO. I'M GOING TO SIT IN THE BACK WITH MY FRIENDS. EVERY TIME SOMEONE ASKS A QUESTION ABOUT EBOOKS, WE'RE GOING TO DRINK A SHOT OF ESPRESSO.
BB

What Would Dewey Do ?

In 2007, as part of a big outreach effort to attract more librarians, Book Expo America asked us to create a comic book for them. The only problem was, neither Gene nor I had ever actually **been** to BEA. So we interviewed a dozen or so librarian friends who had, and gleaned lots of juicy details. We placed our characters against this backdrop, and the result is the second-longest *Unshelved* story ever told (behind *Empire County Strikes Back*, from our book *Library Mascot Cage Match*). We also think it's one of the funniest things we've ever written, and we're thrilled to finally make it available in printed form.

P.S. When we finally did attend BEA that year, we found that we had **totally nailed it**. If you've ever been to a library conference or book festival or other places where book people gather, we think you'll find it all very familiar. And if you haven't, we hope it will tempt you to join in the fun.

@ **bea**
BOOKEXPO AMERICA

Bibliovores

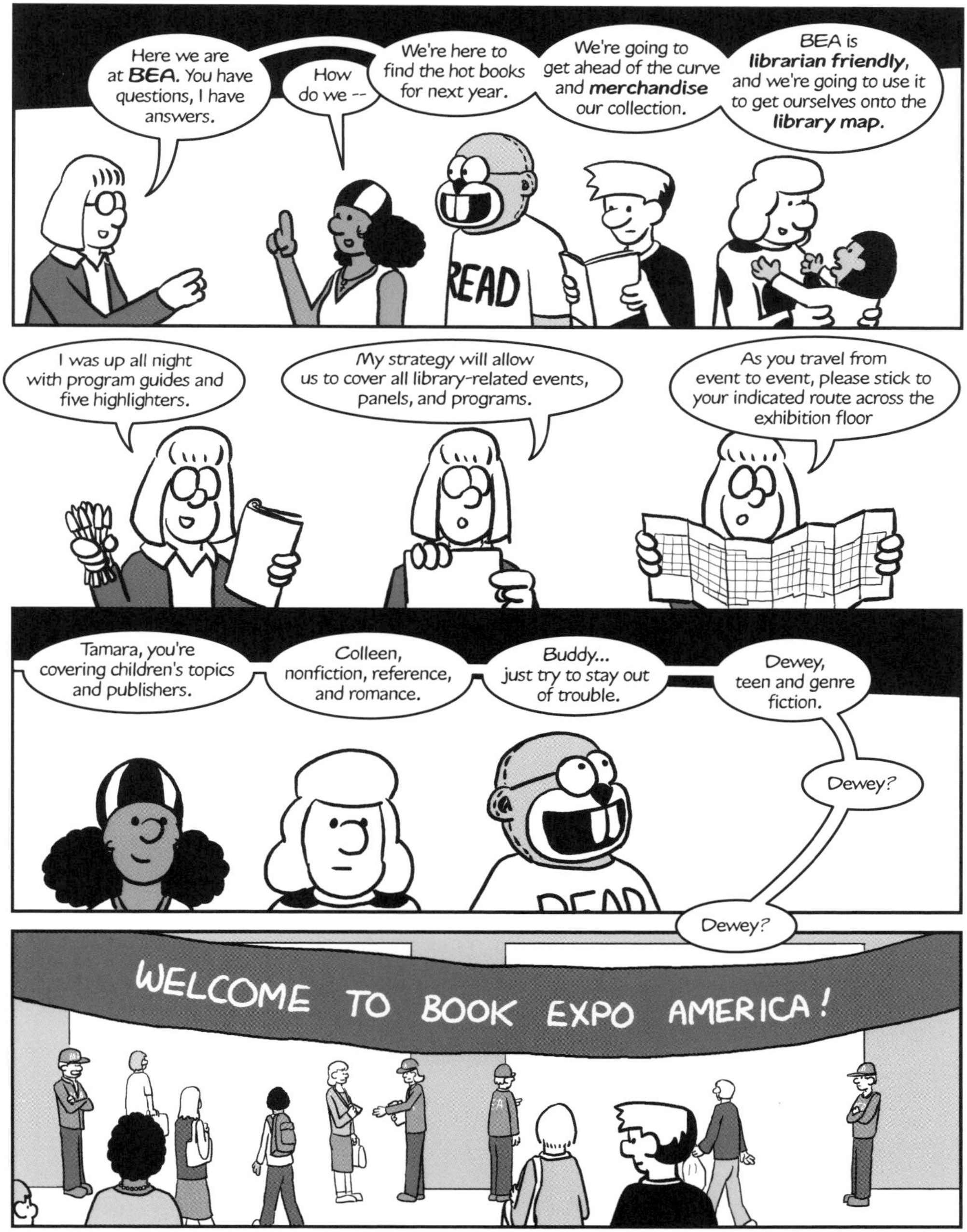
Here we are at **BEA**. You have questions, I have answers.
How do we --
We're here to find the hot books for next year.
We're going to get ahead of the curve and **merchandise** our collection.
BEA is **librarian friendly**, and we're going to use it to get ourselves onto the **library map**.
READ
I was up all night with program guides and five highlighters.
My strategy will allow us to cover all library-related events, panels, and programs.
As you travel from event to event, please stick to your indicated route across the exhibition floor
Tamara, you're covering children's topics and publishers.
Colleen, nonfiction, reference, and romance.
Buddy... just try to stay out of trouble.
Dewey, teen and genre fiction.
Dewey?
Dewey?
WELCOME TO BOOK EXPO AMERICA!

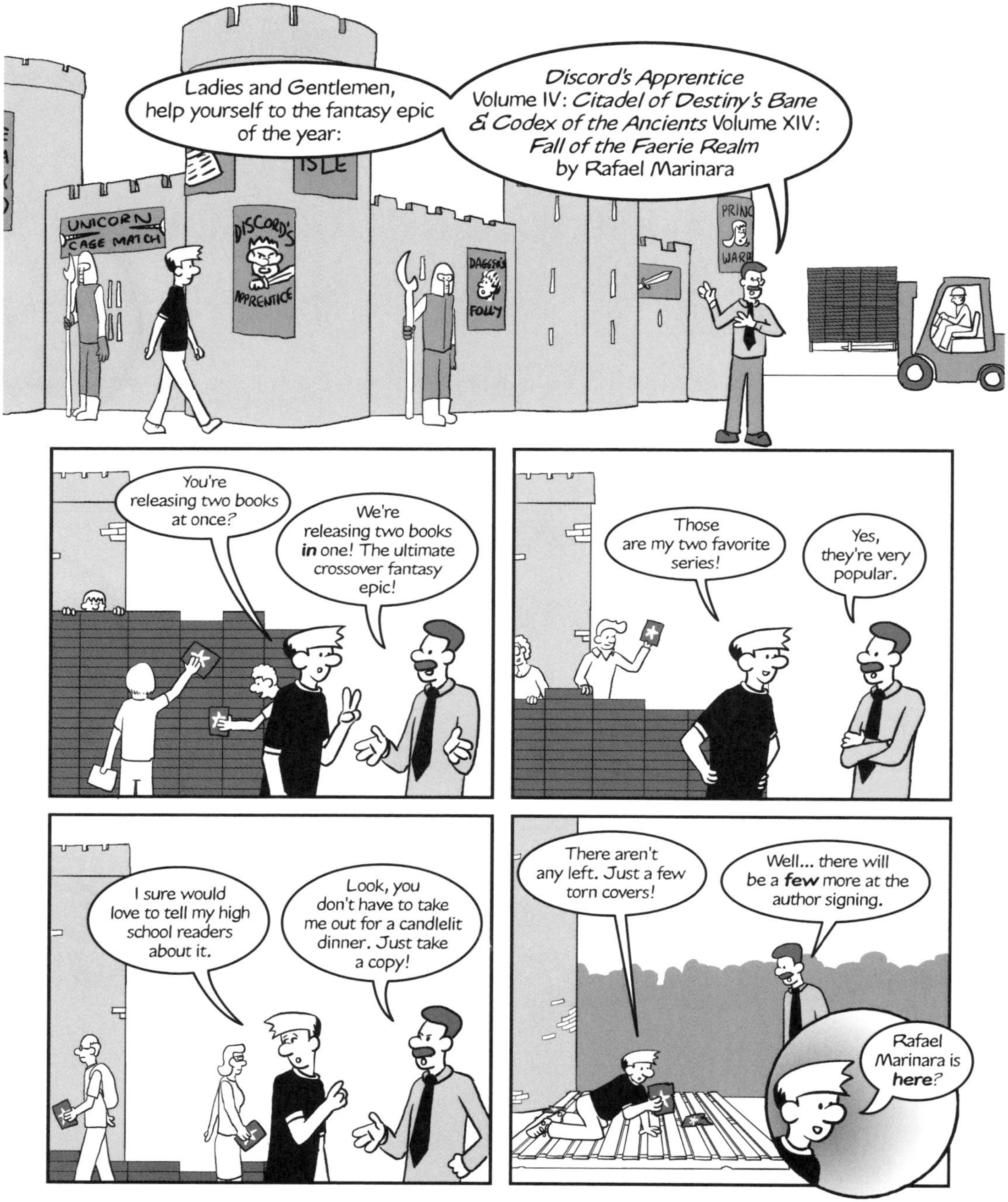
Ladies and Gentlemen, help yourself to the fantasy epic of the year:
Discord's Apprentice Volume IV: Citadel of Destiny's Bane & Codex of the Ancients Volume XIV: Fall of the Faerie Realm by Rafael Marinara
UNICORN CAGE MATCH
DISCORD'S APPRENTICE
DAGGER'S FOLLY
ISLE
You're releasing two books at once?
We're releasing two books in one! The ultimate crossover fantasy epic!
Those are my two favorite series!
Yes, they're very popular.
I sure would love to tell my high school readers about it.
Look, you don't have to take me out for a candlelit dinner. Just take a copy!
There aren't any left. Just a few torn covers!
Well... there will be a few more at the author signing.
Rafael Marinara is here?

Bibliovores

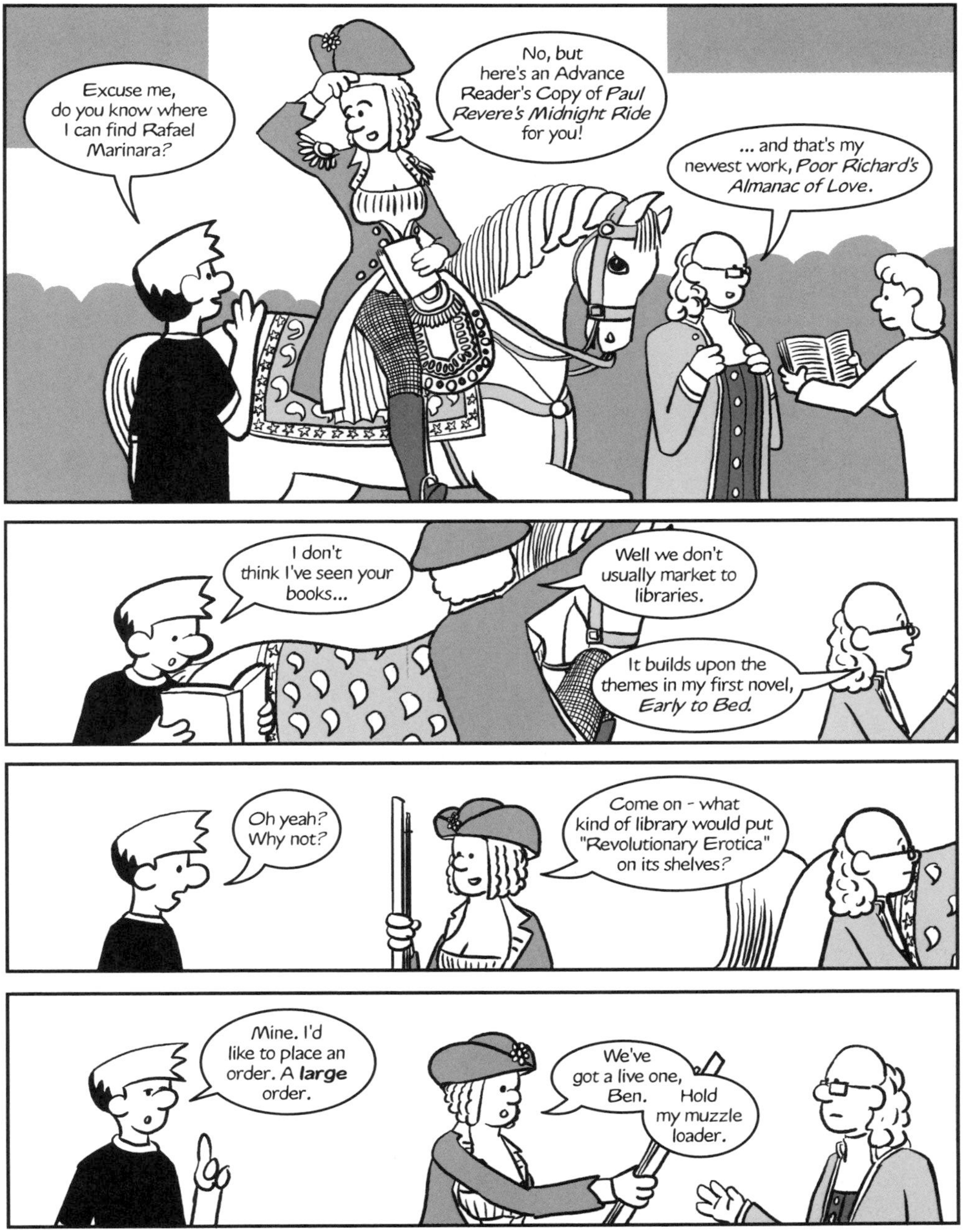
Excuse me, do you know where I can find Rafael Marinara?
No, but here's an Advance Reader's Copy of *Paul Revere's Midnight Ride* for you!
... and that's my newest work, *Poor Richard's Almanac of Love*.
I don't think I've seen your books...
Well we don't usually market to libraries.
It builds upon the themes in my first novel, *Early to Bed*.
Oh yeah? Why not?
Come on - what kind of library would put "Revolutionary Erotica" on its shelves?
Mine. I'd like to place an order. A **large** order.
We've got a live one, Ben. Hold my muzzle loader.

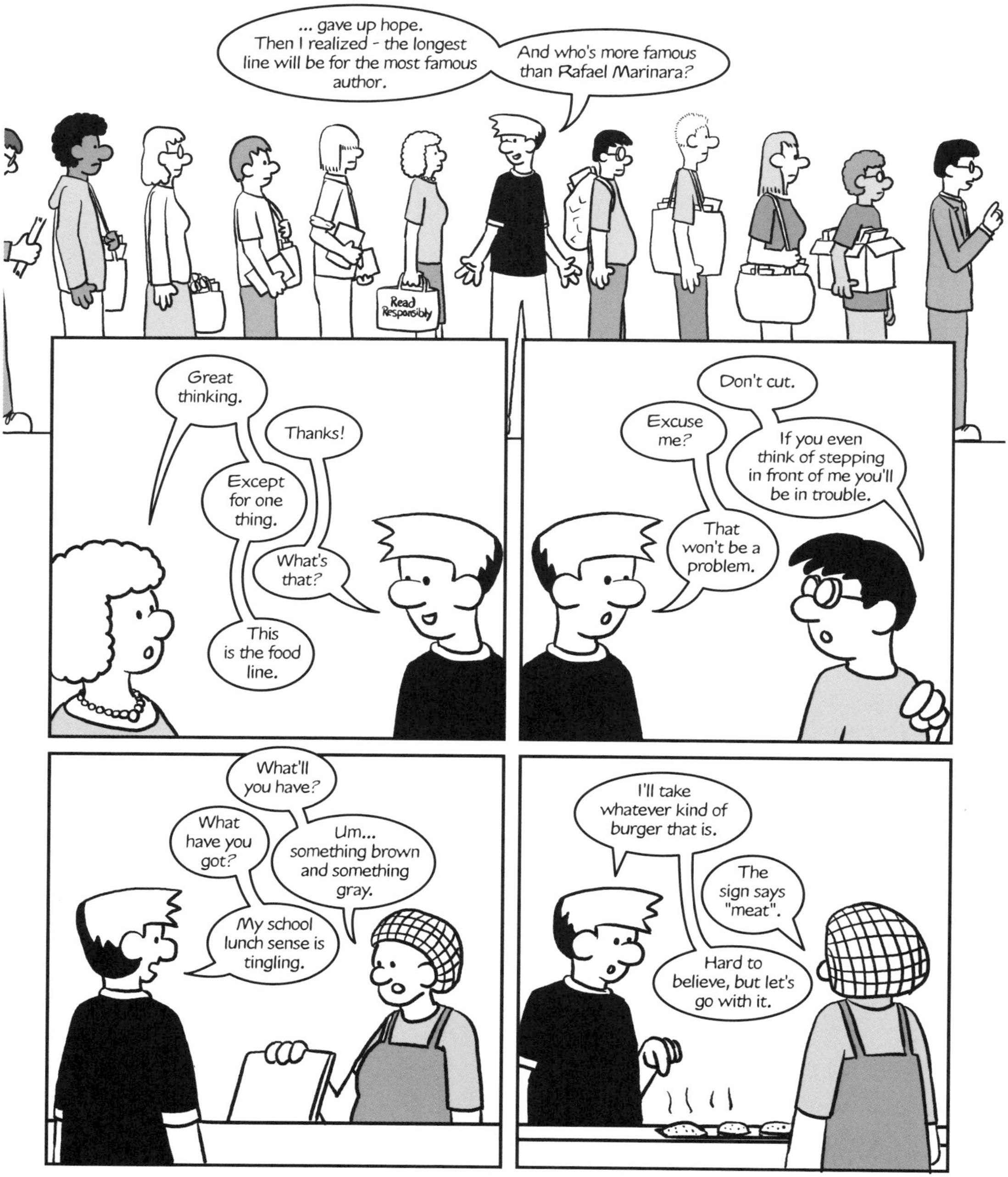
... gave up hope.
Then I realized - the longest line will be for the most famous author.
And who's more famous than Rafael Marinara?
Read Responsibly
Great thinking.
Thanks!
Except for one thing.
What's that?
This is the food line.
Don't cut.
Excuse me?
If you even think of stepping in front of me you'll be in trouble.
That won't be a problem.
What'll you have?
What have you got?
Um... something brown and something gray.
My school lunch sense is tingling.
I'll take whatever kind of burger that is.
The sign says "meat".
Hard to believe, but let's go with it.

Bibliovores

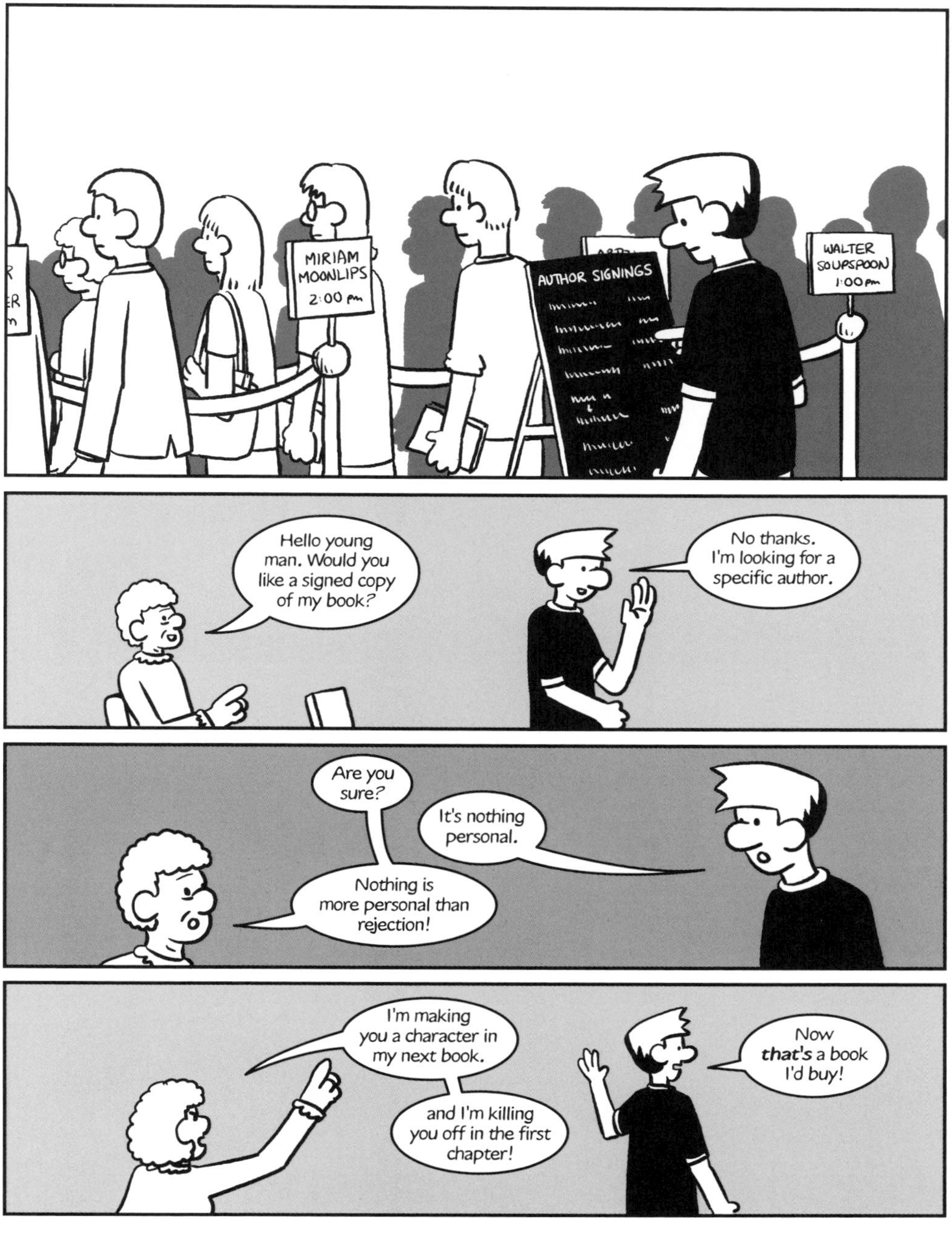
MIRIAM MOONLIPS 2:00 pm
AUTHOR SIGNINGS
WALTER SOUPSPOON 1:00 pm
Hello young man. Would you like a signed copy of my book?
No thanks. I'm looking for a specific author.
Are you sure?
It's nothing personal.
Nothing is more personal than rejection!
I'm making you a character in my next book.
and I'm killing you off in the first chapter!
Now ***that's*** a book I'd buy!

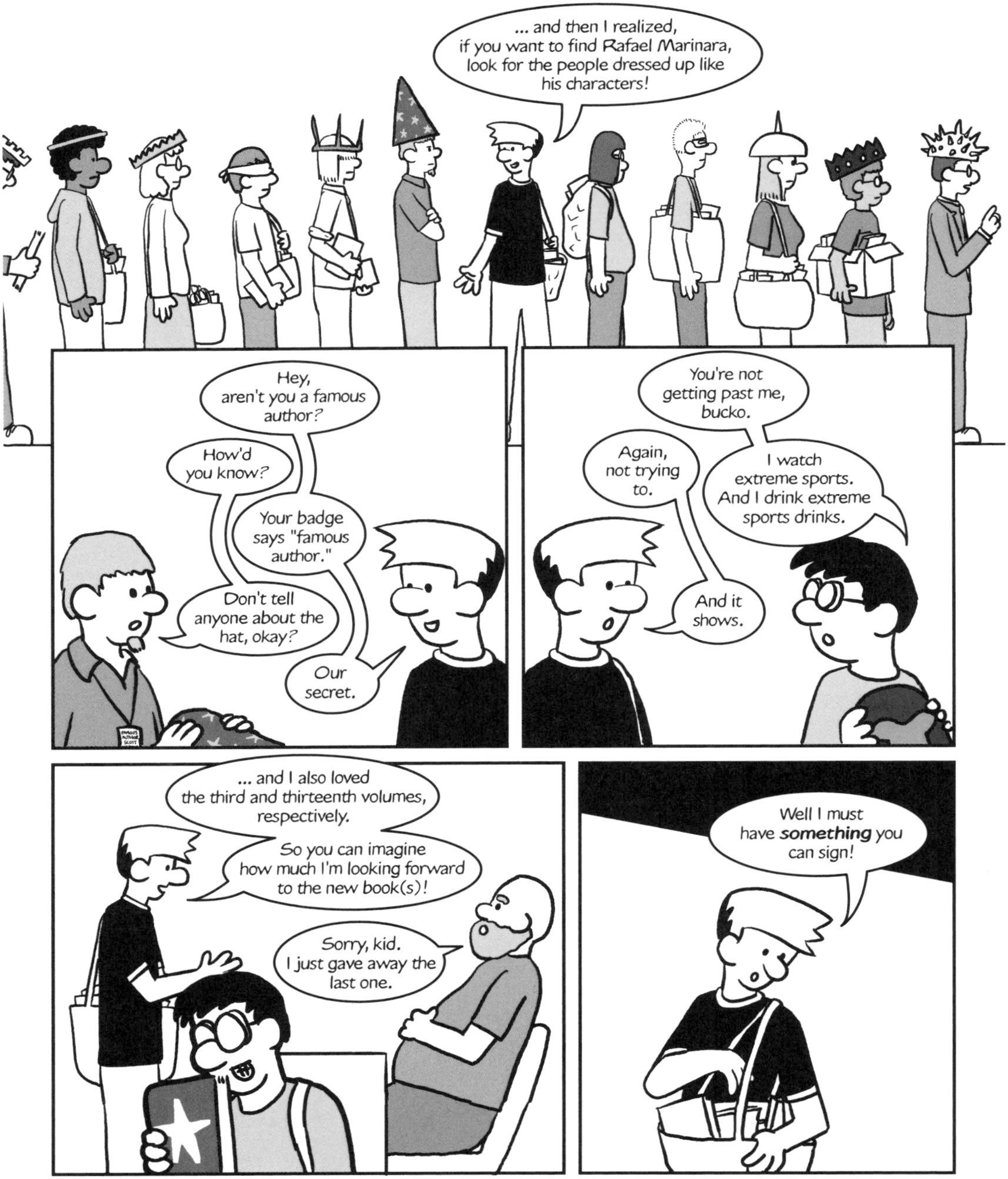
... and then I realized, if you want to find Rafael Marinara, look for the people dressed up like his characters!
Hey, aren't you a famous author?
How'd you know?
Your badge says "famous author."
Don't tell anyone about the hat, okay?
Our secret.
You're not getting past me, bucko.
Again, not trying to.
I watch extreme sports. And I drink extreme sports drinks.
And it shows.
... and I also loved the third and thirteenth volumes, respectively.
So you can imagine how much I'm looking forward to the new book(s)!
Sorry, kid. I just gave away the last one.
Well I must have ***something*** you can sign!

Bibliovores

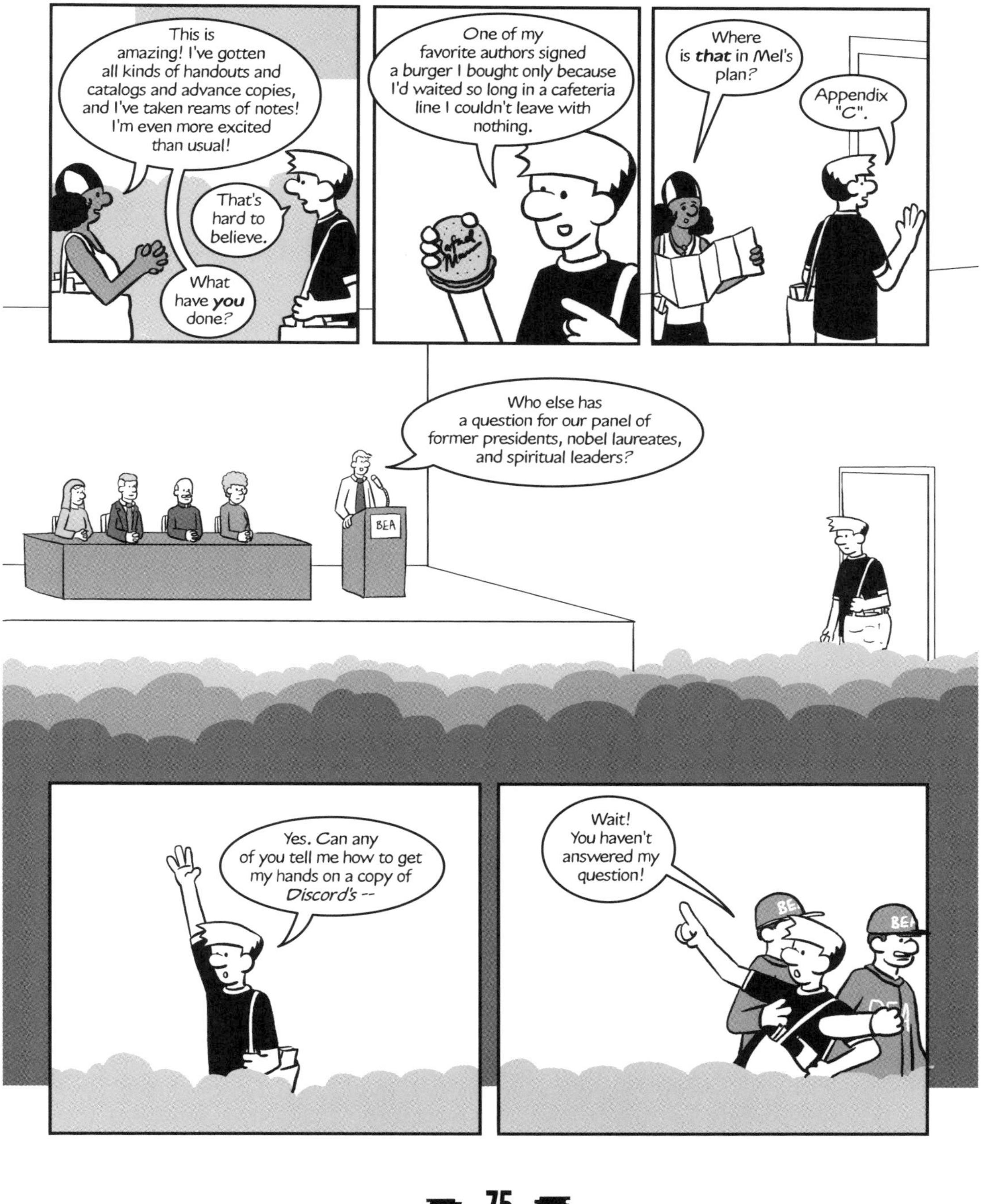

This is amazing! I've gotten all kinds of handouts and catalogs and advance copies, and I've taken reams of notes! I'm even more excited than usual!
That's hard to believe.
What have **you** done?
One of my favorite authors signed a burger I bought only because I'd waited so long in a cafeteria line I couldn't leave with nothing.
Where is **that** in Mel's plan?
Appendix "C".
Who else has a question for our panel of former presidents, nobel laureates, and spiritual leaders?
BEA
Yes. Can any of you tell me how to get my hands on a copy of *Discord's* --
Wait! You haven't answered my question!

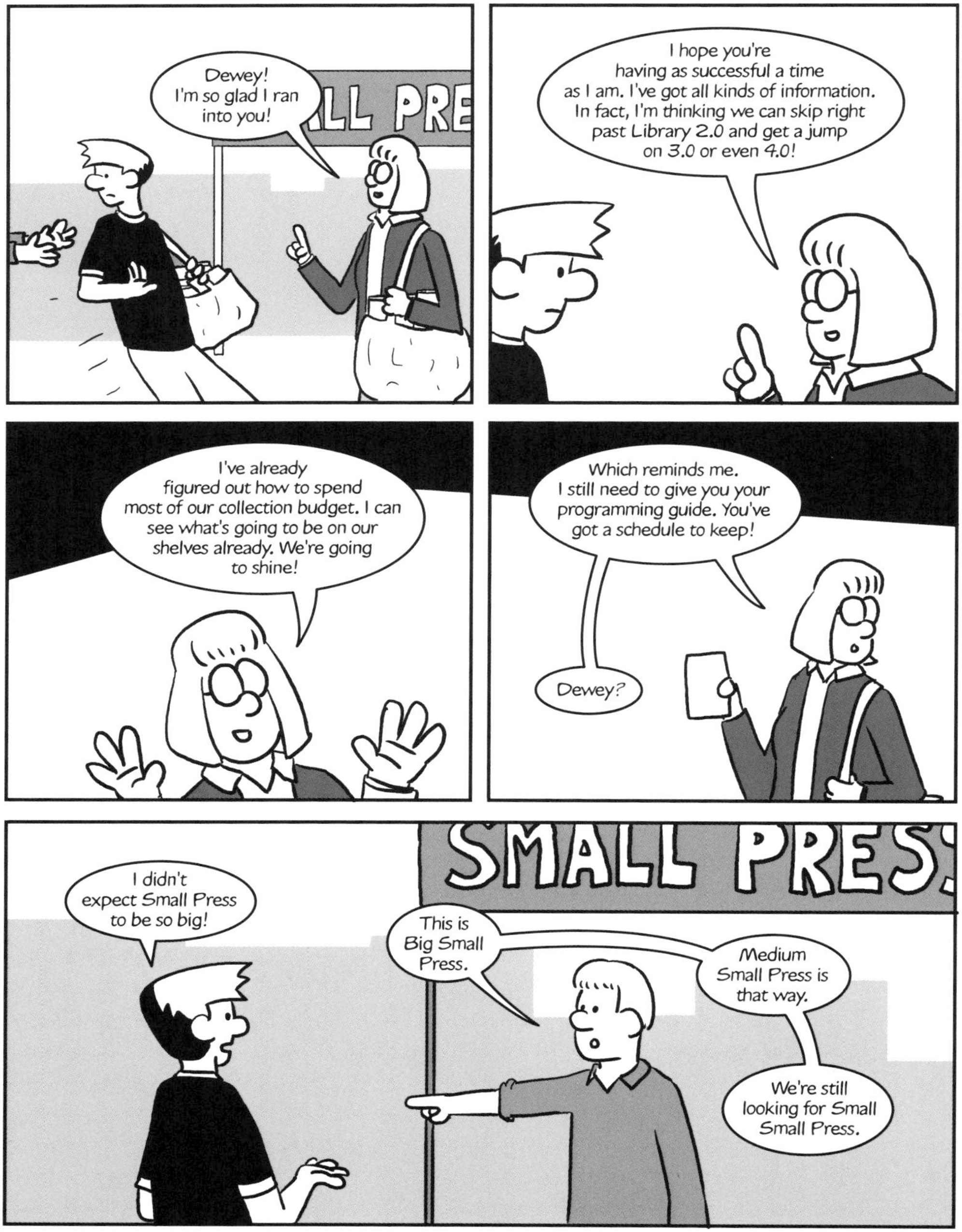
Dewey! I'm so glad I ran into you!
ALL PRE
I hope you're having as successful a time as I am. I've got all kinds of information. In fact, I'm thinking we can skip right past Library 2.0 and get a jump on 3.0 or even 4.0!
I've already figured out how to spend most of our collection budget. I can see what's going to be on our shelves already. We're going to shine!
Which reminds me. I still need to give you your programming guide. You've got a schedule to keep!
Dewey?
SMALL PRES
I didn't expect Small Press to be so big!
This is Big Small Press.
Medium Small Press is that way.
We're still looking for Small Small Press.

Bibliovores

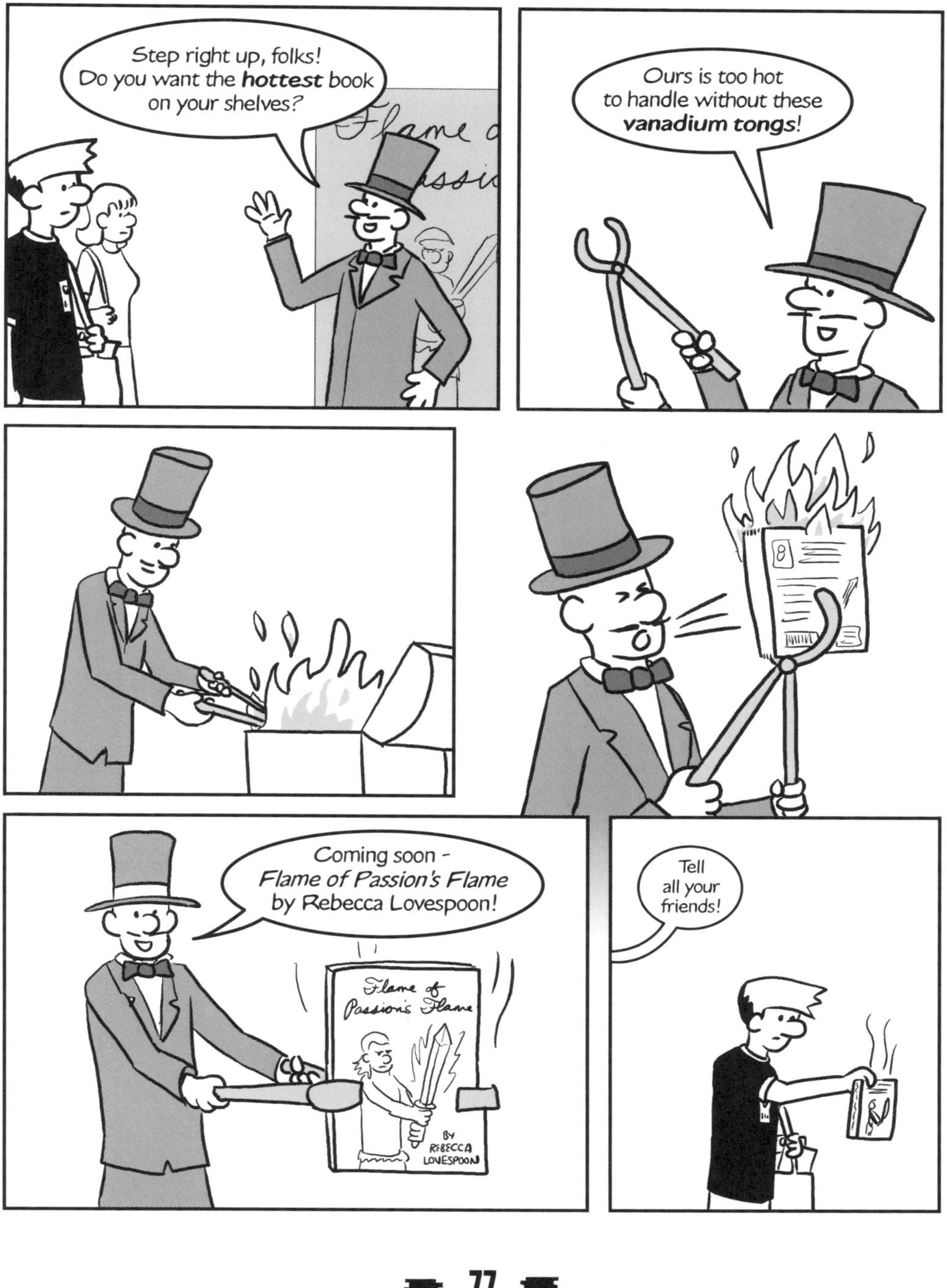
Step right up, folks! Do you want the **hottest** book on your shelves?
Flame of Passion's
Ours is too hot to handle without these **vanadium tongs**!
Coming soon - *Flame of Passion's Flame* by Rebecca Lovespoon!
Flame of Passion's Flame
BY REBECCA LOVESPOON
Tell all your friends!

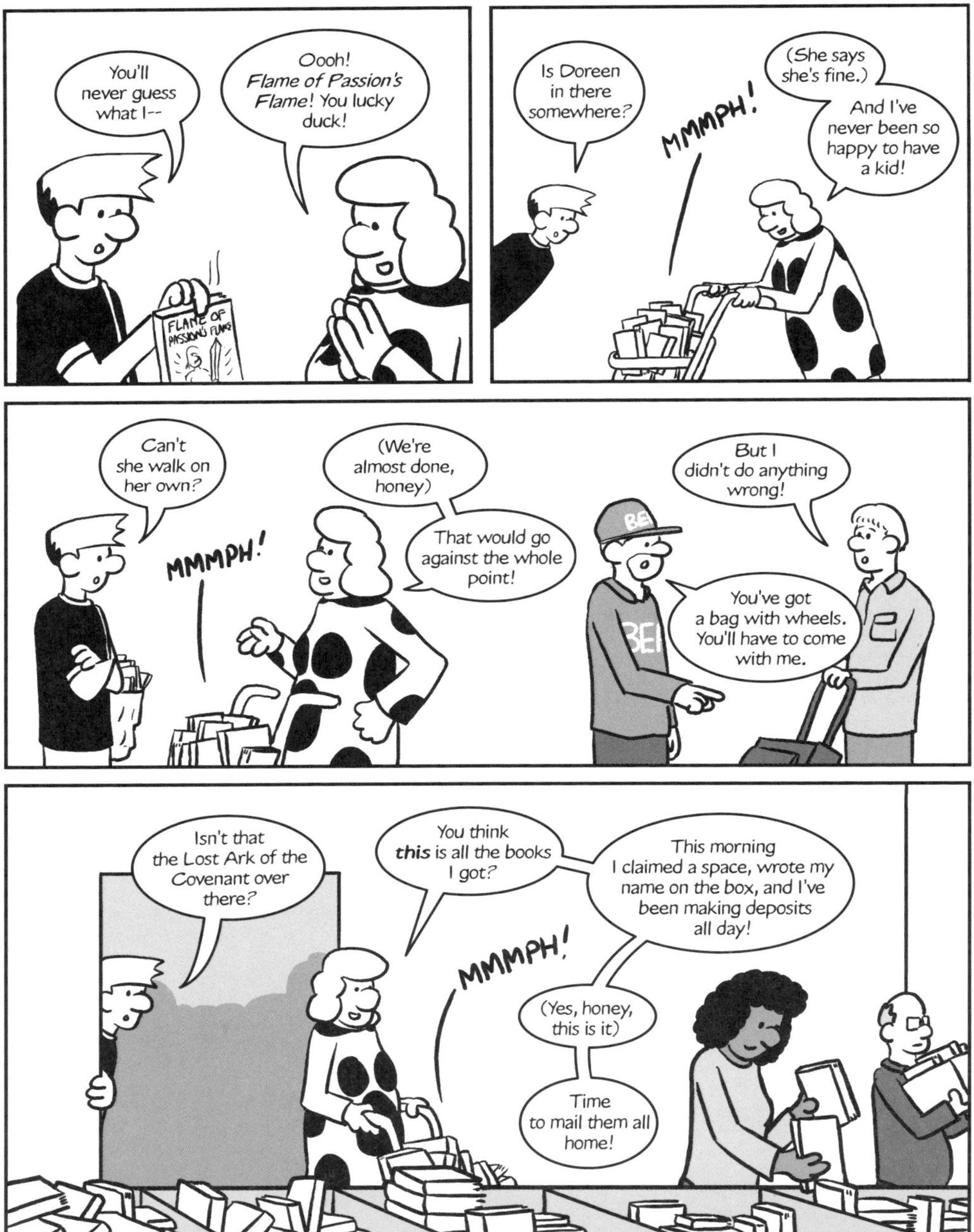
You'll never guess what I--
Oooh! *Flame of Passion's Flame*! You lucky duck!
FLAME OF PASSION'S FLAME
Is Doreen in there somewhere?
MMMPH!
(She says she's fine.)
And I've never been so happy to have a kid!
Can't she walk on her own?
MMMPH!
(We're almost done, honey)
That would go against the whole point!
But I didn't do anything wrong!
You've got a bag with wheels. You'll have to come with me.
Isn't that the Lost Ark of the Covenant over there?
You think **this** is all the books I got?
This morning I claimed a space, wrote my name on the box, and I've been making deposits all day!
MMMPH!
(Yes, honey, this is it)
Time to mail them all home!

Bibliovores

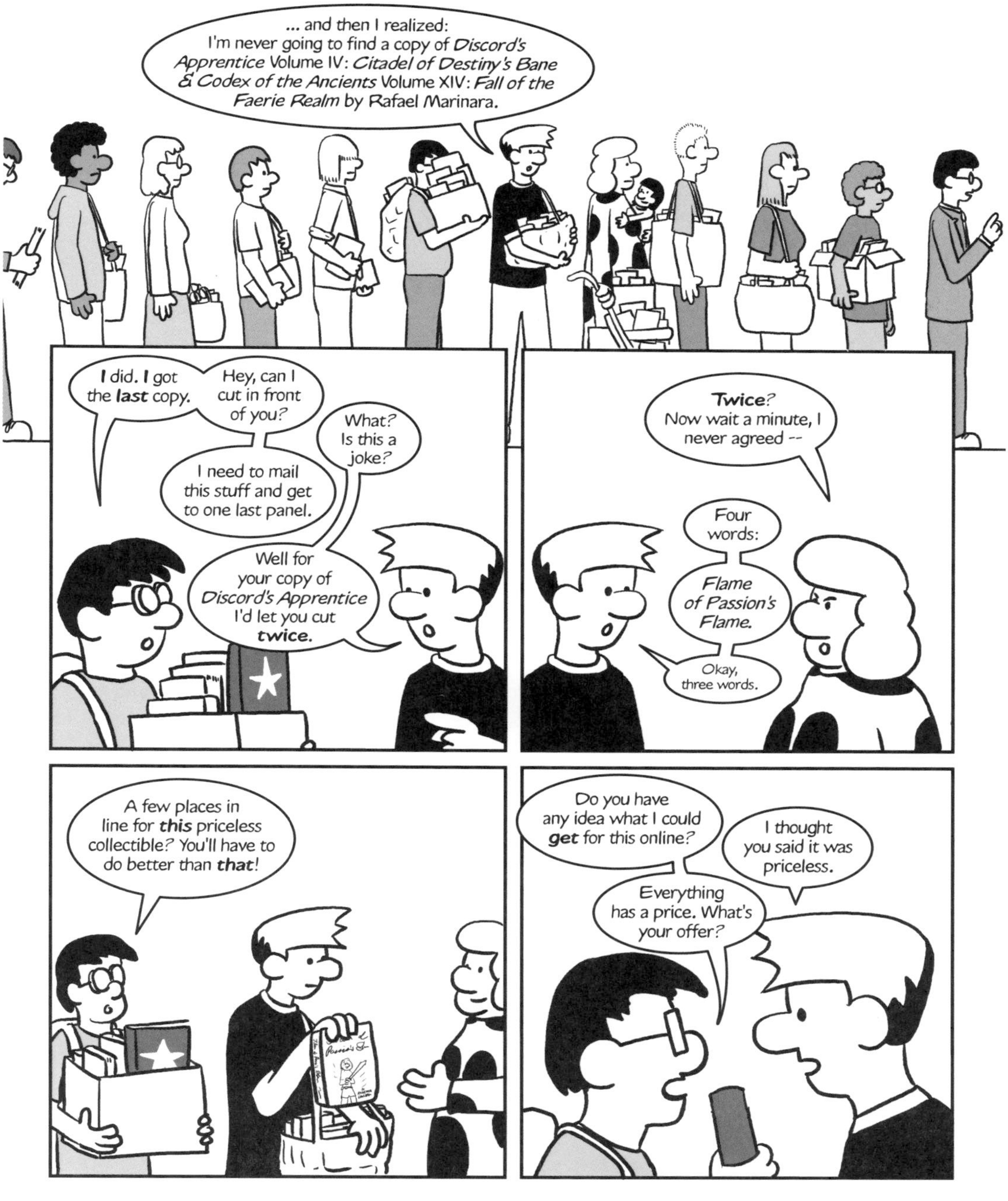

... and then I realized: I'm never going to find a copy of *Discord's Apprentice* Volume IV: *Citadel of Destiny's Bane* & *Codex of the Ancients* Volume XIV: *Fall of the Faerie Realm* by Rafael Marinara.
I did. **I** got the **last** copy.
Hey, can I cut in front of you?
I need to mail this stuff and get to one last panel.
What? Is this a joke?
Well for your copy of *Discord's Apprentice* I'd let you cut **twice**.
Twice? Now wait a minute, I never agreed --
Four words:
Flame of Passion's Flame.
Okay, three words.
A few places in line for **this** priceless collectible? You'll have to do better than **that**!
Do you have any idea what I could **get** for this online?
I thought you said it was priceless.
Everything has a price. What's your offer?

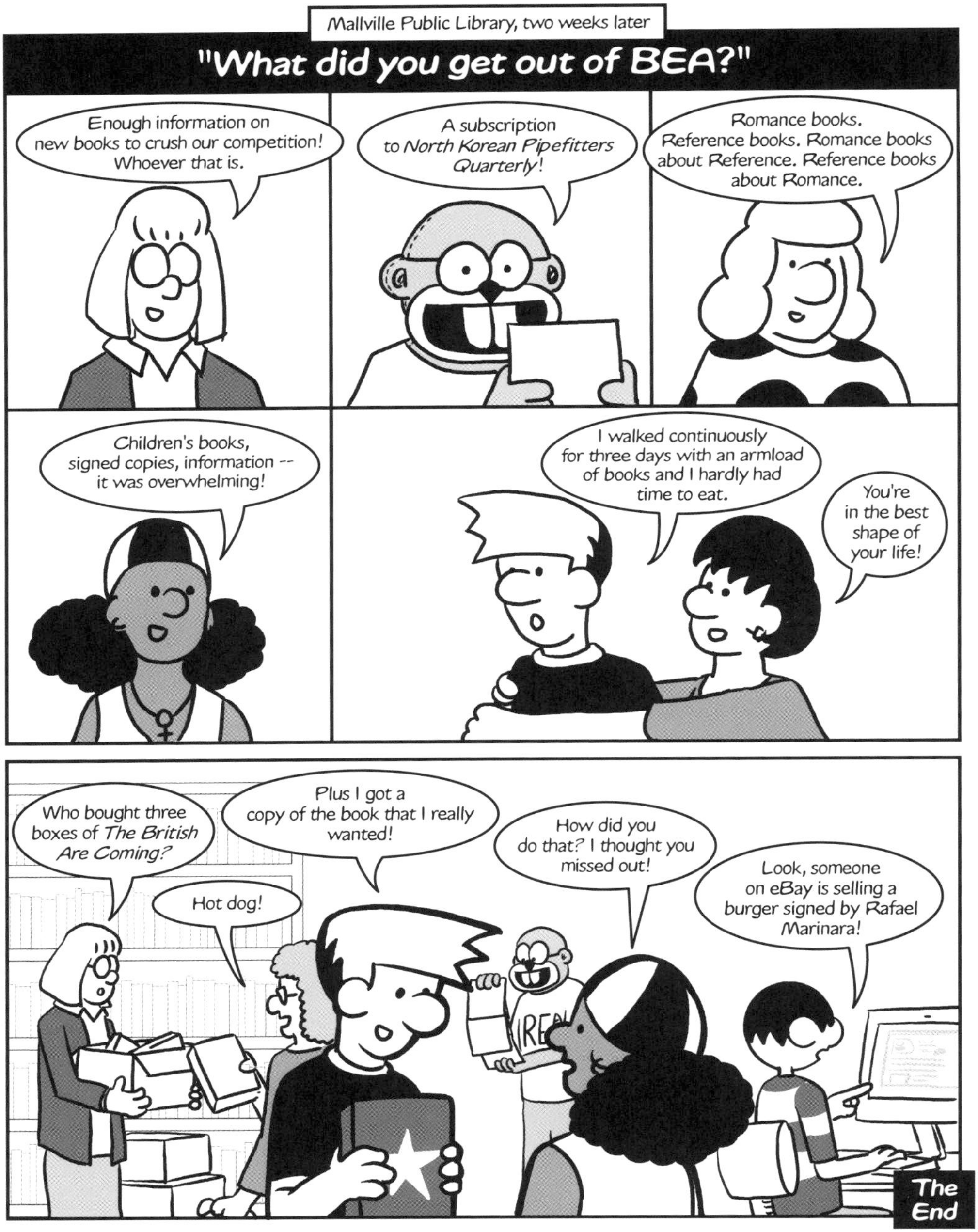
Mallville Public Library, two weeks later
"What did you get out of BEA?"
Enough information on new books to crush our competition! Whoever that is.
A subscription to *North Korean Pipefitters Quarterly*!
Romance books. Reference books. Romance books about Reference. Reference books about Romance.
Children's books, signed copies, information -- it was overwhelming!
I walked continuously for three days with an armload of books and I hardly had time to eat.
You're in the best shape of your life!
Who bought three boxes of *The British Are Coming?*
Plus I got a copy of the book that I really wanted!
Hot dog!
How did you do that? I thought you missed out!
Look, someone on eBay is selling a burger signed by Rafael Marinara!
The End

Bibliovores

In 2010 our friend Josh Elder put together an anthology called *Reading With Pictures*, to promote the use of comics in the classroom. We contributed this three-page secret origin story for Dewey. Find out more about Josh's organization at **www.readingwithpictures.org**

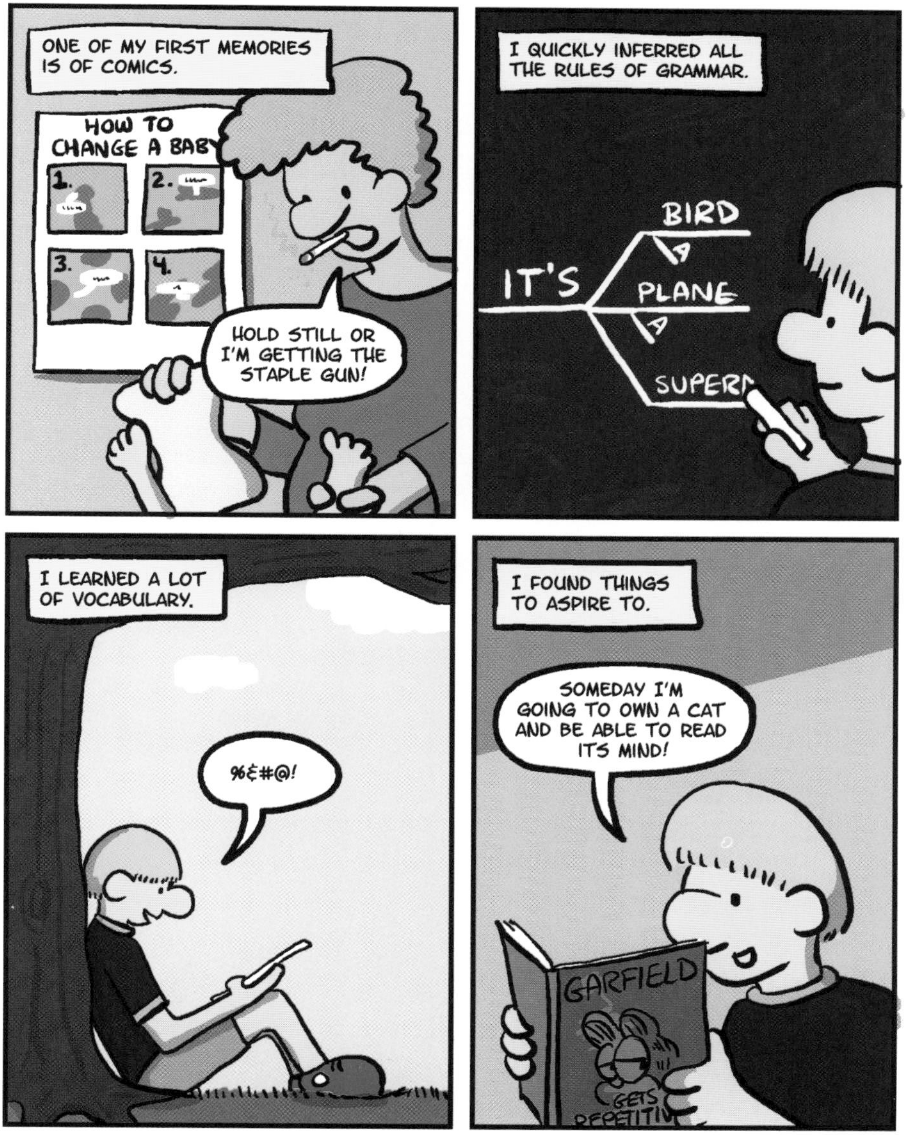

ONE OF MY FIRST MEMORIES IS OF COMICS.
HOW TO CHANGE A BABY
1.
2.
3.
4.
HOLD STILL OR I'M GETTING THE STAPLE GUN!
I QUICKLY INFERRED ALL THE RULES OF GRAMMAR.
IT'S
BIRD
A
PLANE
A
SUPERM
I LEARNED A LOT OF VOCABULARY.
%&#@!
I FOUND THINGS TO ASPIRE TO.
SOMEDAY I'M GOING TO OWN A CAT AND BE ABLE TO READ ITS MIND!
GARFIELD
GETS

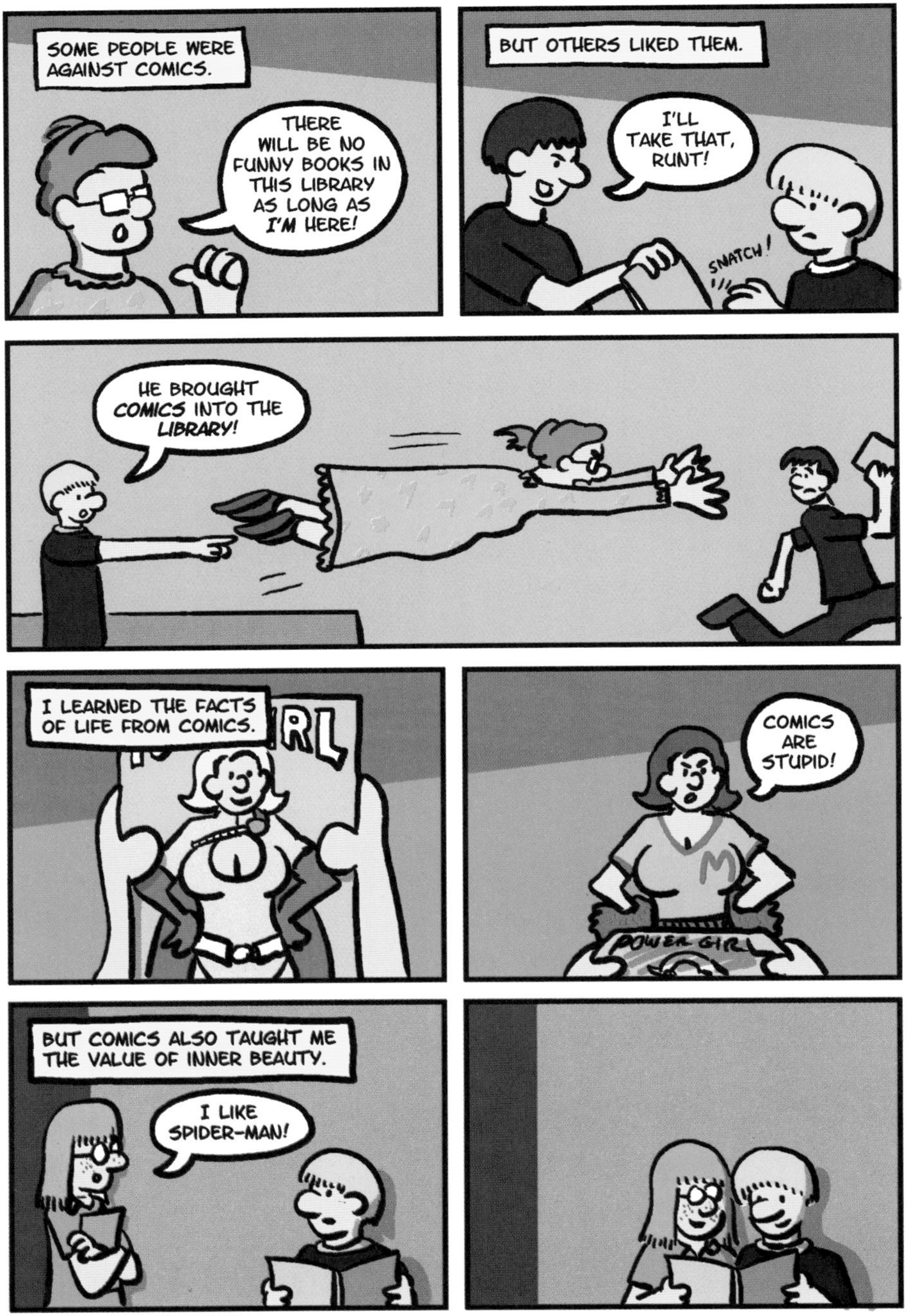
SOME PEOPLE WERE AGAINST COMICS.
THERE WILL BE NO FUNNY BOOKS IN THIS LIBRARY AS LONG AS I'M HERE!
BUT OTHERS LIKED THEM.
I'LL TAKE THAT, RUNT!
SNATCH!
HE BROUGHT COMICS INTO THE LIBRARY!
I LEARNED THE FACTS OF LIFE FROM COMICS.
COMICS ARE STUPID!
POWER GIRL
BUT COMICS ALSO TAUGHT ME THE VALUE OF INNER BEAUTY.
I LIKE SPIDER-MAN!

Bibliovores

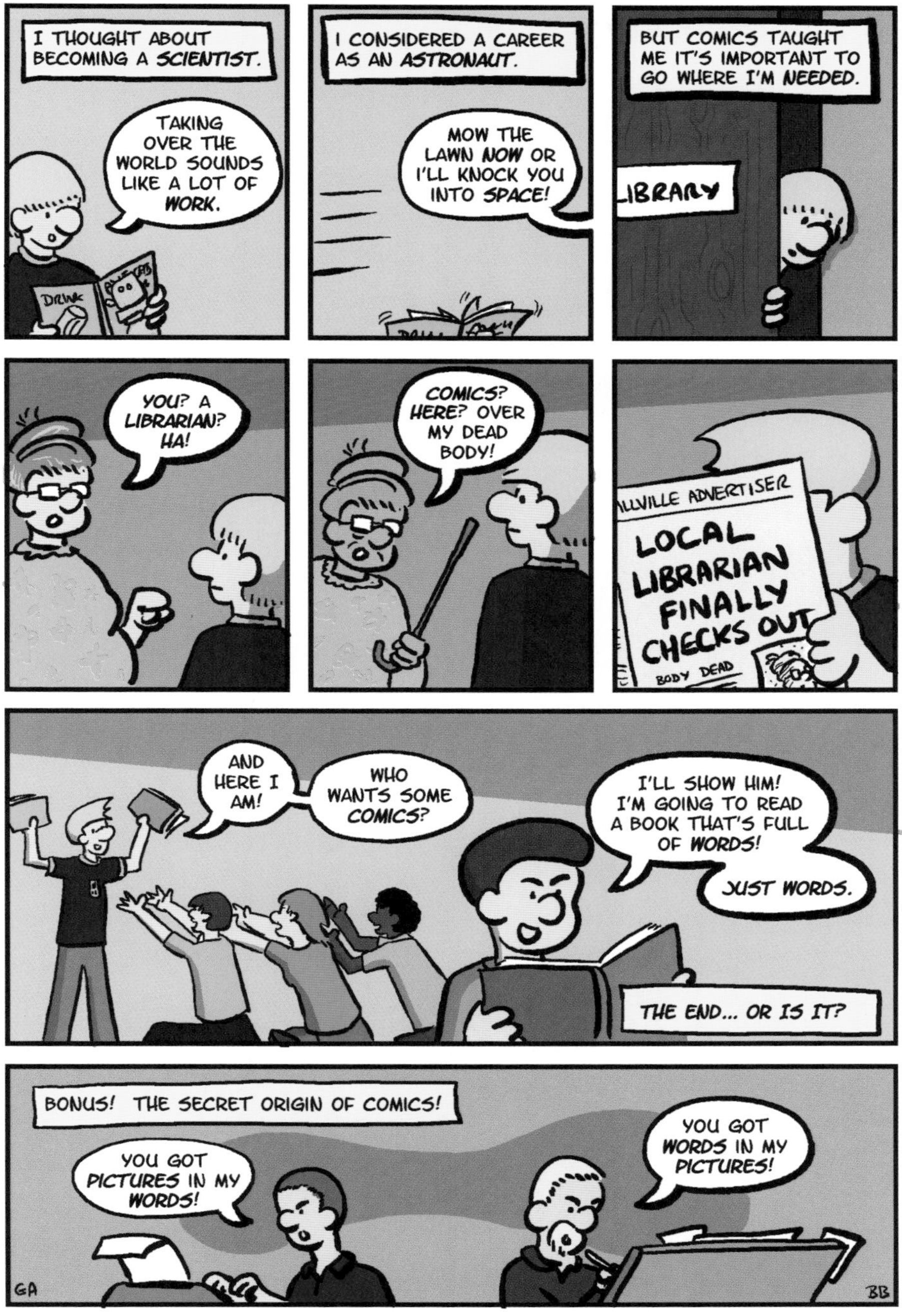
I THOUGHT ABOUT BECOMING A SCIENTIST.
TAKING OVER THE WORLD SOUNDS LIKE A LOT OF WORK.
DRINK
I CONSIDERED A CAREER AS AN ASTRONAUT.
MOW THE LAWN NOW OR I'LL KNOCK YOU INTO SPACE!
BUT COMICS TAUGHT ME IT'S IMPORTANT TO GO WHERE I'M NEEDED.
LIBRARY
YOU? A LIBRARIAN? HA!
COMICS? HERE? OVER MY DEAD BODY!
LLVILLE ADVERTISER
LOCAL LIBRARIAN FINALLY CHECKS OUT
BODY DEAD
AND HERE I AM!
WHO WANTS SOME COMICS?
I'LL SHOW HIM! I'M GOING TO READ A BOOK THAT'S FULL OF WORDS!
JUST WORDS.
THE END... OR IS IT?
BONUS! THE SECRET ORIGIN OF COMICS!
YOU GOT PICTURES IN MY WORDS!
YOU GOT WORDS IN MY PICTURES!
GA
BB

On October 1, 2012, after ten and a half years of drawing daily *Unshelved* strips almost exclusively in black and white, Bill upgraded to color. A few traditionalists complained, but most folks seemed to appreciate the change. Bill also took the opportunity to add some texture to the background, and tweaked the colors we had been using in our weekend *Unshelved Book Club* book recommendation strips. Next up: holograms!

DON'T GET ME ANGRY. YOU WOULDN'T LIKE ME WHEN I'M ANGRY.
I DON'T LIKE YOU NOW.
BB

I WANT TO SHARE MY GREAT IDEAS.
AND BY "SHARE" YOU MEAN...
I WANT TO MAKE MONEY.
TELL ME MORE ABOUT THESE IDEAS OF YOURS.
THEY AREN'T EXACTLY MINE...
SO BASICALLY YOU JUST WANT SOME CASH.
YOU REALLY GET ME.
BB

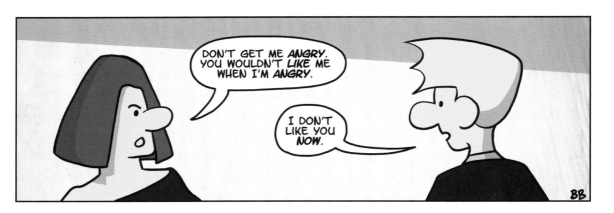

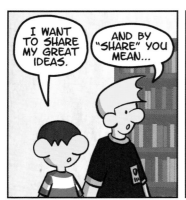

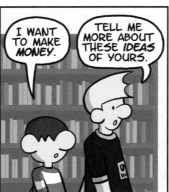

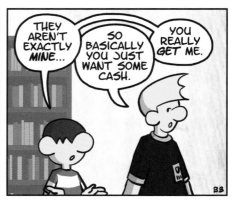

Bibliovores

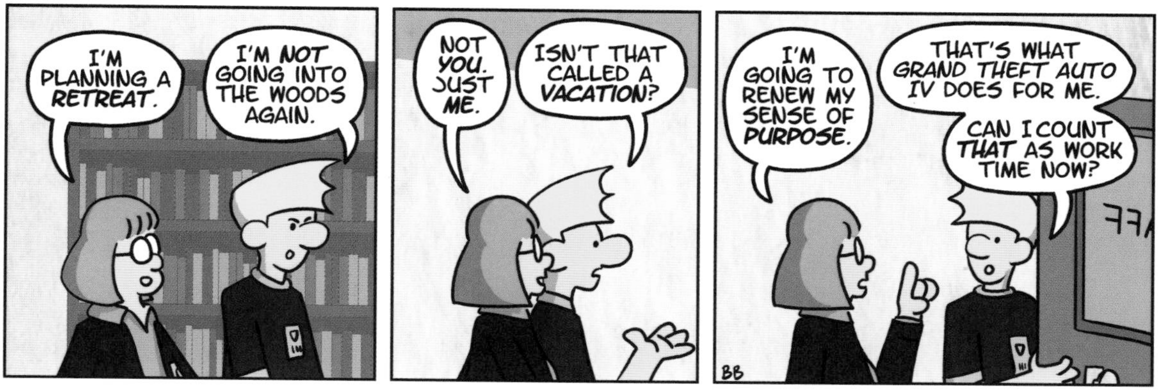

I'M PLANNING A RETREAT.
I'M NOT GOING INTO THE WOODS AGAIN.
NOT YOU. JUST ME.
ISN'T THAT CALLED A VACATION?
I'M GOING TO RENEW MY SENSE OF PURPOSE.
THAT'S WHAT GRAND THEFT AUTO IV DOES FOR ME.
CAN I COUNT THAT AS WORK TIME NOW?
BB

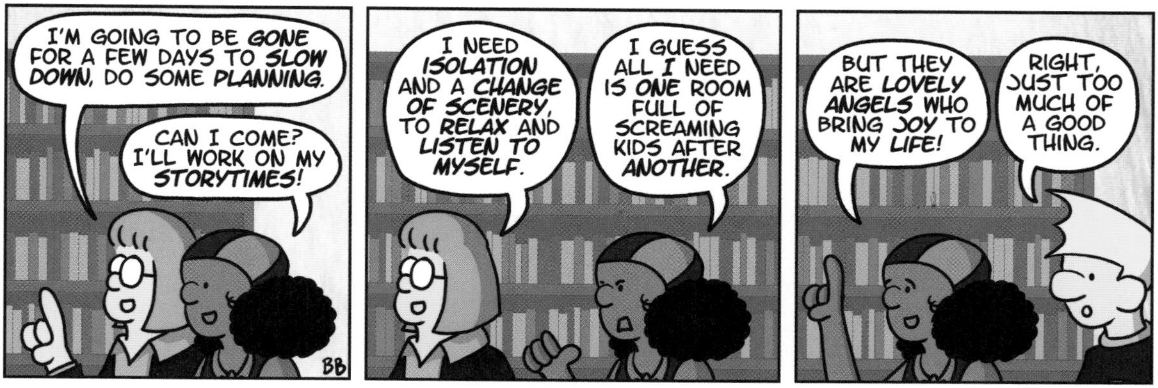

I'M GOING TO BE GONE FOR A FEW DAYS TO SLOW DOWN, DO SOME PLANNING.
CAN I COME? I'LL WORK ON MY STORYTIMES!
BB
I NEED ISOLATION AND A CHANGE OF SCENERY, TO RELAX AND LISTEN TO MYSELF.
I GUESS ALL I NEED IS ONE ROOM FULL OF SCREAMING KIDS AFTER ANOTHER.
BUT THEY ARE LOVELY ANGELS WHO BRING JOY TO MY LIFE!
RIGHT, JUST TOO MUCH OF A GOOD THING.

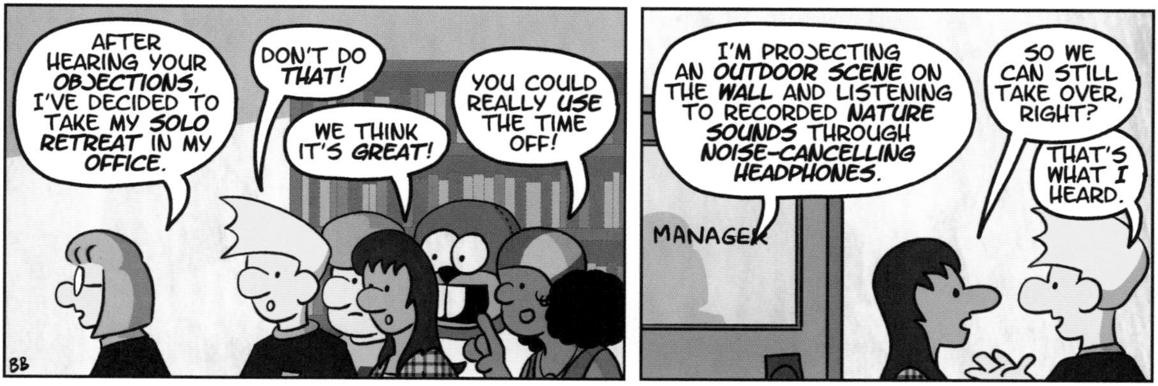

AFTER HEARING YOUR OBJECTIONS, I'VE DECIDED TO TAKE MY SOLO RETREAT IN MY OFFICE.
DON'T DO THAT!
WE THINK IT'S GREAT!
YOU COULD REALLY USE THE TIME OFF!
BB
I'M PROJECTING AN OUTDOOR SCENE ON THE WALL AND LISTENING TO RECORDED NATURE SOUNDS THROUGH NOISE-CANCELLING HEADPHONES.
MANAGE
SO WE CAN STILL TAKE OVER, RIGHT?
THAT'S WHAT I HEARD.

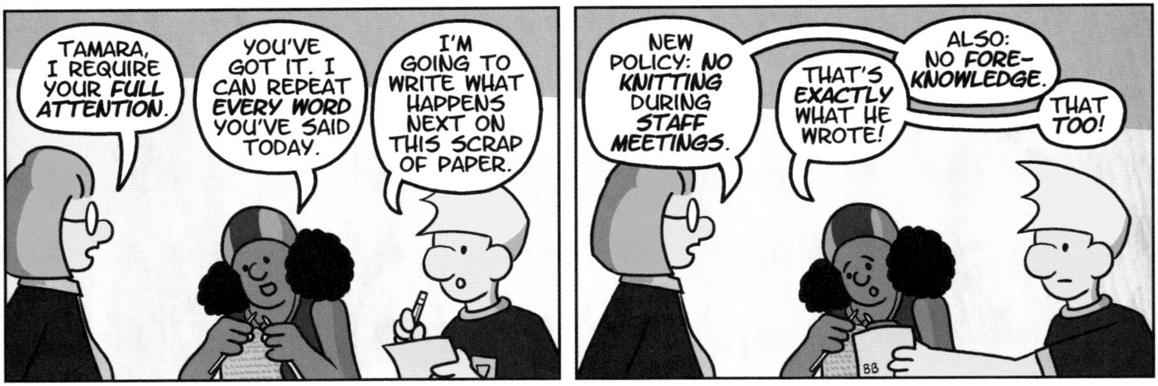
TAMARA, I REQUIRE YOUR FULL ATTENTION.
YOU'VE GOT IT. I CAN REPEAT EVERY WORD YOU'VE SAID TODAY.
I'M GOING TO WRITE WHAT HAPPENS NEXT ON THIS SCRAP OF PAPER.
NEW POLICY: NO KNITTING DURING STAFF MEETINGS.
ALSO: NO FORE-KNOWLEDGE.
THAT'S EXACTLY WHAT HE WROTE!
THAT TOO!
BB

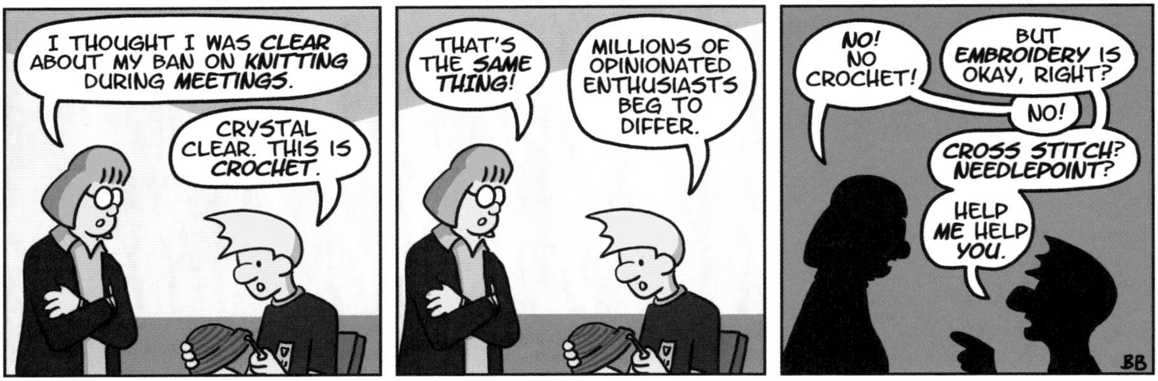
I THOUGHT I WAS CLEAR ABOUT MY BAN ON KNITTING DURING MEETINGS.
CRYSTAL CLEAR. THIS IS CROCHET.
THAT'S THE SAME THING!
MILLIONS OF OPINIONATED ENTHUSIASTS BEG TO DIFFER.
NO! NO CROCHET!
BUT EMBROIDERY IS OKAY, RIGHT?
NO!
CROSS STITCH? NEEDLEPOINT?
HELP ME HELP YOU.
BB

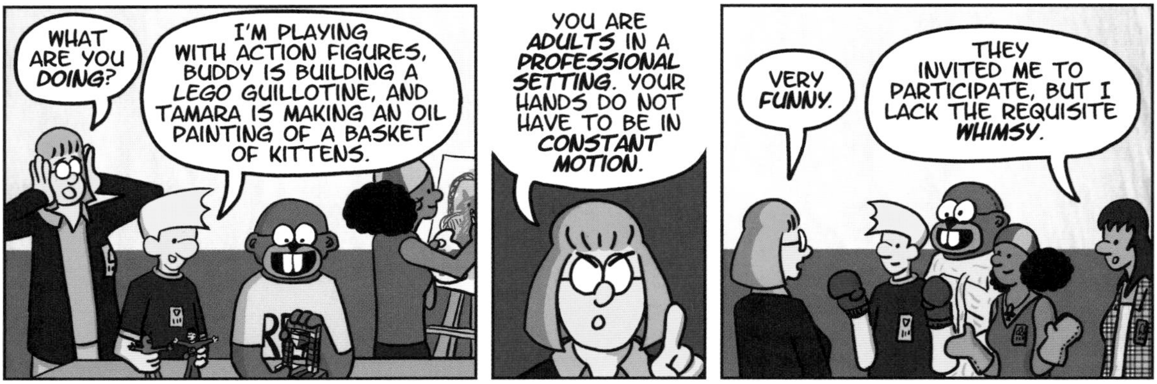
WHAT ARE YOU DOING?
I'M PLAYING WITH ACTION FIGURES, BUDDY IS BUILDING A LEGO GUILLOTINE, AND TAMARA IS MAKING AN OIL PAINTING OF A BASKET OF KITTENS.
YOU ARE ADULTS IN A PROFESSIONAL SETTING. YOUR HANDS DO NOT HAVE TO BE IN CONSTANT MOTION.
VERY FUNNY.
THEY INVITED ME TO PARTICIPATE, BUT I LACK THE REQUISITE WHIMSY.

Bibliovores

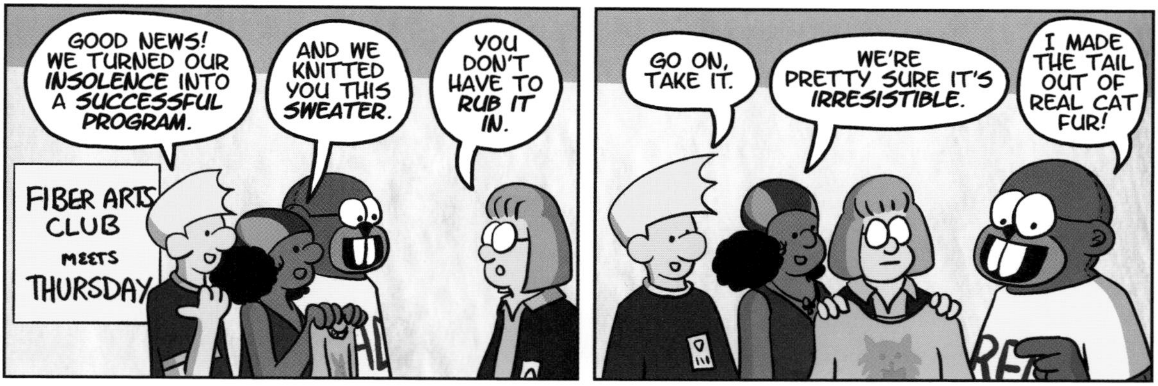
GOOD NEWS! WE TURNED OUR INSOLENCE INTO A SUCCESSFUL PROGRAM.
AND WE KNITTED YOU THIS SWEATER.
YOU DON'T HAVE TO RUB IT IN.
FIBER ARTS CLUB MEETS THURSDAY
GO ON, TAKE IT.
WE'RE PRETTY SURE IT'S IRRESISTIBLE.
I MADE THE TAIL OUT OF REAL CAT FUR!

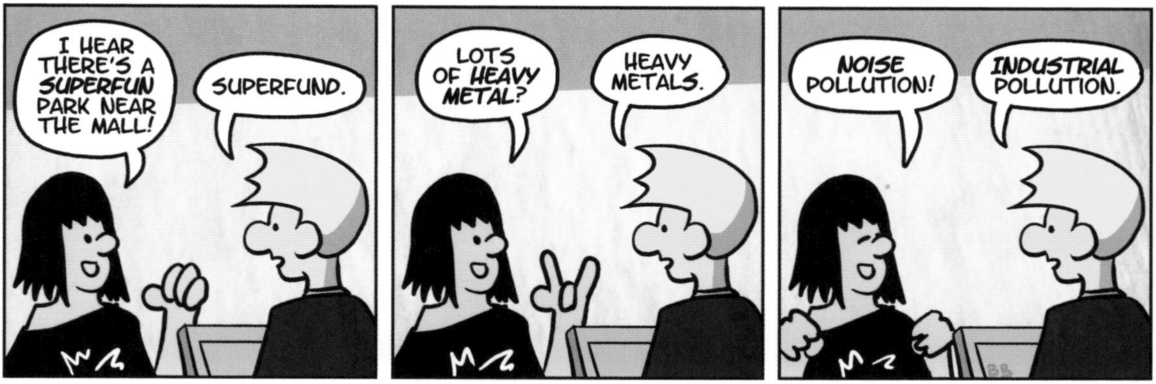
I HEAR THERE'S A SUPERFUN PARK NEAR THE MALL!
SUPERFUND.
LOTS OF HEAVY METAL?
HEAVY METALS.
NOISE POLLUTION!
INDUSTRIAL POLLUTION.

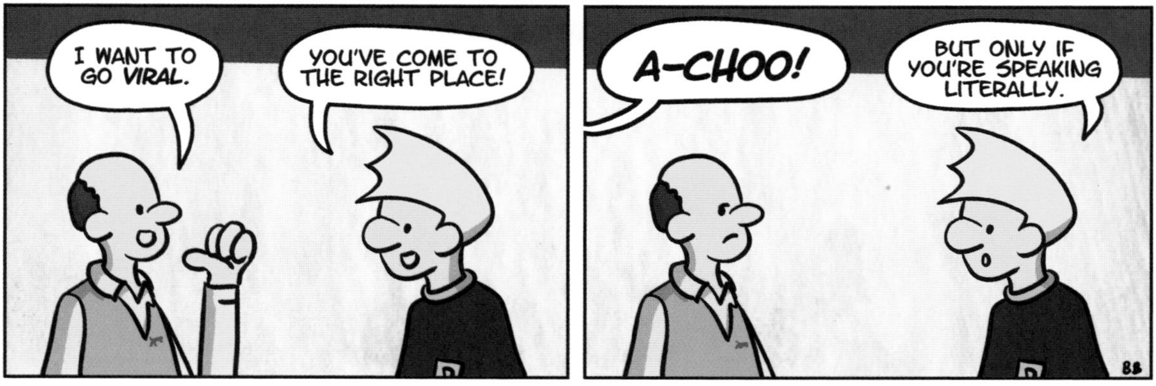
I WANT TO GO VIRAL.
YOU'VE COME TO THE RIGHT PLACE!
A-CHOO!
BUT ONLY IF YOU'RE SPEAKING LITERALLY.

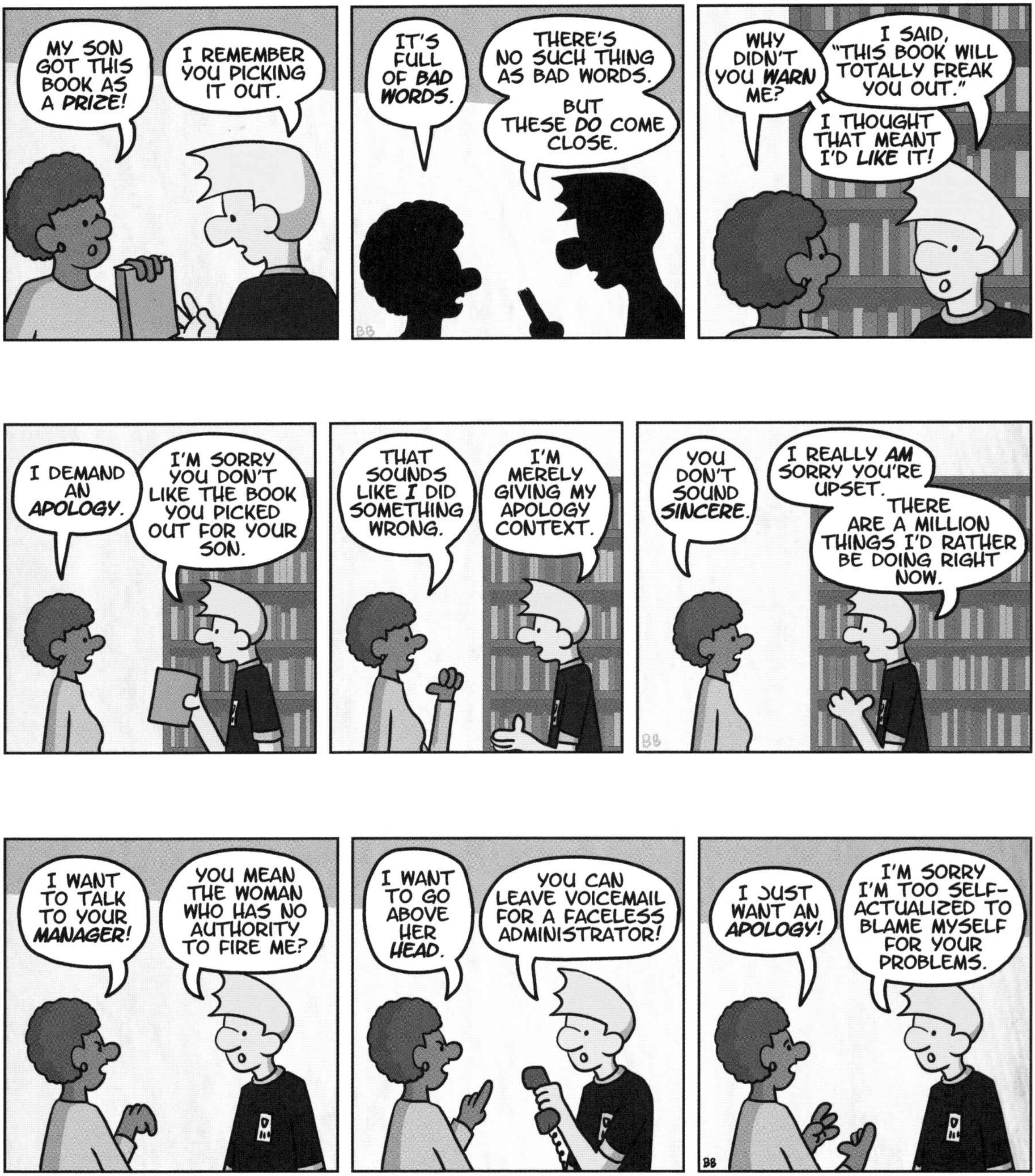
MY SON GOT THIS BOOK AS A *PRIZE*!
I REMEMBER YOU PICKING IT OUT.
IT'S FULL OF *BAD WORDS*.
THERE'S NO SUCH THING AS BAD WORDS.
BUT THESE *DO* COME CLOSE.
WHY DIDN'T YOU *WARN* ME?
I SAID, "THIS BOOK WILL TOTALLY FREAK YOU OUT."
I THOUGHT THAT MEANT I'D *LIKE* IT!
I DEMAND AN *APOLOGY*.
I'M SORRY YOU DON'T LIKE THE BOOK YOU PICKED OUT FOR YOUR SON.
THAT SOUNDS LIKE *I* DID SOMETHING WRONG.
I'M MERELY GIVING MY APOLOGY CONTEXT.
YOU DON'T SOUND *SINCERE*.
I REALLY *AM* SORRY YOU'RE UPSET.
THERE ARE A MILLION THINGS I'D RATHER BE DOING RIGHT NOW.
I WANT TO TALK TO YOUR *MANAGER*!
YOU MEAN THE WOMAN WHO HAS NO AUTHORITY TO FIRE ME?
I WANT TO GO ABOVE HER *HEAD*.
YOU CAN LEAVE VOICEMAIL FOR A FACELESS ADMINISTRATOR!
I JUST WANT AN *APOLOGY*!
I'M SORRY I'M TOO SELF-ACTUALIZED TO BLAME MYSELF FOR YOUR PROBLEMS.

Bibliovores

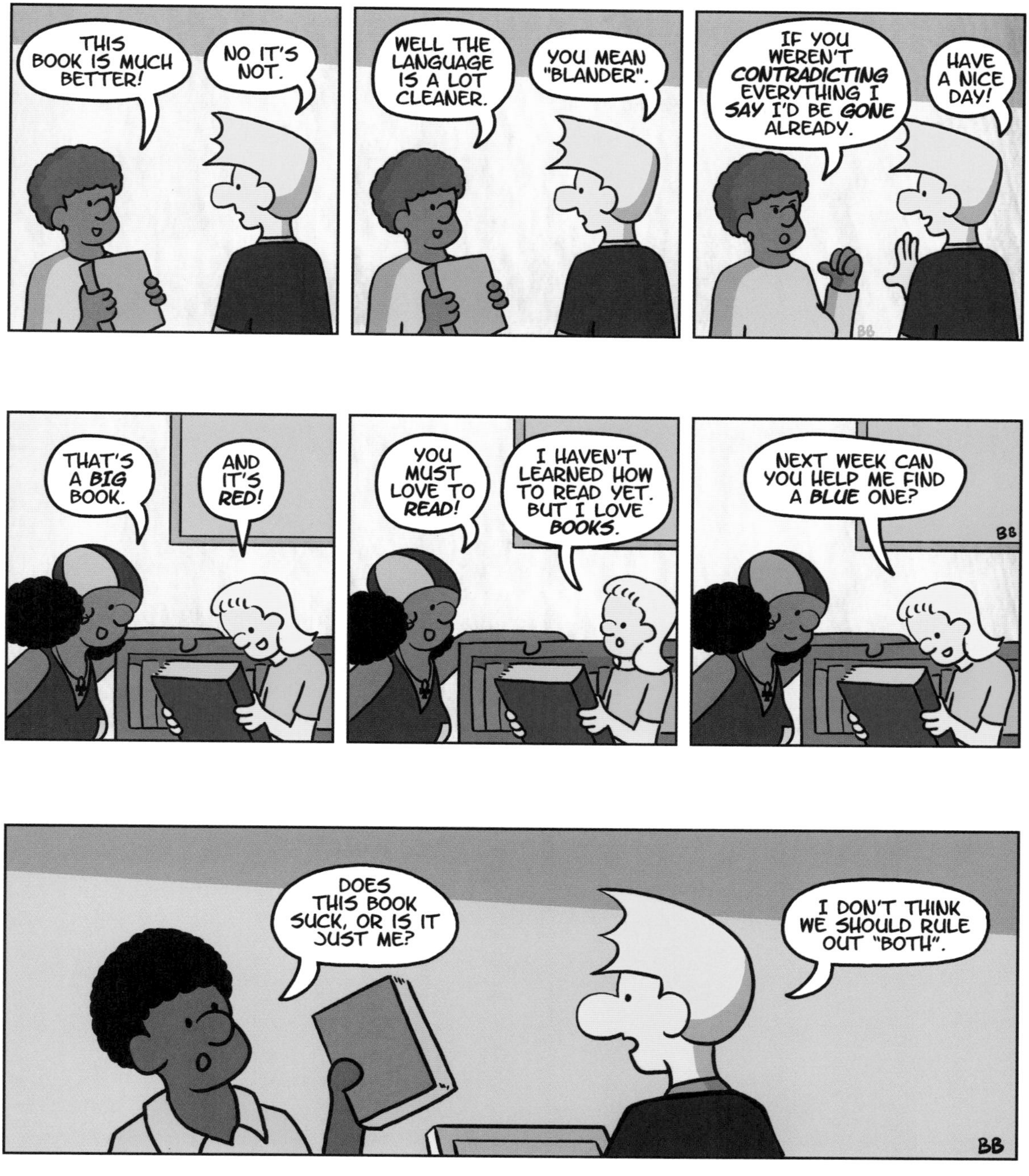

THIS BOOK IS MUCH BETTER!
NO IT'S NOT.
WELL THE LANGUAGE IS A LOT CLEANER.
YOU MEAN "BLANDER".
IF YOU WEREN'T CONTRADICTING EVERYTHING I SAY I'D BE GONE ALREADY.
HAVE A NICE DAY!
BB
THAT'S A BIG BOOK.
AND IT'S RED!
YOU MUST LOVE TO READ!
I HAVEN'T LEARNED HOW TO READ YET. BUT I LOVE BOOKS.
NEXT WEEK CAN YOU HELP ME FIND A BLUE ONE?
BB
DOES THIS BOOK SUCK, OR IS IT JUST ME?
I DON'T THINK WE SHOULD RULE OUT "BOTH".
BB

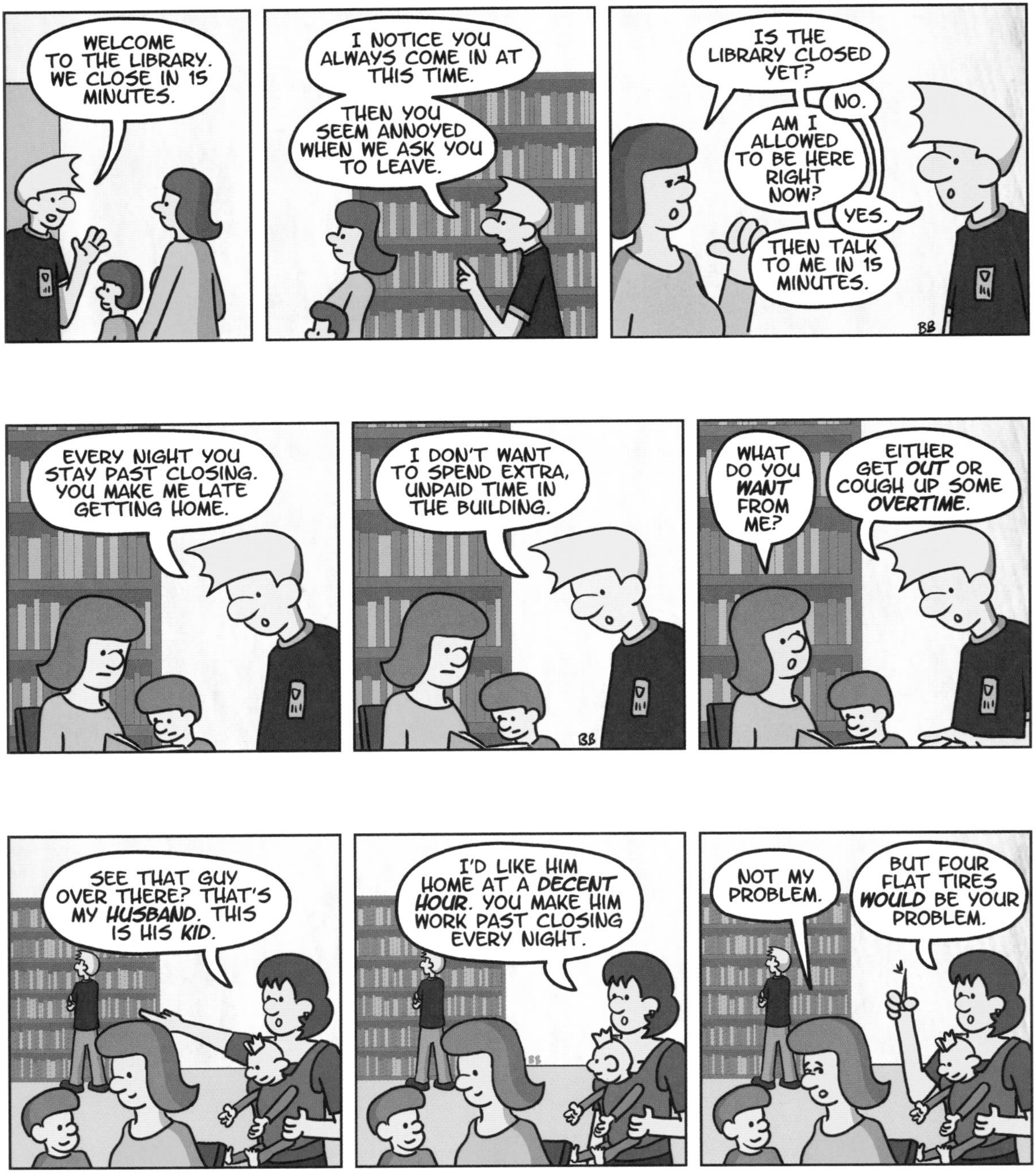
WELCOME TO THE LIBRARY. WE CLOSE IN 15 MINUTES.
I NOTICE YOU ALWAYS COME IN AT THIS TIME.
THEN YOU SEEM ANNOYED WHEN WE ASK YOU TO LEAVE.
IS THE LIBRARY CLOSED YET?
NO.
AM I ALLOWED TO BE HERE RIGHT NOW?
YES.
THEN TALK TO ME IN 15 MINUTES.
BB
EVERY NIGHT YOU STAY PAST CLOSING. YOU MAKE ME LATE GETTING HOME.
I DON'T WANT TO SPEND EXTRA, UNPAID TIME IN THE BUILDING.
BB
WHAT DO YOU *WANT* FROM ME?
EITHER GET *OUT* OR COUGH UP SOME *OVERTIME*.
SEE THAT GUY OVER THERE? THAT'S MY *HUSBAND*. THIS IS HIS *KID*.
I'D LIKE HIM HOME AT A *DECENT HOUR*. YOU MAKE HIM WORK PAST CLOSING EVERY NIGHT.
BB
NOT MY PROBLEM.
BUT FOUR FLAT TIRES *WOULD* BE YOUR PROBLEM.

Bibliovores

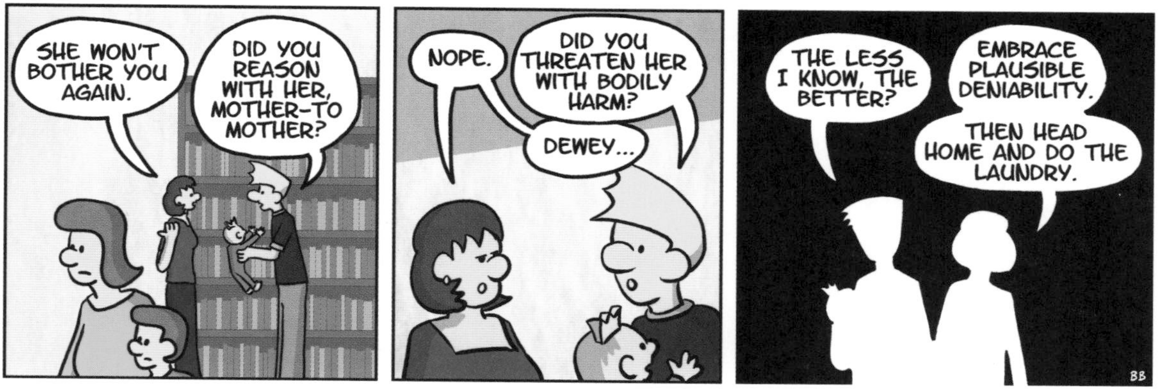
SHE WON'T BOTHER YOU AGAIN.
DID YOU REASON WITH HER, MOTHER-TO MOTHER?
NOPE.
DID YOU THREATEN HER WITH BODILY HARM?
DEWEY...
THE LESS I KNOW, THE BETTER?
EMBRACE PLAUSIBLE DENIABILITY.
THEN HEAD HOME AND DO THE LAUNDRY.

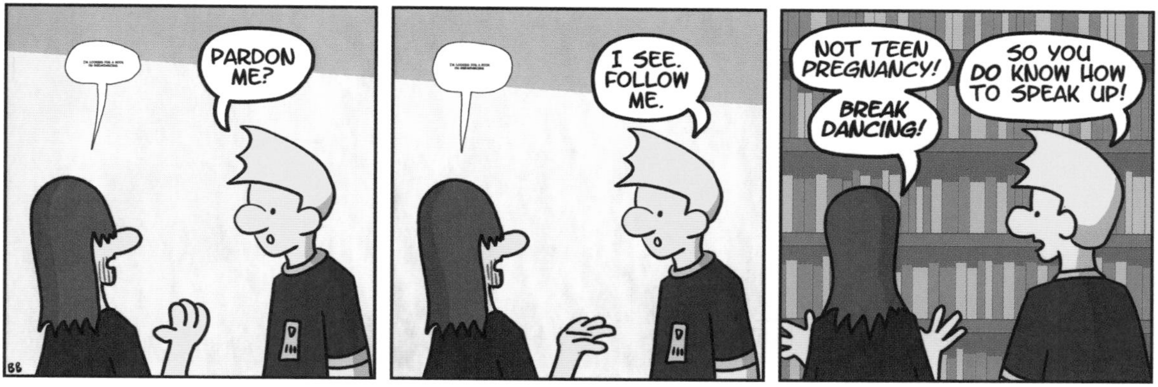
PARDON ME?
I SEE. FOLLOW ME.
NOT TEEN PREGNANCY!
BREAK DANCING!
SO YOU DO KNOW HOW TO SPEAK UP!

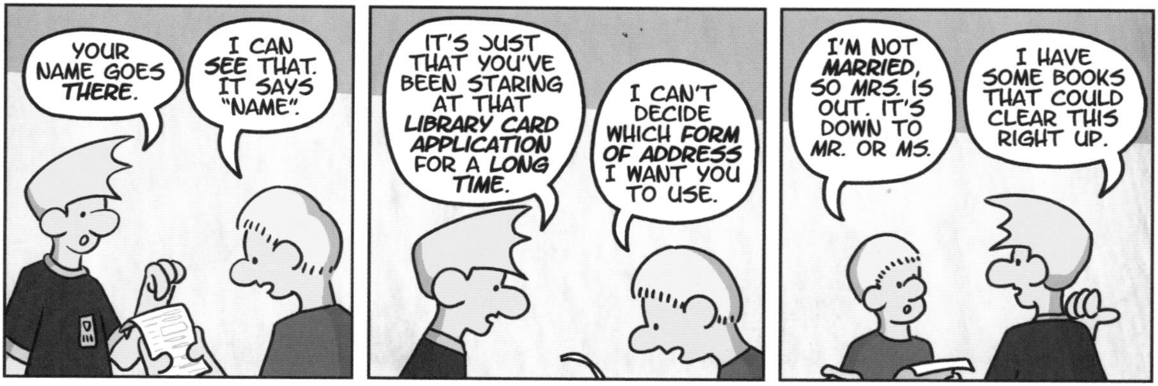
YOUR NAME GOES THERE.
I CAN SEE THAT. IT SAYS "NAME".
IT'S JUST THAT YOU'VE BEEN STARING AT THAT LIBRARY CARD APPLICATION FOR A LONG TIME.
I CAN'T DECIDE WHICH FORM OF ADDRESS I WANT YOU TO USE.
I'M NOT MARRIED, SO MRS. IS OUT. IT'S DOWN TO MR. OR MS.
I HAVE SOME BOOKS THAT COULD CLEAR THIS RIGHT UP.

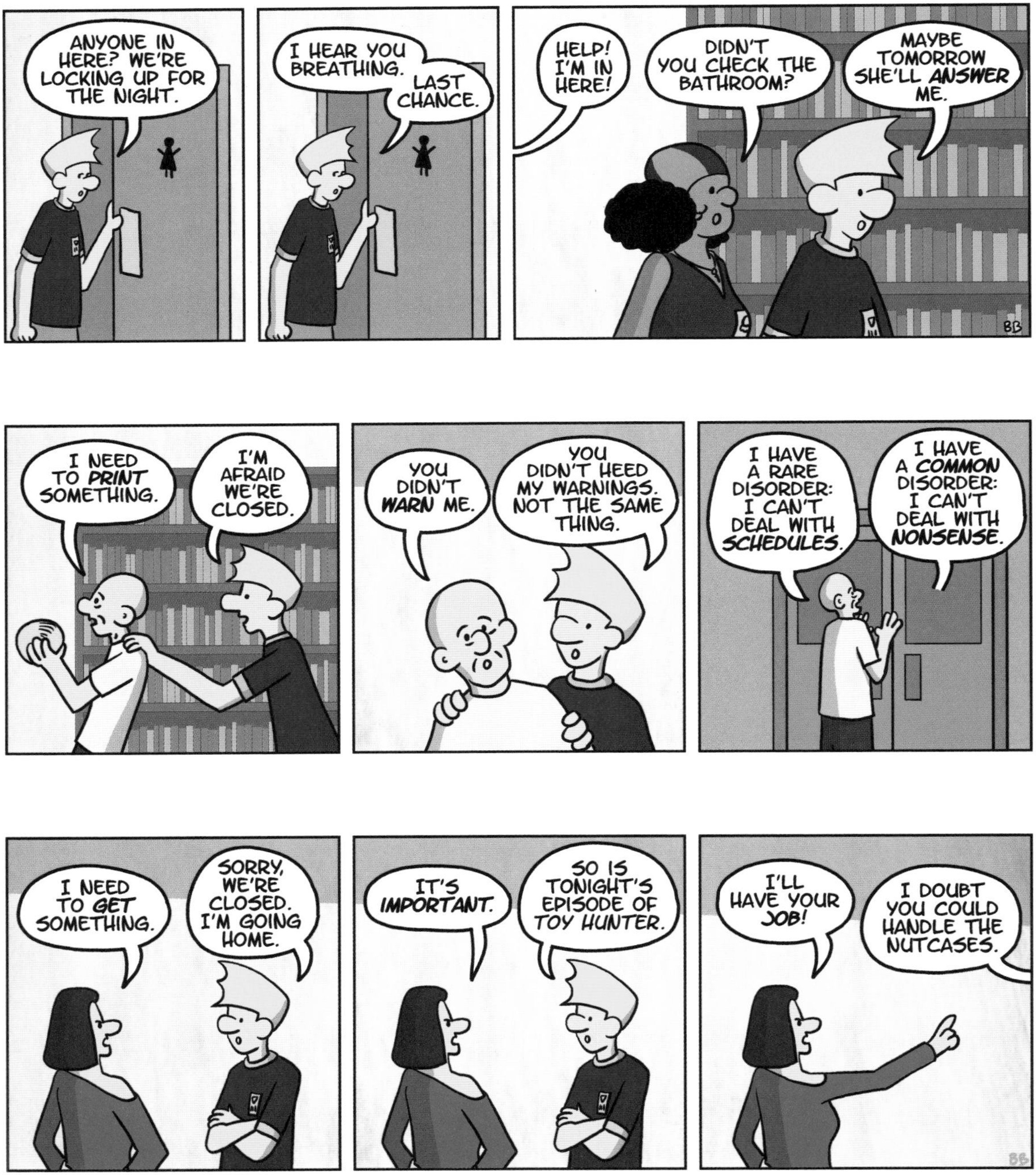
ANYONE IN HERE? WE'RE LOCKING UP FOR THE NIGHT.
I HEAR YOU BREATHING.
LAST CHANCE.
HELP! I'M IN HERE!
DIDN'T YOU CHECK THE BATHROOM?
MAYBE TOMORROW SHE'LL ANSWER ME.
BB
I NEED TO PRINT SOMETHING.
I'M AFRAID WE'RE CLOSED.
YOU DIDN'T WARN ME.
YOU DIDN'T HEED MY WARNINGS. NOT THE SAME THING.
I HAVE A RARE DISORDER: I CAN'T DEAL WITH SCHEDULES.
I HAVE A COMMON DISORDER: I CAN'T DEAL WITH NONSENSE.
I NEED TO GET SOMETHING.
SORRY, WE'RE CLOSED. I'M GOING HOME.
IT'S IMPORTANT.
SO IS TONIGHT'S EPISODE OF TOY HUNTER.
I'LL HAVE YOUR JOB!
I DOUBT YOU COULD HANDLE THE NUTCASES.
BB

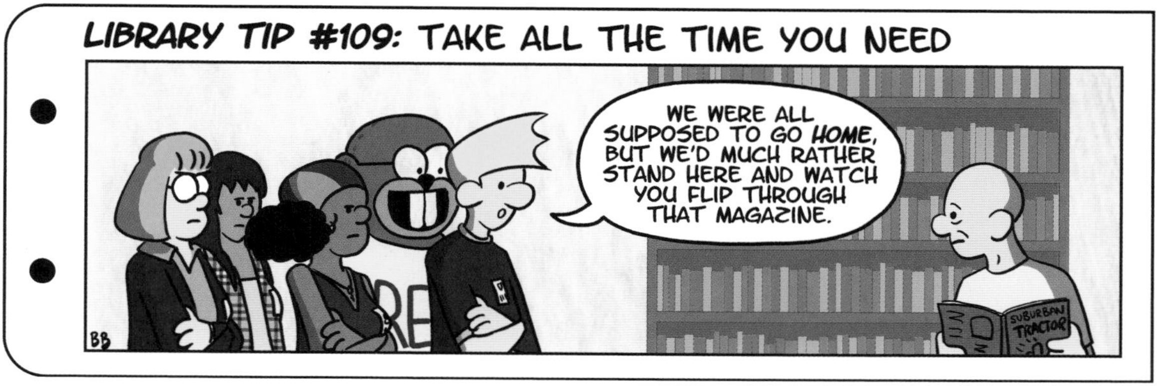
LIBRARY TIP #109: TAKE ALL THE TIME YOU NEED
WE WERE ALL SUPPOSED TO GO HOME, BUT WE'D MUCH RATHER STAND HERE AND WATCH YOU FLIP THROUGH THAT MAGAZINE.
SUBURBAN TRACTOR
BB

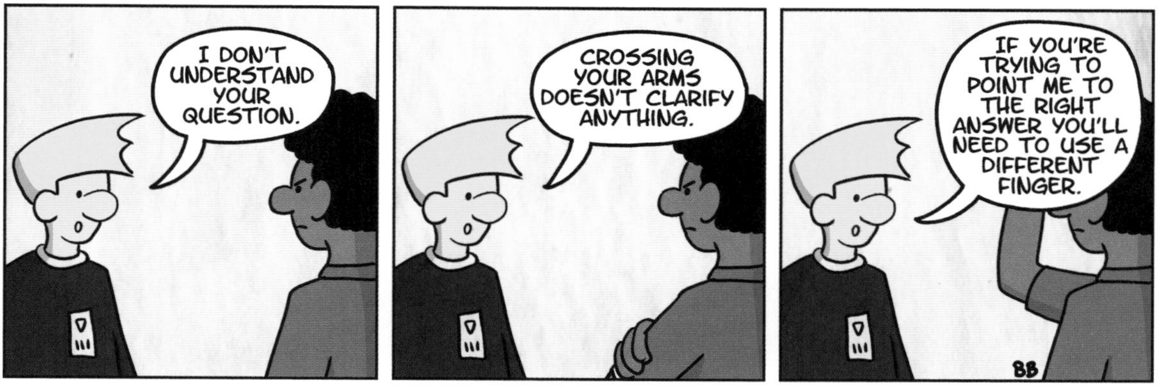
I DON'T UNDERSTAND YOUR QUESTION.
CROSSING YOUR ARMS DOESN'T CLARIFY ANYTHING.
IF YOU'RE TRYING TO POINT ME TO THE RIGHT ANSWER YOU'LL NEED TO USE A DIFFERENT FINGER.
BB

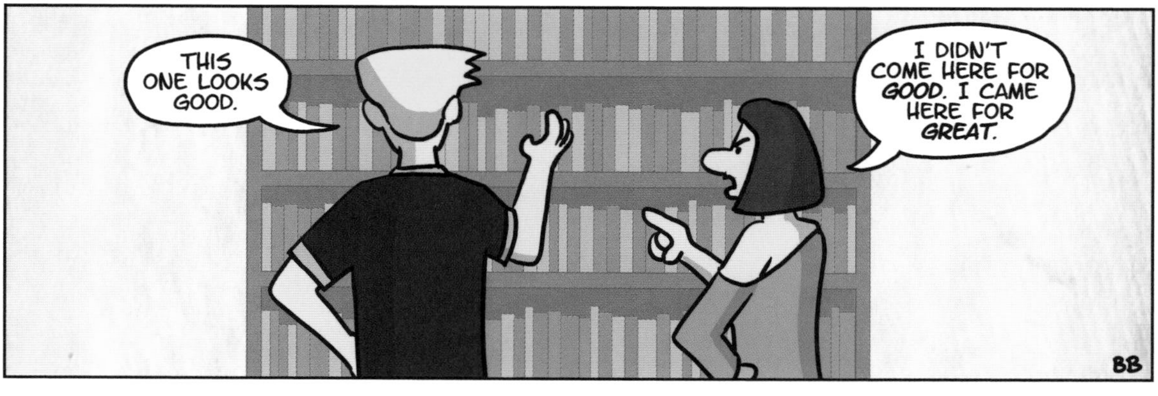
THIS ONE LOOKS GOOD.
I DIDN'T COME HERE FOR GOOD. I CAME HERE FOR GREAT.
BB

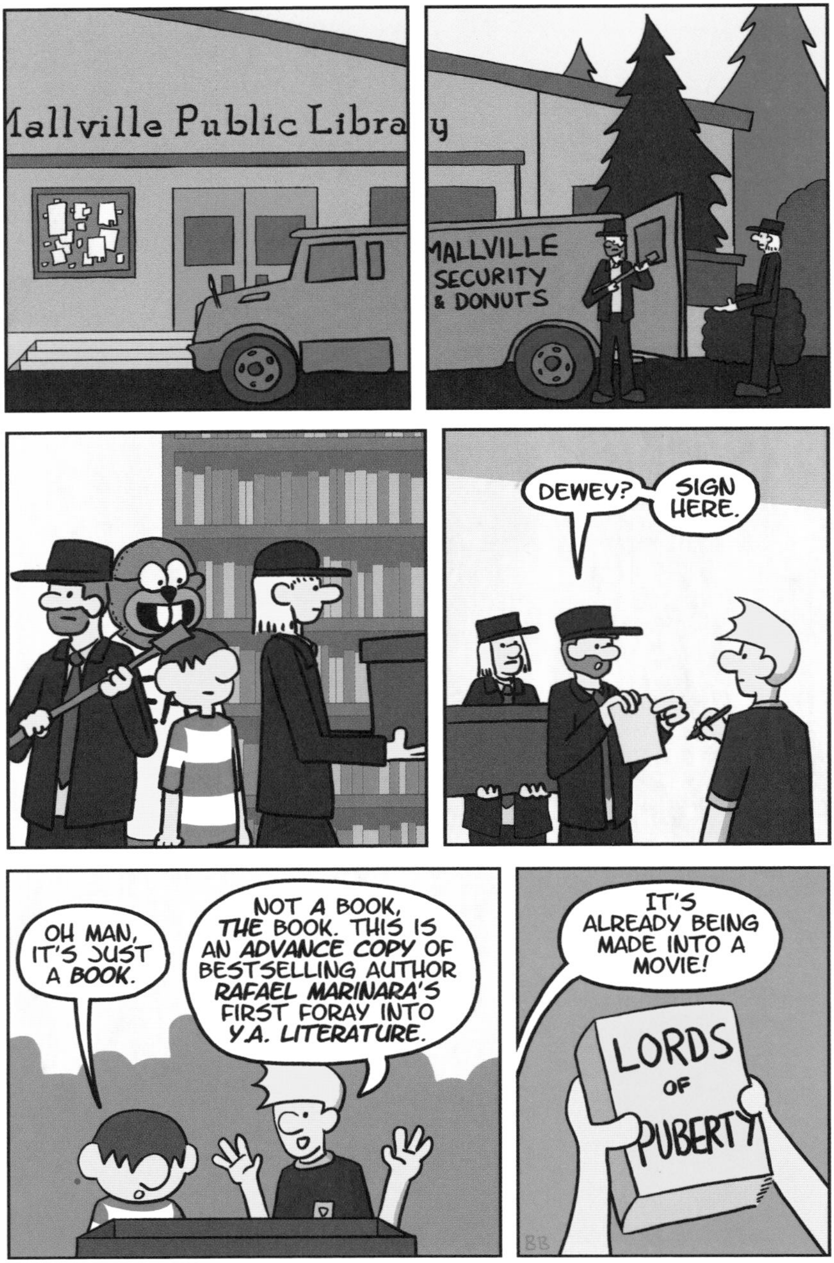
Mallville Public Library
MALLVILLE SECURITY & DONUTS
DEWEY?
SIGN HERE.
OH MAN, IT'S JUST A BOOK.
NOT A BOOK, THE BOOK. THIS IS AN ADVANCE COPY OF BESTSELLING AUTHOR RAFAEL MARINARA'S FIRST FORAY INTO Y.A. LITERATURE.
IT'S ALREADY BEING MADE INTO A MOVIE!
LORDS OF PUBERTY
BB

Bibliovores

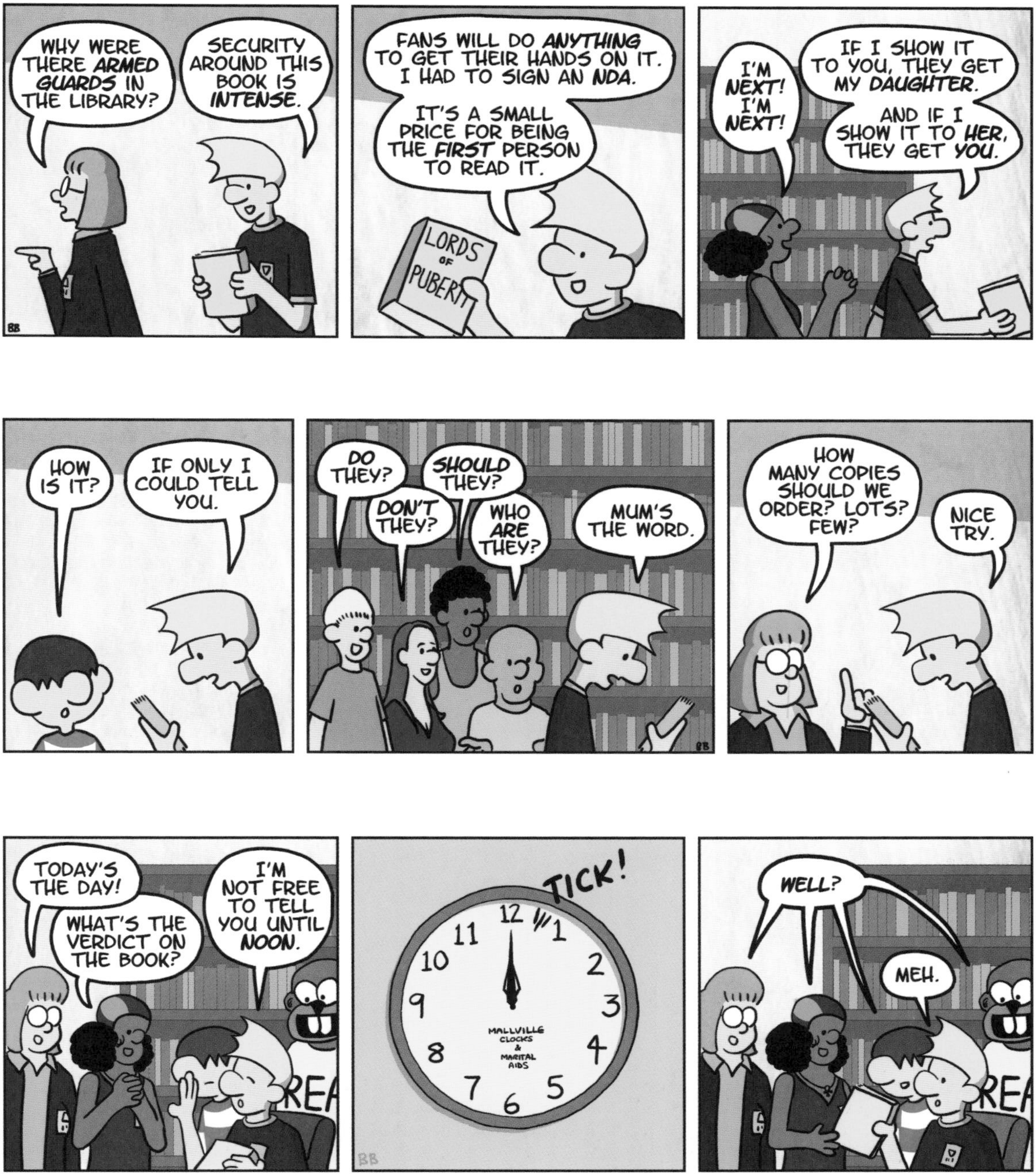

WHY WERE THERE ARMED GUARDS IN THE LIBRARY?
SECURITY AROUND THIS BOOK IS INTENSE.
FANS WILL DO ANYTHING TO GET THEIR HANDS ON IT. I HAD TO SIGN AN NDA.
IT'S A SMALL PRICE FOR BEING THE FIRST PERSON TO READ IT.
LORDS OF PUBERTY
I'M NEXT! I'M NEXT!
IF I SHOW IT TO YOU, THEY GET MY DAUGHTER.
AND IF I SHOW IT TO HER, THEY GET YOU.
HOW IS IT?
IF ONLY I COULD TELL YOU.
DO THEY?
DON'T THEY?
SHOULD THEY?
WHO ARE THEY?
MUM'S THE WORD.
HOW MANY COPIES SHOULD WE ORDER? LOTS? FEW?
NICE TRY.
TODAY'S THE DAY!
WHAT'S THE VERDICT ON THE BOOK?
I'M NOT FREE TO TELL YOU UNTIL NOON.
TICK!
MALLVILLE CLOCKS & MARITAL AIDS
WELL?
MEH.

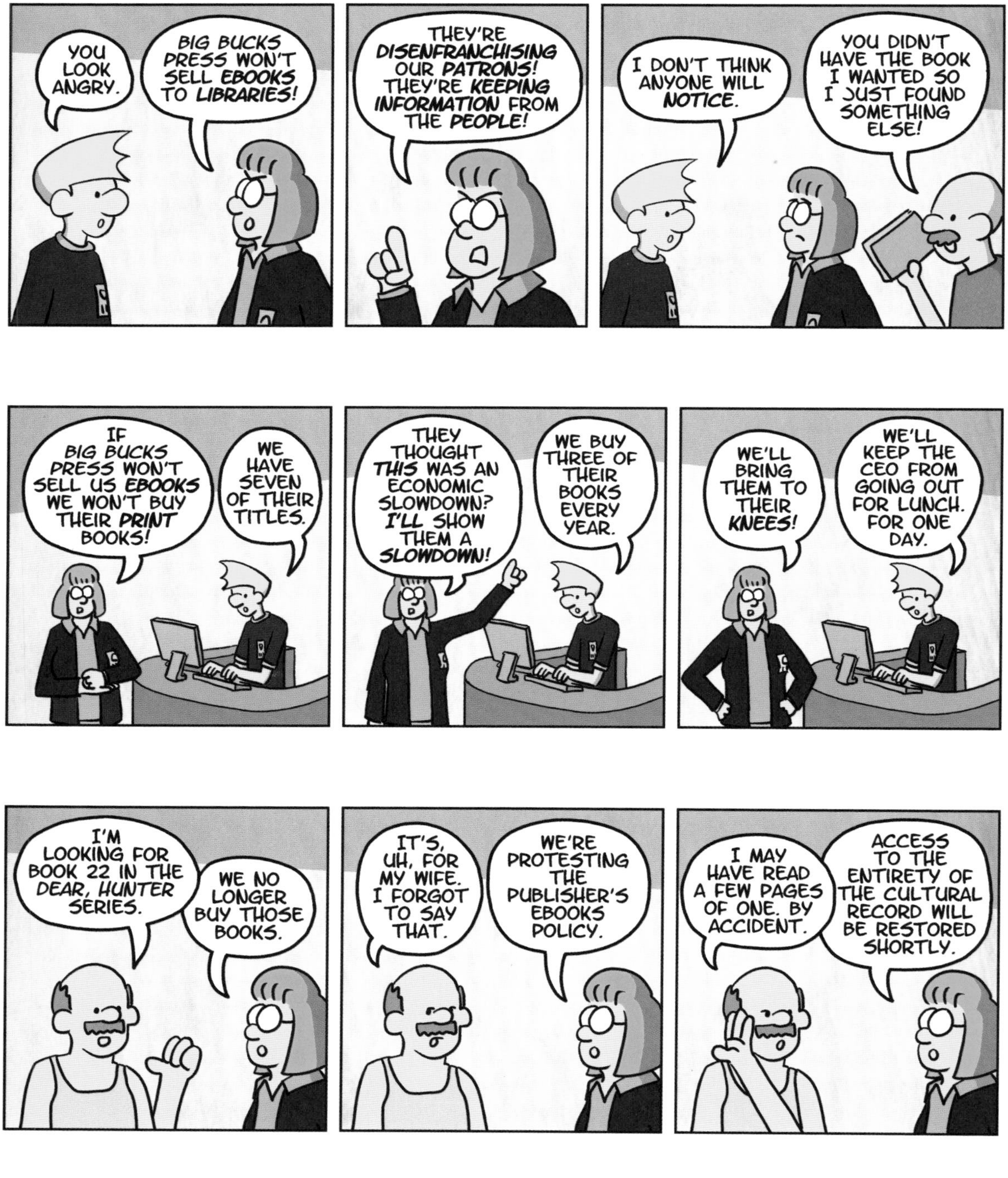
YOU LOOK ANGRY.
BIG BUCKS PRESS WON'T SELL EBOOKS TO LIBRARIES!
THEY'RE DISENFRANCHISING OUR PATRONS! THEY'RE KEEPING INFORMATION FROM THE PEOPLE!
I DON'T THINK ANYONE WILL NOTICE.
YOU DIDN'T HAVE THE BOOK I WANTED SO I JUST FOUND SOMETHING ELSE!
IF BIG BUCKS PRESS WON'T SELL US EBOOKS WE WON'T BUY THEIR PRINT BOOKS!
WE HAVE SEVEN OF THEIR TITLES.
THEY THOUGHT THIS WAS AN ECONOMIC SLOWDOWN? I'LL SHOW THEM A SLOWDOWN!
WE BUY THREE OF THEIR BOOKS EVERY YEAR.
WE'LL BRING THEM TO THEIR KNEES!
WE'LL KEEP THE CEO FROM GOING OUT FOR LUNCH. FOR ONE DAY.
I'M LOOKING FOR BOOK 22 IN THE DEAR, HUNTER SERIES.
WE NO LONGER BUY THOSE BOOKS.
IT'S, UH, FOR MY WIFE. I FORGOT TO SAY THAT.
WE'RE PROTESTING THE PUBLISHER'S EBOOKS POLICY.
I MAY HAVE READ A FEW PAGES OF ONE. BY ACCIDENT.
ACCESS TO THE ENTIRETY OF THE CULTURAL RECORD WILL BE RESTORED SHORTLY.

Bibliovores

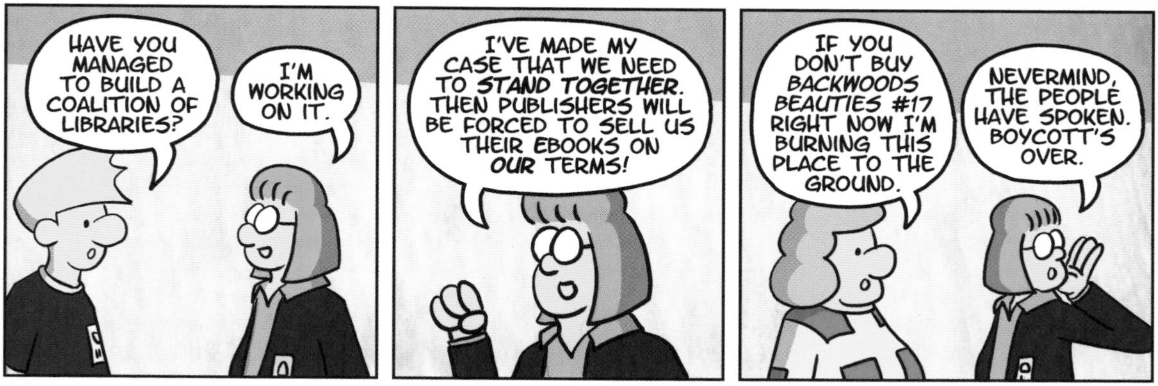
HAVE YOU MANAGED TO BUILD A COALITION OF LIBRARIES?
I'M WORKING ON IT.
I'VE MADE MY CASE THAT WE NEED TO STAND TOGETHER. THEN PUBLISHERS WILL BE FORCED TO SELL US THEIR EBOOKS ON OUR TERMS!
IF YOU DON'T BUY BACKWOODS BEAUTIES #17 RIGHT NOW I'M BURNING THIS PLACE TO THE GROUND.
NEVERMIND, THE PEOPLE HAVE SPOKEN. BOYCOTT'S OVER.

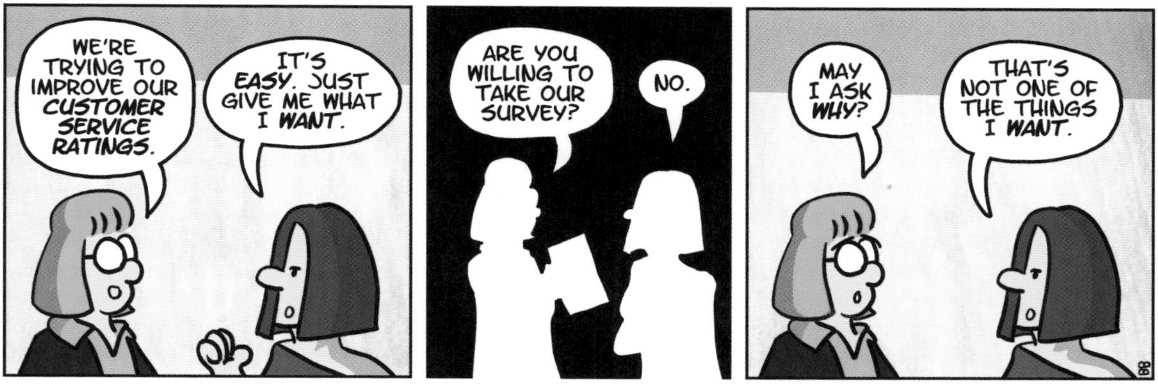
WE'RE TRYING TO IMPROVE OUR CUSTOMER SERVICE RATINGS.
IT'S EASY. JUST GIVE ME WHAT I WANT.
ARE YOU WILLING TO TAKE OUR SURVEY?
NO.
MAY I ASK WHY?
THAT'S NOT ONE OF THE THINGS I WANT.

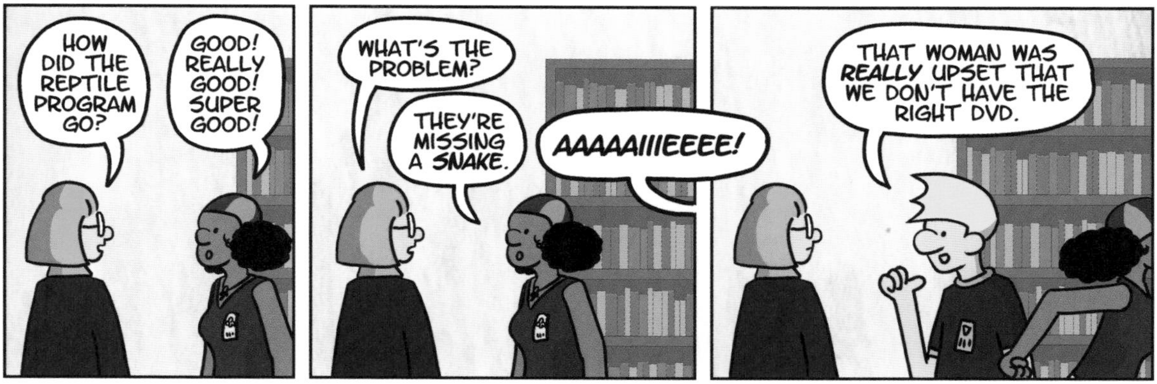
HOW DID THE REPTILE PROGRAM GO?
GOOD! REALLY GOOD! SUPER GOOD!
WHAT'S THE PROBLEM?
THEY'RE MISSING A SNAKE.
AAAAAIIIEEEE!
THAT WOMAN WAS REALLY UPSET THAT WE DON'T HAVE THE RIGHT DVD.

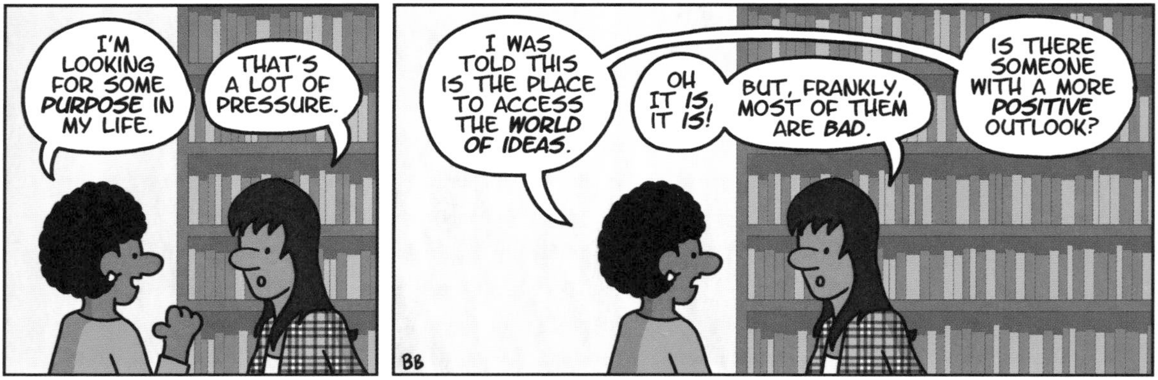
I'M LOOKING FOR SOME PURPOSE IN MY LIFE.
THAT'S A LOT OF PRESSURE.
I WAS TOLD THIS IS THE PLACE TO ACCESS THE WORLD OF IDEAS.
OH IT IS, IT IS!
BUT, FRANKLY, MOST OF THEM ARE BAD.
IS THERE SOMEONE WITH A MORE POSITIVE OUTLOOK?
BB

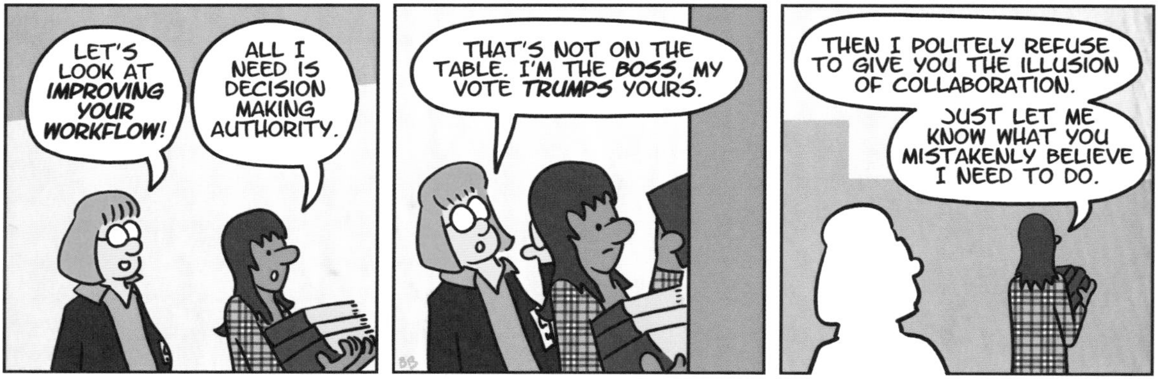
LET'S LOOK AT IMPROVING YOUR WORKFLOW!
ALL I NEED IS DECISION MAKING AUTHORITY.
THAT'S NOT ON THE TABLE. I'M THE BOSS, MY VOTE TRUMPS YOURS.
THEN I POLITELY REFUSE TO GIVE YOU THE ILLUSION OF COLLABORATION.
JUST LET ME KNOW WHAT YOU MISTAKENLY BELIEVE I NEED TO DO.
BB

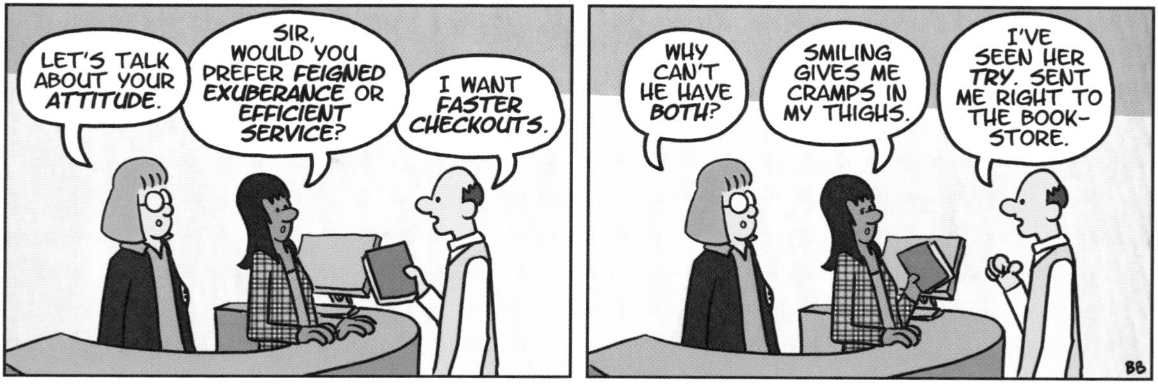
LET'S TALK ABOUT YOUR ATTITUDE.
SIR, WOULD YOU PREFER FEIGNED EXUBERANCE OR EFFICIENT SERVICE?
I WANT FASTER CHECKOUTS.
WHY CAN'T HE HAVE BOTH?
SMILING GIVES ME CRAMPS IN MY THIGHS.
I'VE SEEN HER TRY. SENT ME RIGHT TO THE BOOK-STORE.
BB

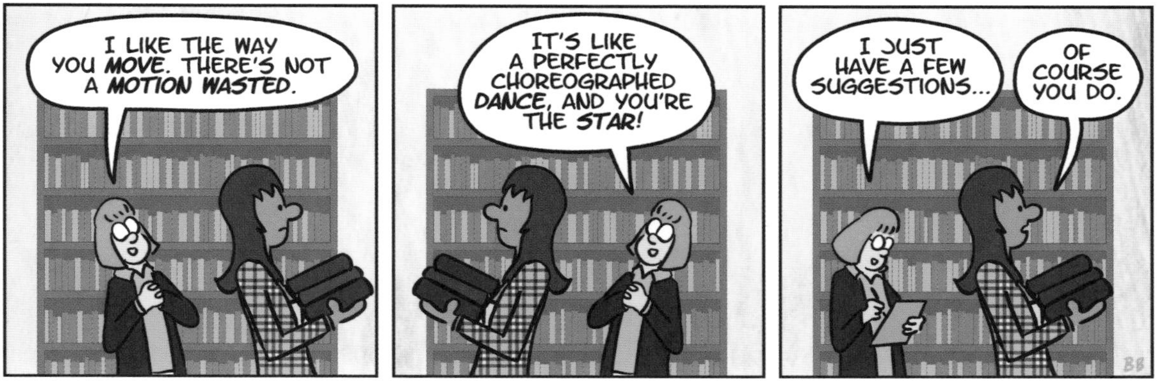
I LIKE THE WAY YOU MOVE. THERE'S NOT A MOTION WASTED.
IT'S LIKE A PERFECTLY CHOREOGRAPHED DANCE, AND YOU'RE THE STAR!
I JUST HAVE A FEW SUGGESTIONS...
OF COURSE YOU DO.
BB

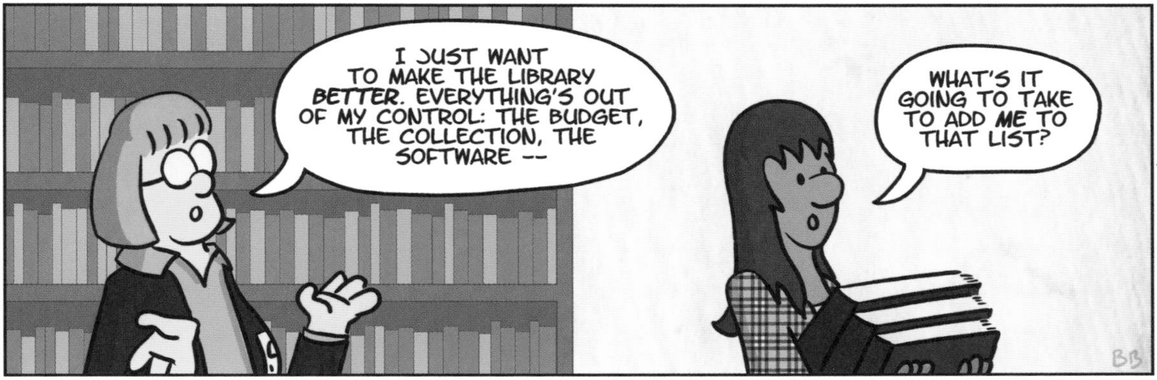
I JUST WANT TO MAKE THE LIBRARY BETTER. EVERYTHING'S OUT OF MY CONTROL: THE BUDGET, THE COLLECTION, THE SOFTWARE --
WHAT'S IT GOING TO TAKE TO ADD ME TO THAT LIST?
BB

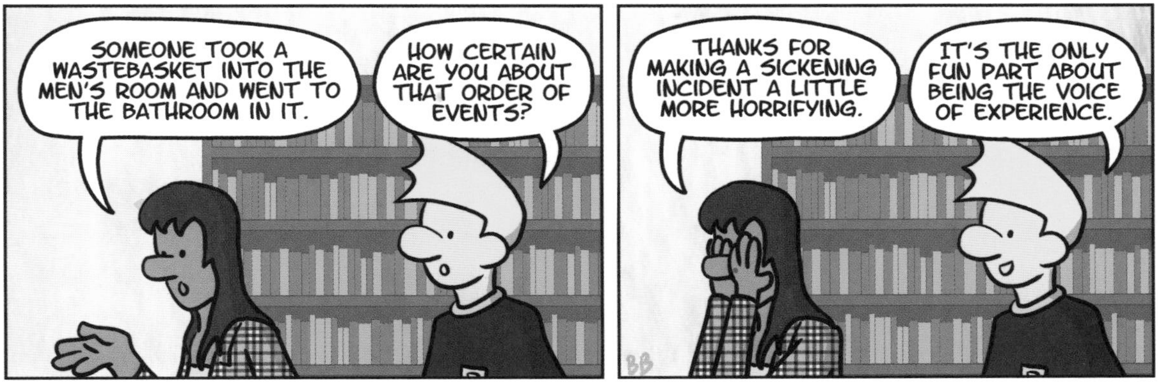
SOMEONE TOOK A WASTEBASKET INTO THE MEN'S ROOM AND WENT TO THE BATHROOM IN IT.
HOW CERTAIN ARE YOU ABOUT THAT ORDER OF EVENTS?
THANKS FOR MAKING A SICKENING INCIDENT A LITTLE MORE HORRIFYING.
IT'S THE ONLY FUN PART ABOUT BEING THE VOICE OF EXPERIENCE.
BB

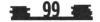

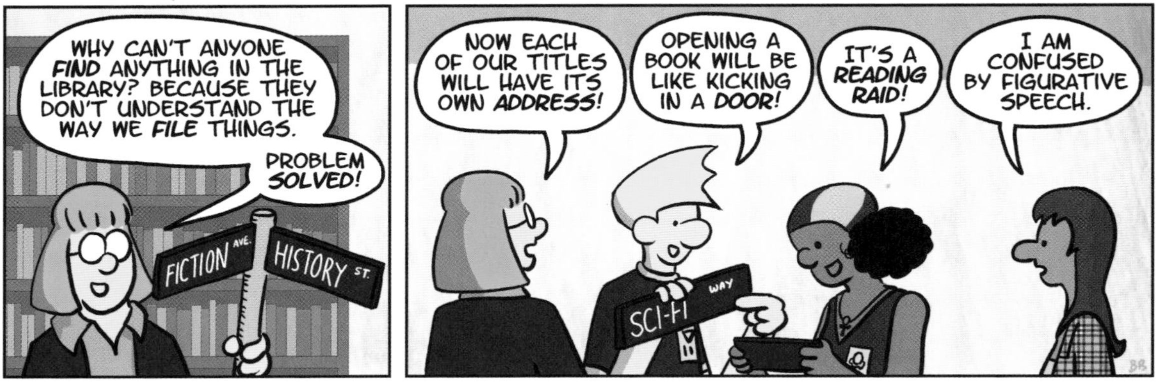
WHY CAN'T ANYONE FIND ANYTHING IN THE LIBRARY? BECAUSE THEY DON'T UNDERSTAND THE WAY WE FILE THINGS.
PROBLEM SOLVED!
FICTION AVE.
HISTORY ST.
NOW EACH OF OUR TITLES WILL HAVE ITS OWN ADDRESS!
OPENING A BOOK WILL BE LIKE KICKING IN A DOOR!
SCI-FI WAY
IT'S A READING RAID!
I AM CONFUSED BY FIGURATIVE SPEECH.
BB

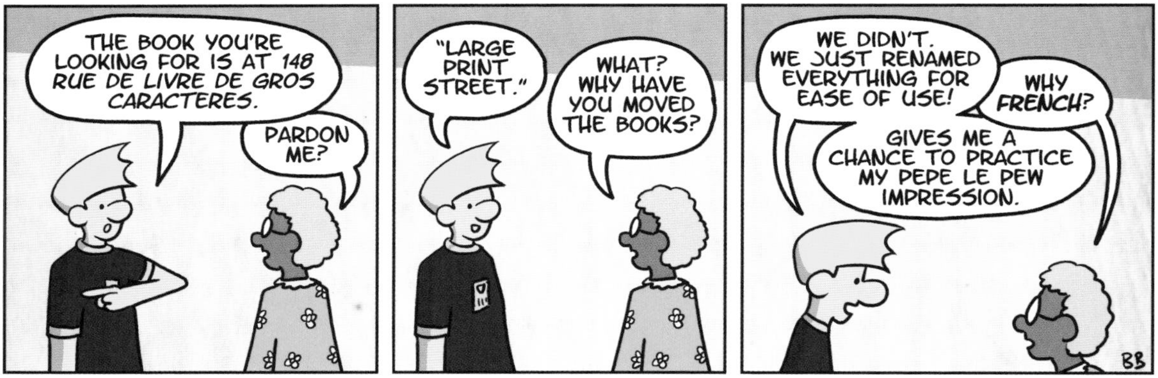
THE BOOK YOU'RE LOOKING FOR IS AT 148 RUE DE LIVRE DE GROS CARACTERES.
PARDON ME?
"LARGE PRINT STREET."
WHAT? WHY HAVE YOU MOVED THE BOOKS?
WE DIDN'T. WE JUST RENAMED EVERYTHING FOR EASE OF USE!
WHY FRENCH?
GIVES ME A CHANCE TO PRACTICE MY PEPE LE PEW IMPRESSION.
BB

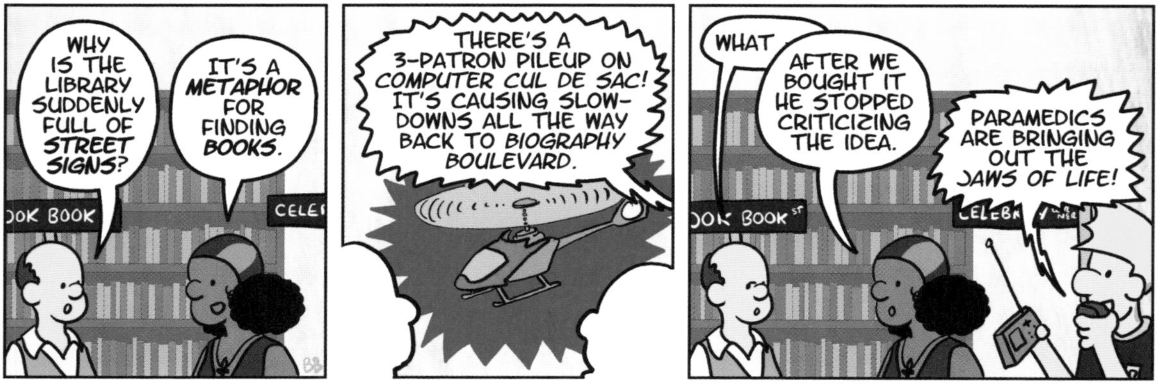
WHY IS THE LIBRARY SUDDENLY FULL OF STREET SIGNS?
IT'S A METAPHOR FOR FINDING BOOKS.
BB
THERE'S A 3-PATRON PILEUP ON COMPUTER CUL DE SAC! IT'S CAUSING SLOW-DOWNS ALL THE WAY BACK TO BIOGRAPHY BOULEVARD.
WHAT
AFTER WE BOUGHT IT HE STOPPED CRITICIZING THE IDEA.
PARAMEDICS ARE BRINGING OUT THE JAWS OF LIFE!

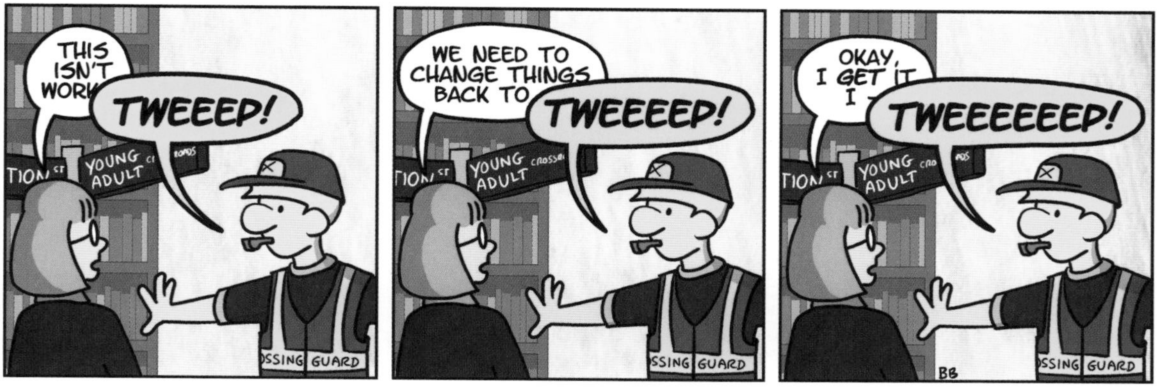
THIS ISN'T WORK
TWEEEP!
YOUNG ADULT
SSING GUARD
WE NEED TO CHANGE THINGS BACK TO
TWEEEEP!
YOUNG ADULT
SSING GUARD
OKAY, I GET IT I
TWEEEEEEP!
YOUNG ADULT
SSING GUARD
BB

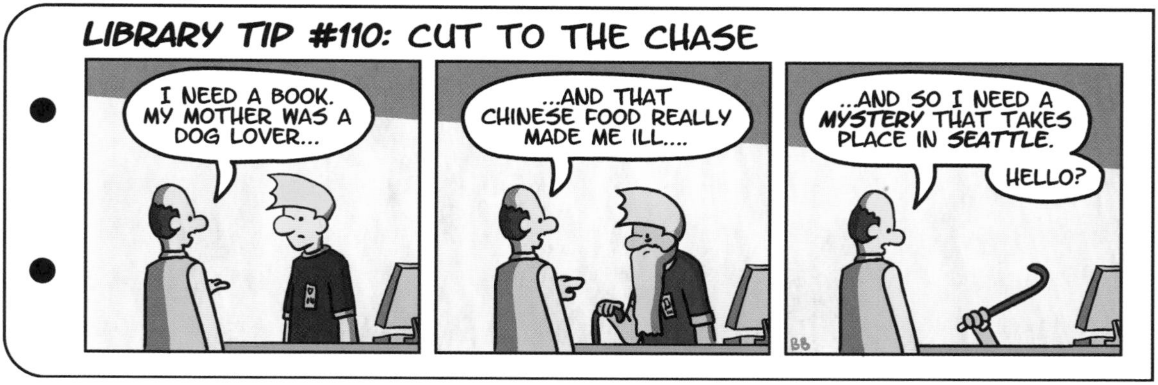
LIBRARY TIP #110: CUT TO THE CHASE
I NEED A BOOK. MY MOTHER WAS A DOG LOVER...
...AND THAT CHINESE FOOD REALLY MADE ME ILL....
...AND SO I NEED A MYSTERY THAT TAKES PLACE IN SEATTLE.
HELLO?
BB

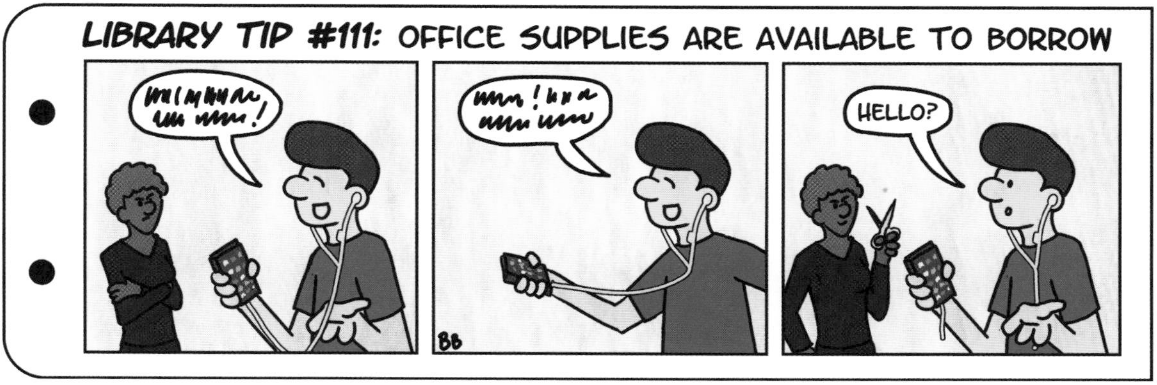
LIBRARY TIP #111: OFFICE SUPPLIES ARE AVAILABLE TO BORROW
HELLO?
BB

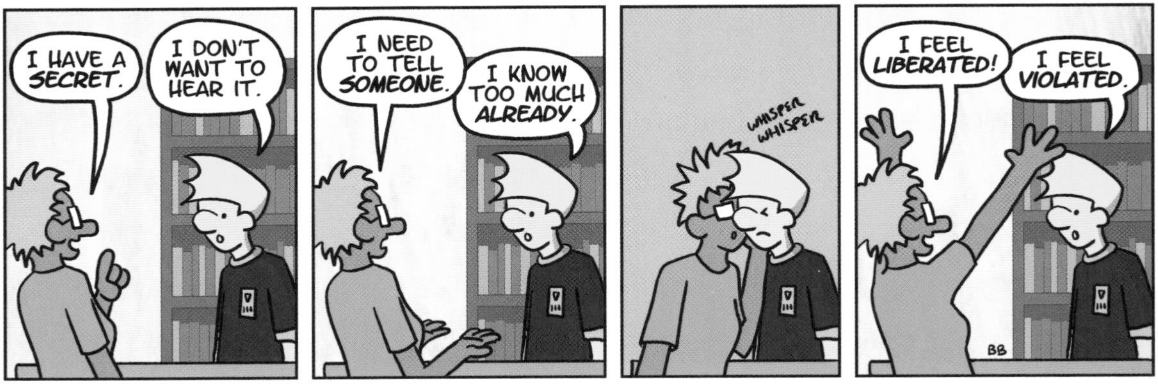
I HAVE A SECRET.
I DON'T WANT TO HEAR IT.
I NEED TO TELL SOMEONE.
I KNOW TOO MUCH ALREADY.
WHISPER WHISPER
I FEEL LIBERATED!
I FEEL VIOLATED.
BB

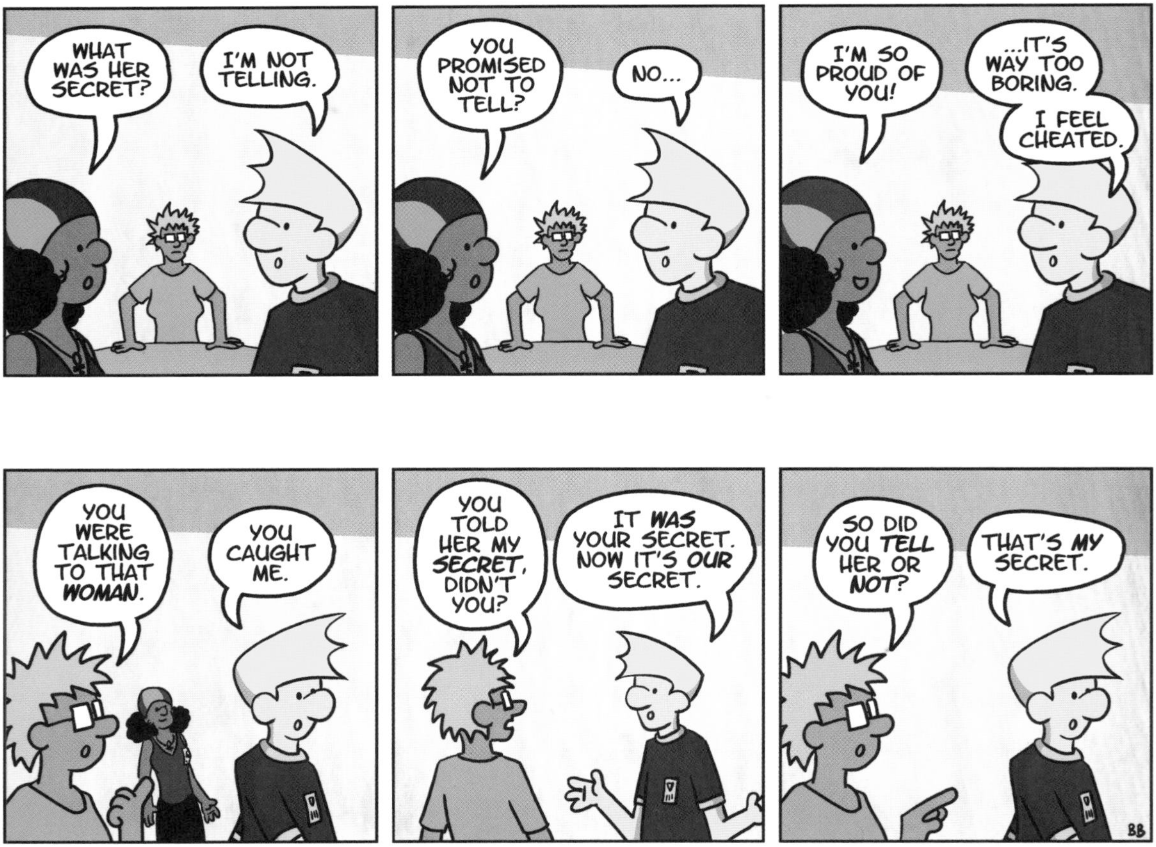
WHAT WAS HER SECRET?
I'M NOT TELLING.
YOU PROMISED NOT TO TELL?
NO...
I'M SO PROUD OF YOU!
...IT'S WAY TOO BORING.
I FEEL CHEATED.
YOU WERE TALKING TO THAT WOMAN.
YOU CAUGHT ME.
YOU TOLD HER MY SECRET, DIDN'T YOU?
IT WAS YOUR SECRET. NOW IT'S OUR SECRET.
SO DID YOU TELL HER OR NOT?
THAT'S MY SECRET.
BB

Bibliovores

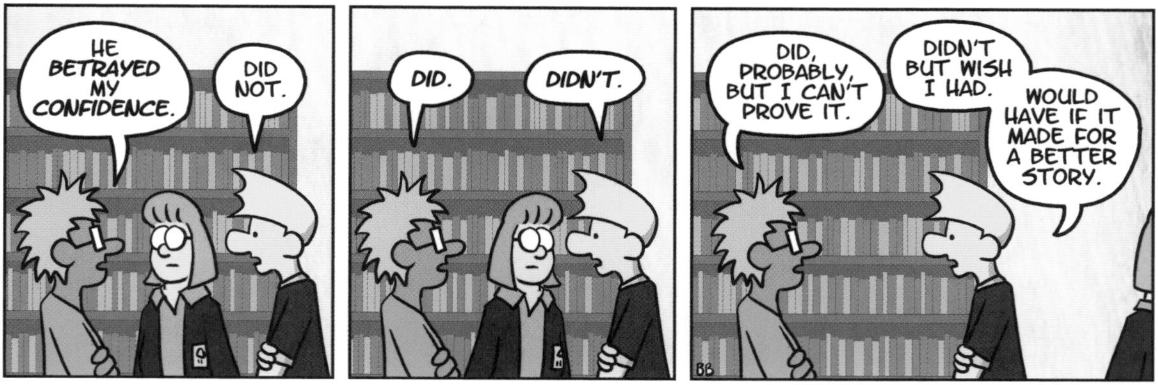

HE **BETRAYED** MY **CONFIDENCE.**
DID NOT.
DID.
DIDN'T.
DID, PROBABLY, BUT I CAN'T PROVE IT.
DIDN'T BUT **WISH** I HAD.
WOULD HAVE IF IT MADE FOR A BETTER STORY.
BB

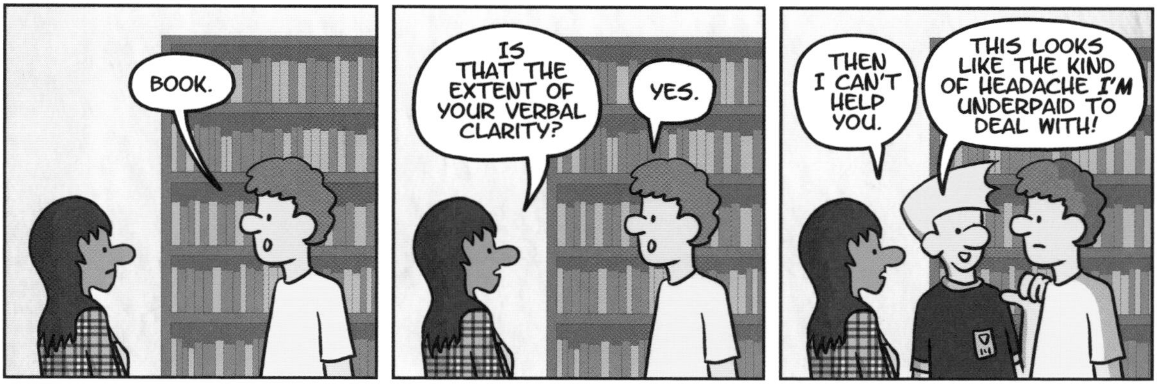

BOOK.
IS THAT THE EXTENT OF YOUR VERBAL CLARITY?
YES.
THEN I CAN'T HELP YOU.
THIS LOOKS LIKE THE KIND OF HEADACHE ***I'M*** UNDERPAID TO DEAL WITH!

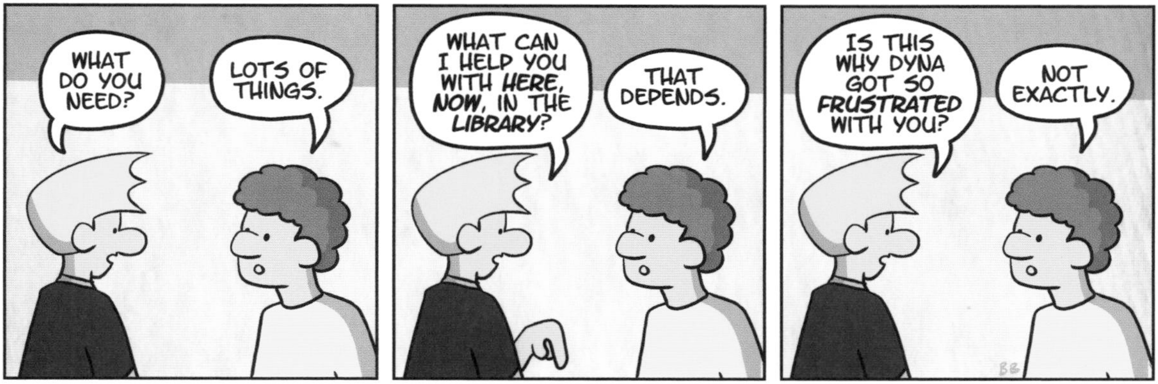

WHAT DO YOU NEED?
LOTS OF THINGS.
WHAT CAN I HELP YOU WITH ***HERE, NOW,*** IN THE ***LIBRARY?***
THAT DEPENDS.
IS THIS WHY DYNA GOT SO ***FRUSTRATED*** WITH YOU?
NOT EXACTLY.
BB

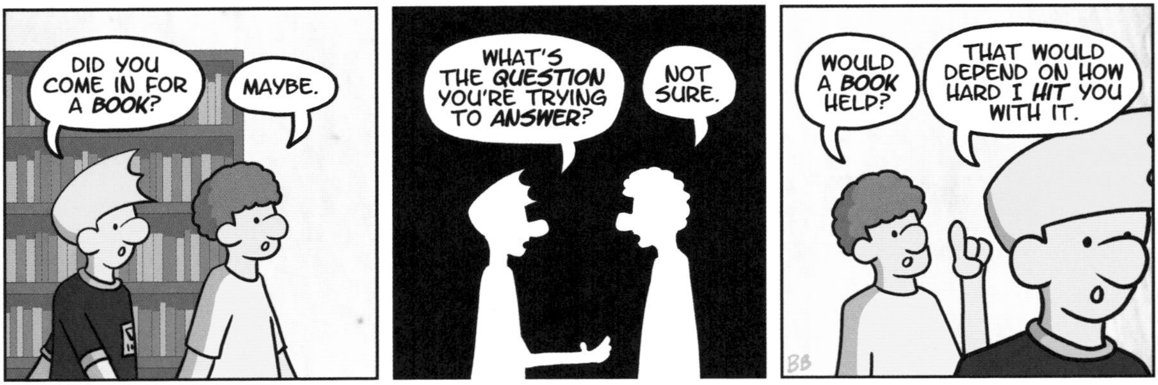
DID YOU COME IN FOR A BOOK?
MAYBE.
WHAT'S THE QUESTION YOU'RE TRYING TO ANSWER?
NOT SURE.
WOULD A BOOK HELP?
THAT WOULD DEPEND ON HOW HARD I HIT YOU WITH IT.
BB

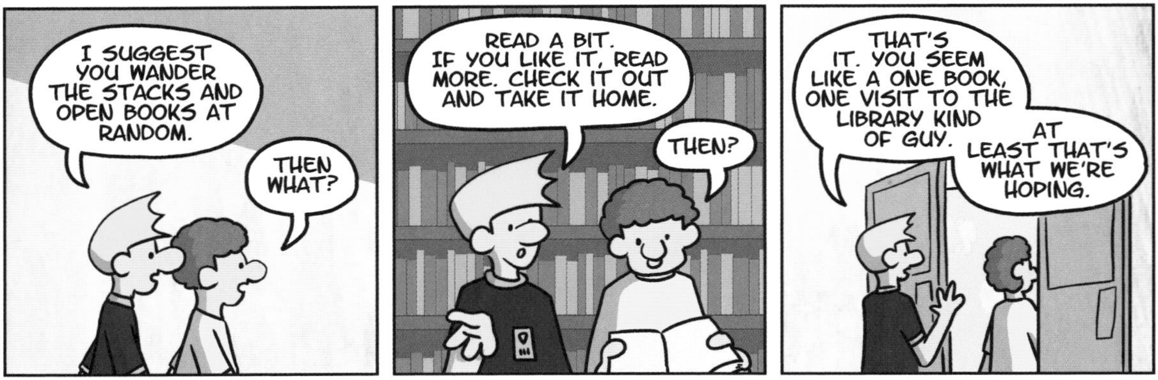
I SUGGEST YOU WANDER THE STACKS AND OPEN BOOKS AT RANDOM.
THEN WHAT?
READ A BIT. IF YOU LIKE IT, READ MORE. CHECK IT OUT AND TAKE IT HOME.
THEN?
THAT'S IT. YOU SEEM LIKE A ONE BOOK, ONE VISIT TO THE LIBRARY KIND OF GUY.
AT LEAST THAT'S WHAT WE'RE HOPING.

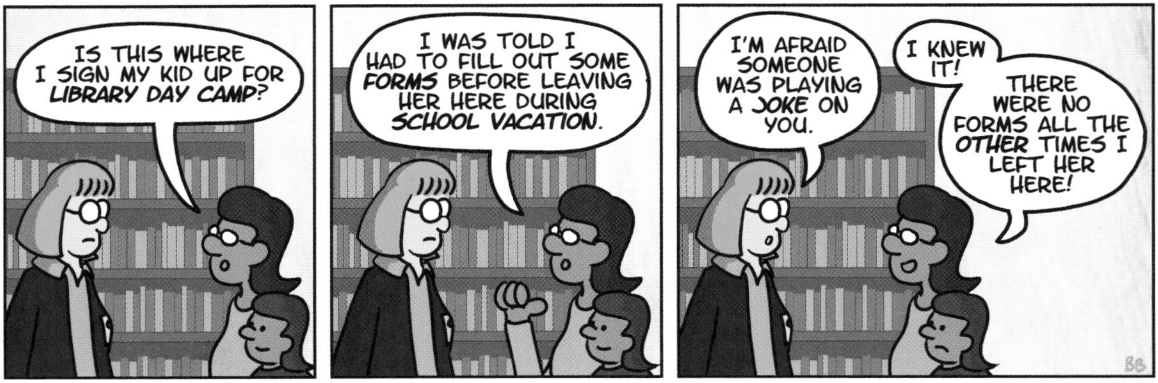
IS THIS WHERE I SIGN MY KID UP FOR LIBRARY DAY CAMP?
I WAS TOLD I HAD TO FILL OUT SOME FORMS BEFORE LEAVING HER HERE DURING SCHOOL VACATION.
I'M AFRAID SOMEONE WAS PLAYING A JOKE ON YOU.
I KNEW IT!
THERE WERE NO FORMS ALL THE OTHER TIMES I LEFT HER HERE!
BB

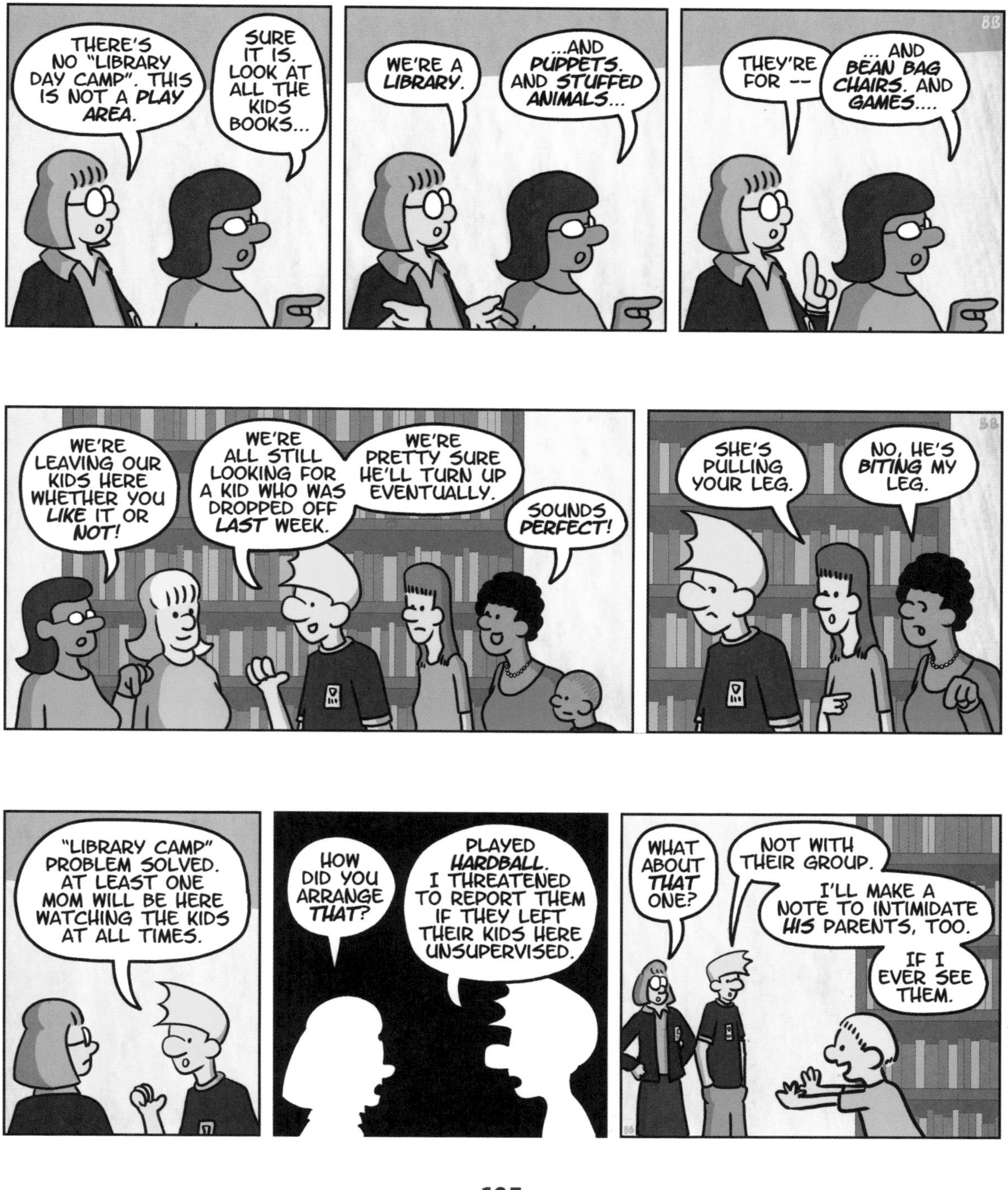
THERE'S NO "LIBRARY DAY CAMP". THIS IS NOT A PLAY AREA.
SURE IT IS. LOOK AT ALL THE KIDS BOOKS...
WE'RE A LIBRARY.
...AND PUPPETS. AND STUFFED ANIMALS...
THEY'RE FOR --
... AND BEAN BAG CHAIRS. AND GAMES....
WE'RE LEAVING OUR KIDS HERE WHETHER YOU LIKE IT OR NOT!
WE'RE ALL STILL LOOKING FOR A KID WHO WAS DROPPED OFF LAST WEEK.
WE'RE PRETTY SURE HE'LL TURN UP EVENTUALLY.
SOUNDS PERFECT!
SHE'S PULLING YOUR LEG.
NO, HE'S BITING MY LEG.
"LIBRARY CAMP" PROBLEM SOLVED. AT LEAST ONE MOM WILL BE HERE WATCHING THE KIDS AT ALL TIMES.
HOW DID YOU ARRANGE THAT?
PLAYED HARDBALL. I THREATENED TO REPORT THEM IF THEY LEFT THEIR KIDS HERE UNSUPERVISED.
WHAT ABOUT THAT ONE?
NOT WITH THEIR GROUP.
I'LL MAKE A NOTE TO INTIMIDATE HIS PARENTS, TOO.
IF I EVER SEE THEM.

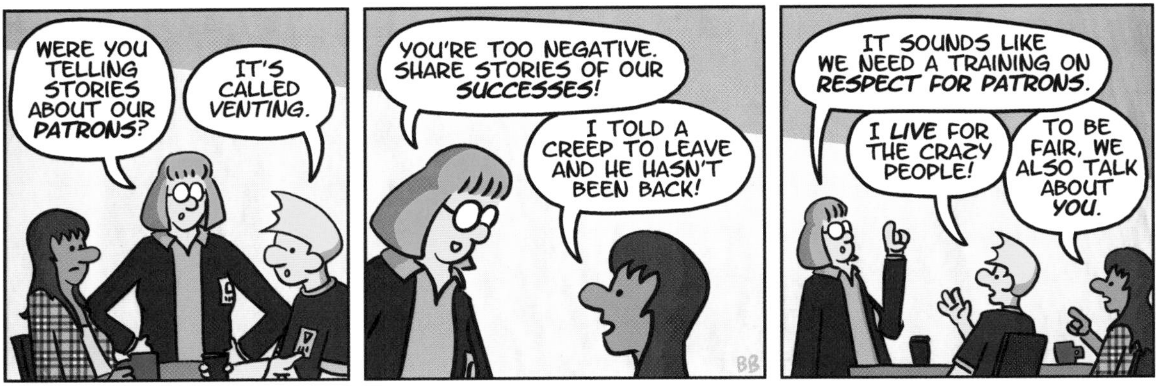
WERE YOU TELLING STORIES ABOUT OUR PATRONS?
IT'S CALLED VENTING.
YOU'RE TOO NEGATIVE. SHARE STORIES OF OUR SUCCESSES!
I TOLD A CREEP TO LEAVE AND HE HASN'T BEEN BACK!
IT SOUNDS LIKE WE NEED A TRAINING ON RESPECT FOR PATRONS.
I LIVE FOR THE CRAZY PEOPLE!
TO BE FAIR, WE ALSO TALK ABOUT YOU.
BB

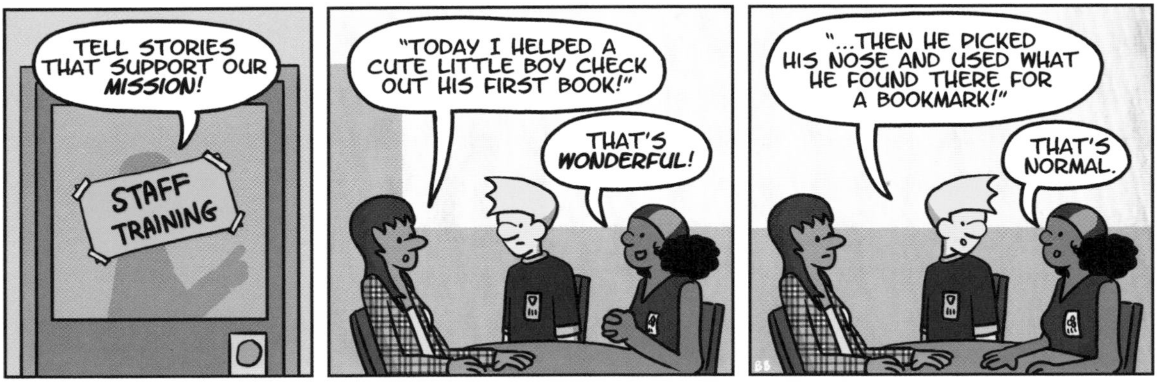
TELL STORIES THAT SUPPORT OUR MISSION!
STAFF TRAINING
"TODAY I HELPED A CUTE LITTLE BOY CHECK OUT HIS FIRST BOOK!"
THAT'S WONDERFUL!
"...THEN HE PICKED HIS NOSE AND USED WHAT HE FOUND THERE FOR A BOOKMARK!"
THAT'S NORMAL.
BB

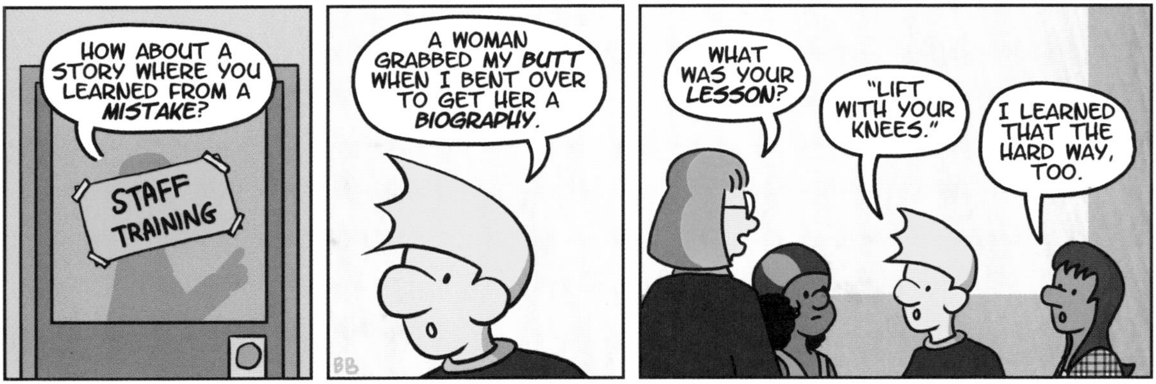
HOW ABOUT A STORY WHERE YOU LEARNED FROM A MISTAKE?
STAFF TRAINING
A WOMAN GRABBED MY BUTT WHEN I BENT OVER TO GET HER A BIOGRAPHY.
BB
WHAT WAS YOUR LESSON?
"LIFT WITH YOUR KNEES."
I LEARNED THAT THE HARD WAY, TOO.

Bibliovores

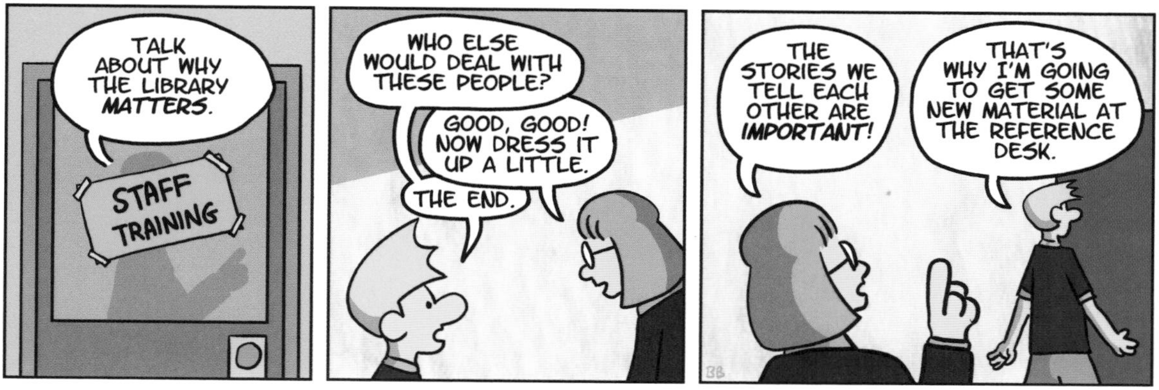
TALK ABOUT WHY THE LIBRARY *MATTERS*.
STAFF TRAINING
WHO ELSE WOULD DEAL WITH THESE PEOPLE?
GOOD, GOOD! NOW DRESS IT UP A LITTLE.
THE END.
THE STORIES WE TELL EACH OTHER ARE *IMPORTANT*!
THAT'S WHY I'M GOING TO GET SOME NEW MATERIAL AT THE REFERENCE DESK.

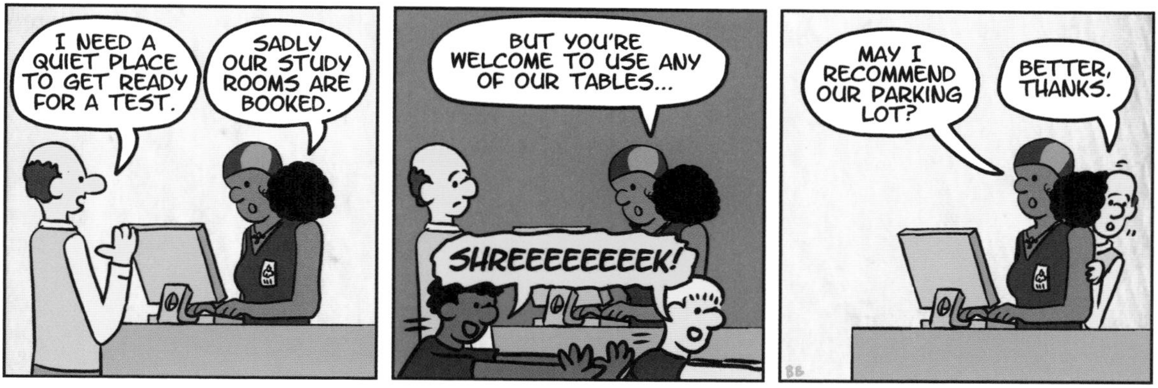
I NEED A QUIET PLACE TO GET READY FOR A TEST.
SADLY OUR STUDY ROOMS ARE BOOKED.
BUT YOU'RE WELCOME TO USE ANY OF OUR TABLES...
SHREEEEEEEEK!
MAY I RECOMMEND OUR PARKING LOT?
BETTER, THANKS.

Drawing the strip is Gene's annual birthday present to Bill, and to humanity as a whole.

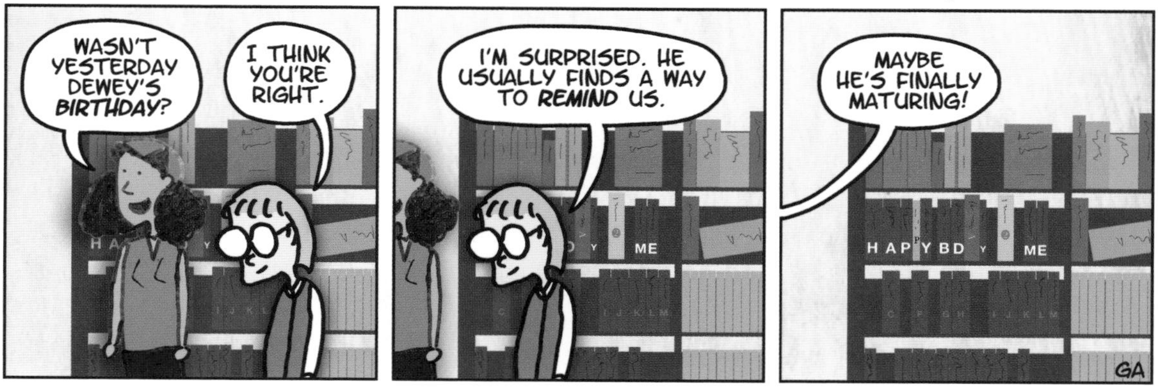
WASN'T YESTERDAY DEWEY'S *BIRTHDAY*?
I THINK YOU'RE RIGHT.
I'M SURPRISED. HE USUALLY FINDS A WAY TO *REMIND* US.
MAYBE HE'S FINALLY MATURING!

LIBRARY TIP #112: READ THE SIGNALS

ARE YOU FANNING ME?
NO, I'M WAVING GOODBYE. OUR BUSINESS IS DONE.
SHOULDN'T A GOODBYE WAVE BE HIGHER UP? LIKE THIS?
IT'S TIME FOR YOU TO MOVE ALONG, DEAR.
I'M NOT GOING ANYWHERE UNTIL I UNDERSTAND WHAT HE'S TRYING TO SAY.
BB

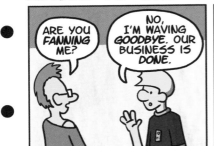

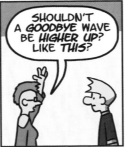

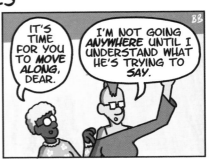

LIBRARY TIP #113: YIELD TO PEDESTRIANS

AREN'T YOU DONE SHELVING THOSE BOOKS YET?
WE'RE SO CROWDED TODAY! I'VE BEEN STUCK HERE FOR HOURS.
WHY DON'T YOU JUST GO?
THE CUSTOMER ALWAYS HAS THE RIGHT OF WAY.

LIBRARY TIP #114: IDENTIFY THE PROBLEM

IT'LL BE TOUGH TO ANSWER YOUR QUESTION.
WITH THAT KIND OF ATTITUDE, SURE.
GET ME A CAN-DO LIBRARIAN WHO BELIEVES IN THEMSELF AND THEIR RESOURCES!
WILL DO.
HE'S BEEN GONE A LONG TIME.
TRUST ME, WE'RE BETTER OFF.
BB

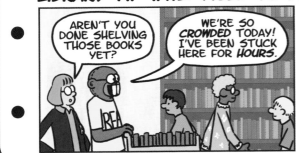

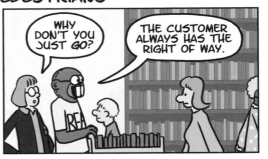

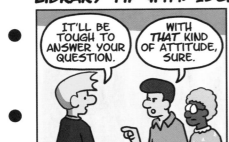

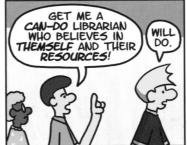

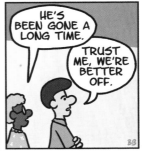

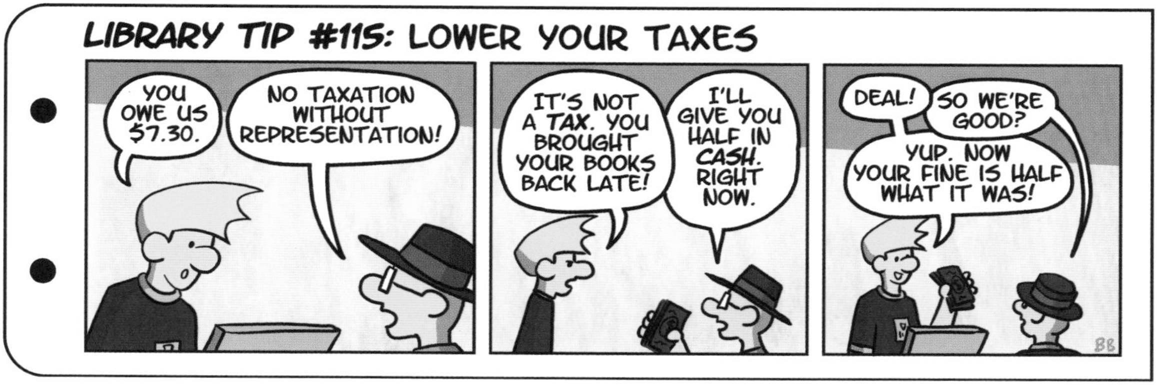
LIBRARY TIP #115: LOWER YOUR TAXES
YOU OWE US $7.30.
NO TAXATION WITHOUT REPRESENTATION!
IT'S NOT A TAX. YOU BROUGHT YOUR BOOKS BACK LATE!
I'LL GIVE YOU HALF IN CASH. RIGHT NOW.
DEAL!
SO WE'RE GOOD?
YUP. NOW YOUR FINE IS HALF WHAT IT WAS!
BB

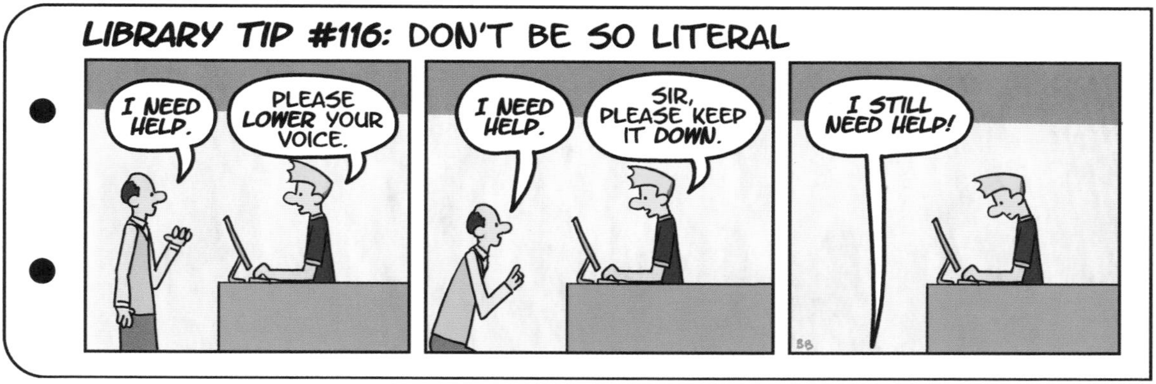
LIBRARY TIP #116: DON'T BE SO LITERAL
I NEED HELP.
PLEASE LOWER YOUR VOICE.
I NEED HELP.
SIR, PLEASE KEEP IT DOWN.
I STILL NEED HELP!
BB

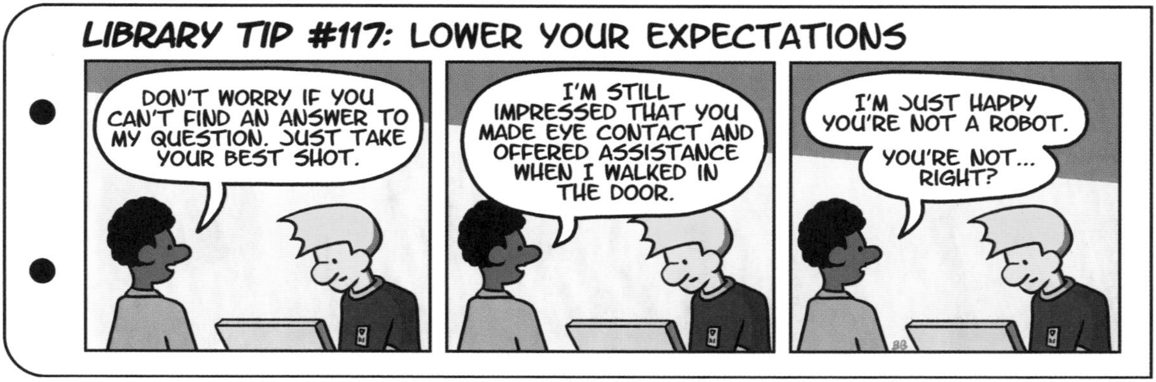
LIBRARY TIP #117: LOWER YOUR EXPECTATIONS
DON'T WORRY IF YOU CAN'T FIND AN ANSWER TO MY QUESTION. JUST TAKE YOUR BEST SHOT.
I'M STILL IMPRESSED THAT YOU MADE EYE CONTACT AND OFFERED ASSISTANCE WHEN I WALKED IN THE DOOR.
I'M JUST HAPPY YOU'RE NOT A ROBOT.
YOU'RE NOT... RIGHT?
BB

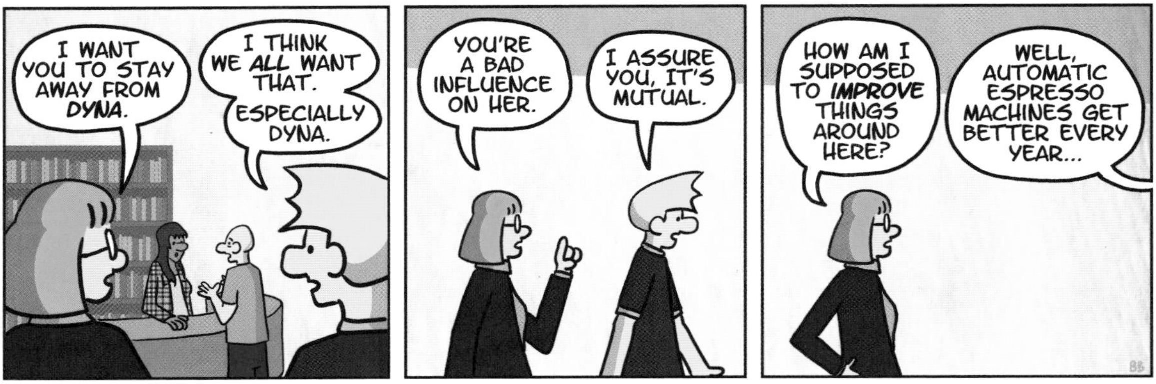
I WANT YOU TO STAY AWAY FROM DYNA.
I THINK WE ALL WANT THAT.
ESPECIALLY DYNA.
YOU'RE A BAD INFLUENCE ON HER.
I ASSURE YOU, IT'S MUTUAL.
HOW AM I SUPPOSED TO IMPROVE THINGS AROUND HERE?
WELL, AUTOMATIC ESPRESSO MACHINES GET BETTER EVERY YEAR...
BB

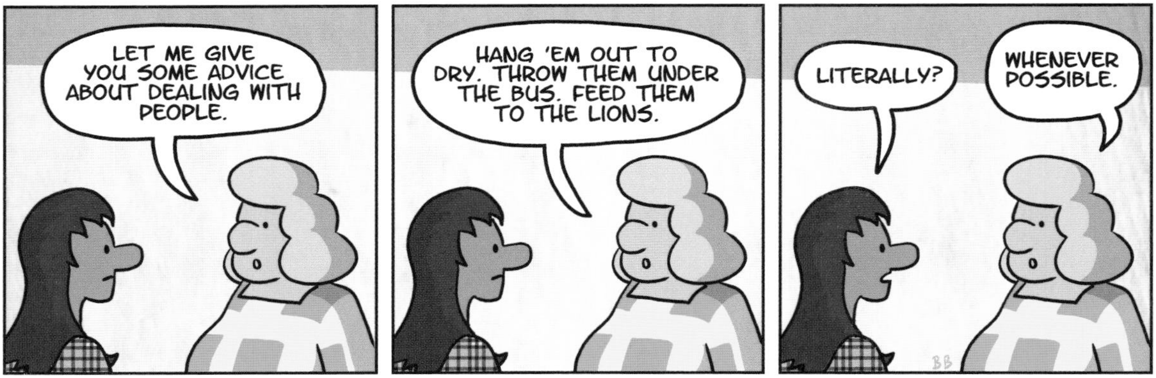
LET ME GIVE YOU SOME ADVICE ABOUT DEALING WITH PEOPLE.
HANG 'EM OUT TO DRY. THROW THEM UNDER THE BUS. FEED THEM TO THE LIONS.
LITERALLY?
WHENEVER POSSIBLE.
BB

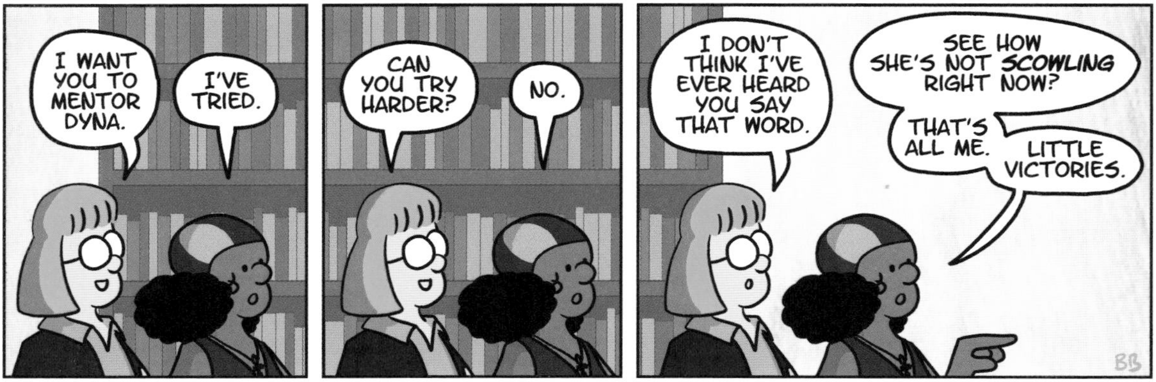
I WANT YOU TO MENTOR DYNA.
I'VE TRIED.
CAN YOU TRY HARDER?
NO.
I DON'T THINK I'VE EVER HEARD YOU SAY THAT WORD.
SEE HOW SHE'S NOT SCOWLING RIGHT NOW?
THAT'S ALL ME.
LITTLE VICTORIES.
BB

Bibliovores

We have been speaking professionally for over a decade now, keynoting library conferences, book festivals, and comic conventions in over 40 states and provinces. But in October 2012, at Kitsap Regional Library's annual staff development day, we did something new: we produced a comic strip live on site, from conception to final inks.

Prior to our keynote, the staff wrote down dozens of true stories they had personally experienced. Some were funny, some were disturbing, all were awesome. We triaged them based on which ones would make the best comic strip, then finally chose one about a guy who wanted help "reproducing." Of course he was talking about the copy machine, but we took it in a different direction.

EXCUSE ME, CAN YOU HELP ME REPRODUCE?
SIR, THE COPY MACHINE IS
NO, NO, NO. I WANT TO ASK HER ON

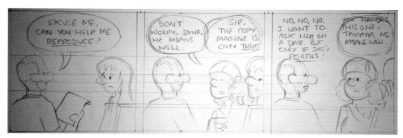

Bill pencilled out roughs and dialog (Gene modeled for the creepy guy), then inked with a marker and brush pen.

EXCUSE ME, CAN YOU HELP ME REPRODUCE?
DON'T WORRY, DYNA. HE MEANS WELL.
SIR, THE COPY MACHINE IS OVER THERE.
NO, NO, NO. I WANT TO ASK HER ON A DATE. BUT ONLY IF SHE'S FERTILE.
YOU HANDLE THIS ONE, TAMARA. HE MEANS WELL.

We presented this version to the staff, and donated the original art to the library system for display. Back at home Bill did some postproduction and posted to the site.

This is the closest to a reality show we may ever come. It was super fun, and we plan to do it again!

EXCUSE ME, CAN YOU HELP ME REPRODUCE?
DON'T WORRY, DYNA. HE MEANS WELL.
SIR, THE COPY MACHINE IS OVER THERE.
NO, NO, NO. I WANT TO ASK HER ON A DATE. BUT ONLY IF SHE'S FERTILE.
YOU HANDLE THIS ONE, TAMARA. HE MEANS WELL.

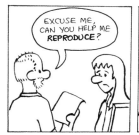

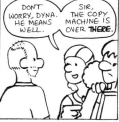

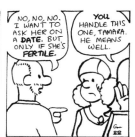

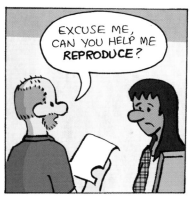

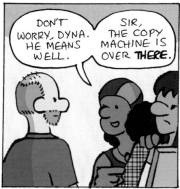

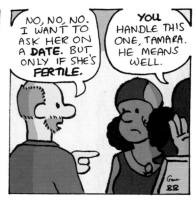

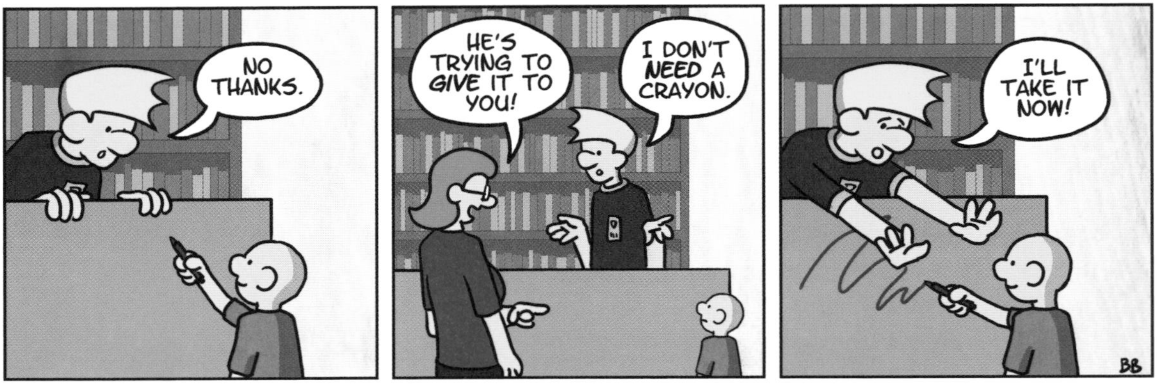
NO THANKS.
HE'S TRYING TO GIVE IT TO YOU!
I DON'T NEED A CRAYON.
I'LL TAKE IT NOW!
BB

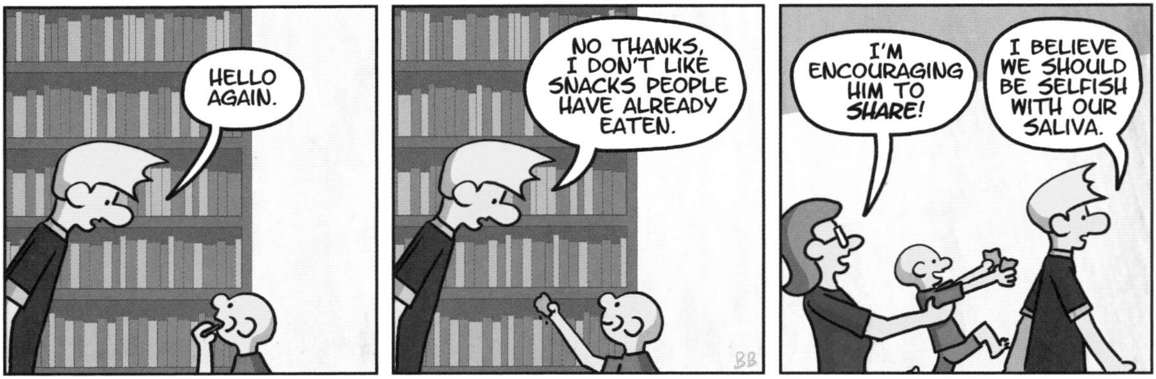
HELLO AGAIN.
NO THANKS, I DON'T LIKE SNACKS PEOPLE HAVE ALREADY EATEN.
I'M ENCOURAGING HIM TO SHARE!
I BELIEVE WE SHOULD BE SELFISH WITH OUR SALIVA.
BB

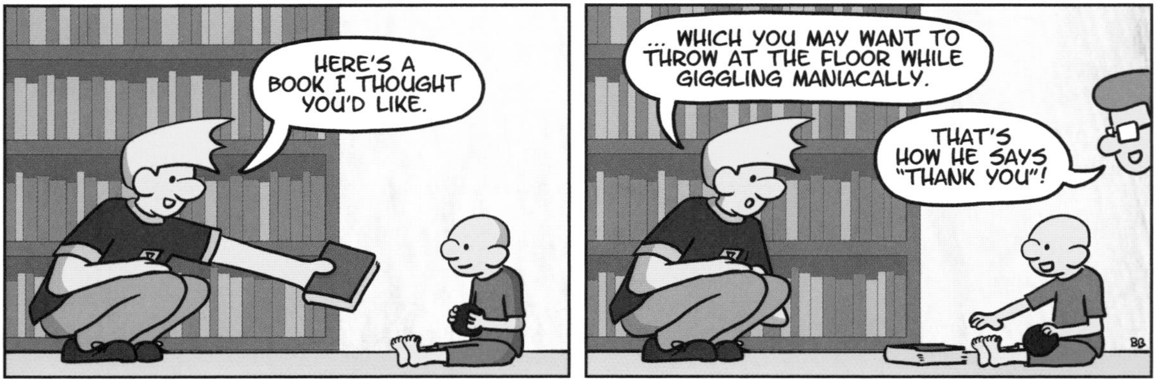
HERE'S A BOOK I THOUGHT YOU'D LIKE.
... WHICH YOU MAY WANT TO THROW AT THE FLOOR WHILE GIGGLING MANIACALLY.
THAT'S HOW HE SAYS "THANK YOU"!
BB

Bibliovores

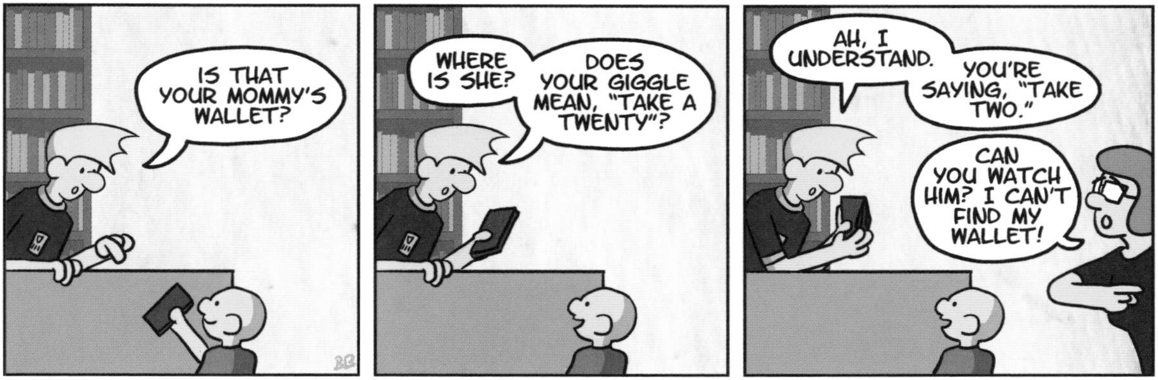

IS THAT YOUR MOMMY'S WALLET?
WHERE IS SHE?
DOES YOUR GIGGLE MEAN, "TAKE A TWENTY"?
AH, I UNDERSTAND.
YOU'RE SAYING, "TAKE TWO."
CAN YOU WATCH HIM? I CAN'T FIND MY WALLET!
BB

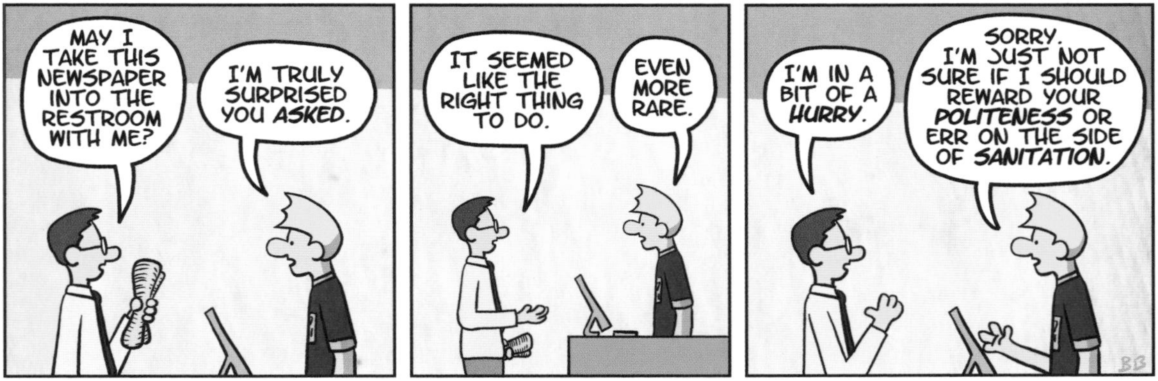

MAY I TAKE THIS NEWSPAPER INTO THE RESTROOM WITH ME?
I'M TRULY SURPRISED YOU ***ASKED***.
IT SEEMED LIKE THE RIGHT THING TO DO.
EVEN MORE RARE.
I'M IN A BIT OF A ***HURRY***.
SORRY. I'M JUST NOT SURE IF I SHOULD REWARD YOUR ***POLITENESS*** OR ERR ON THE SIDE OF ***SANITATION***.
BB

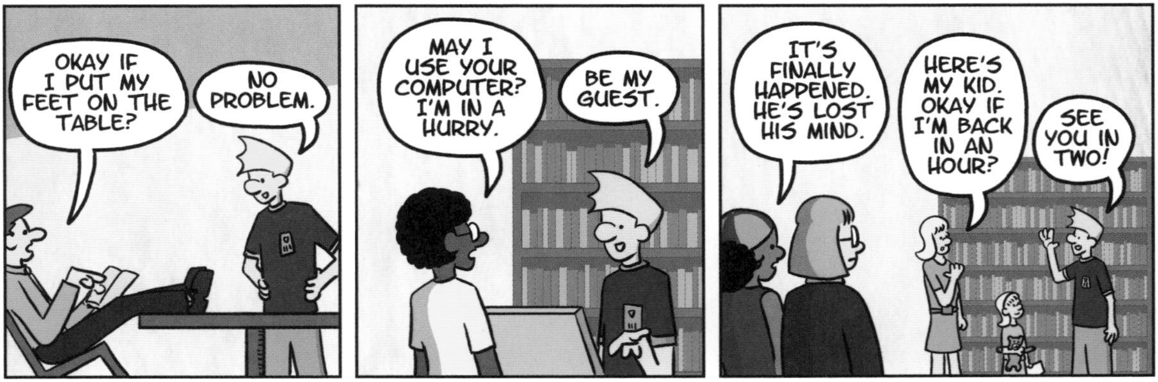

OKAY IF I PUT MY FEET ON THE TABLE?
NO PROBLEM.
MAY I USE YOUR COMPUTER? I'M IN A HURRY.
BE MY GUEST.
IT'S FINALLY HAPPENED. HE'S LOST HIS MIND.
HERE'S MY KID. OKAY IF I'M BACK IN AN HOUR?
SEE YOU IN TWO!

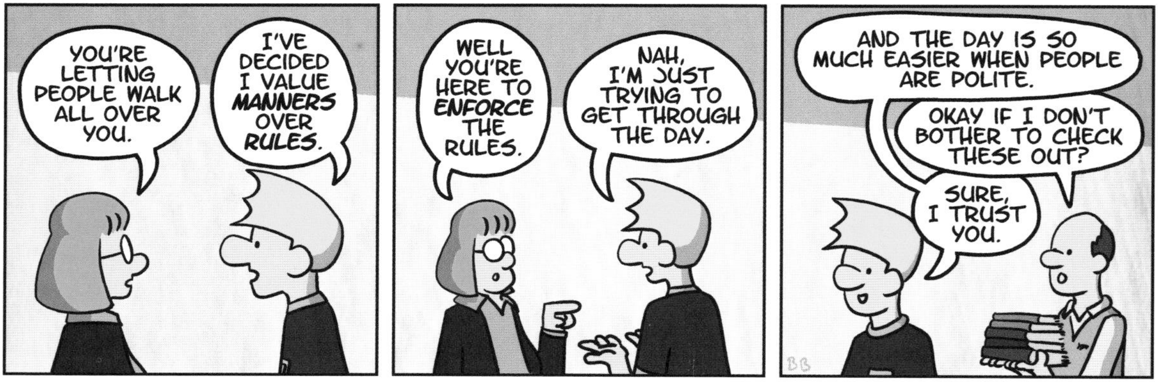
YOU'RE LETTING PEOPLE WALK ALL OVER YOU.
I'VE DECIDED I VALUE **MANNERS** OVER **RULES**.
WELL YOU'RE HERE TO **ENFORCE** THE RULES.
NAH, I'M JUST TRYING TO GET THROUGH THE DAY.
AND THE DAY IS SO MUCH EASIER WHEN PEOPLE ARE POLITE.
OKAY IF I DON'T BOTHER TO CHECK THESE OUT?
SURE, I TRUST YOU.
BB

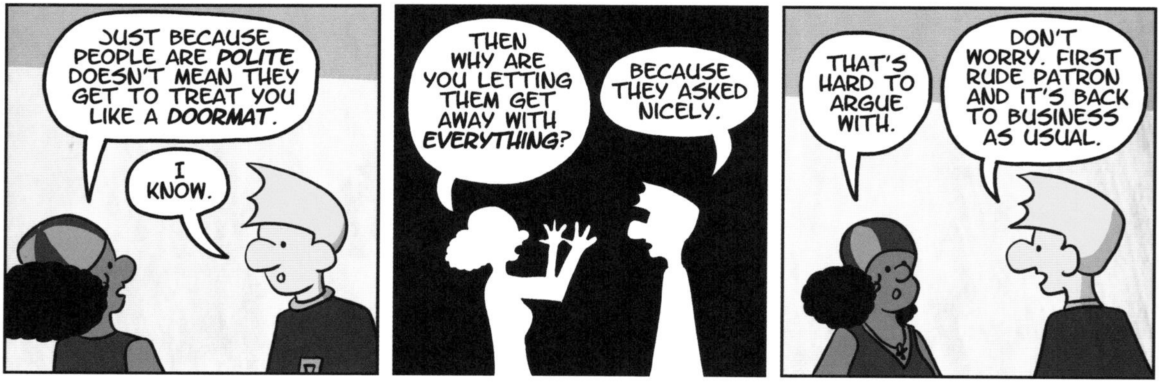
JUST BECAUSE PEOPLE ARE **POLITE** DOESN'T MEAN THEY GET TO TREAT YOU LIKE A **DOORMAT**.
I KNOW.
THEN WHY ARE YOU LETTING THEM GET AWAY WITH **EVERYTHING**?
BECAUSE THEY ASKED NICELY.
THAT'S HARD TO ARGUE WITH.
DON'T WORRY. FIRST RUDE PATRON AND IT'S BACK TO BUSINESS AS USUAL.

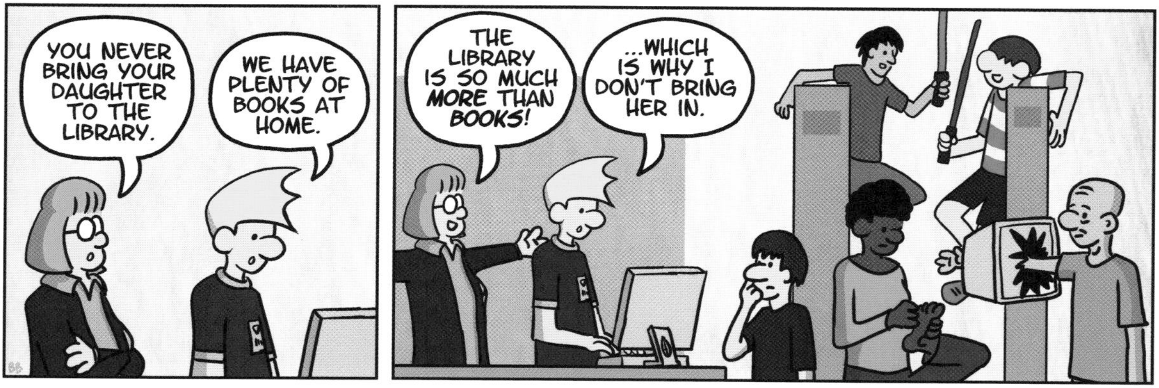
YOU NEVER BRING YOUR DAUGHTER TO THE LIBRARY.
WE HAVE PLENTY OF BOOKS AT HOME.
THE LIBRARY IS SO MUCH **MORE** THAN **BOOKS**!
...WHICH IS WHY I DON'T BRING HER IN.
BB

Bibliovores

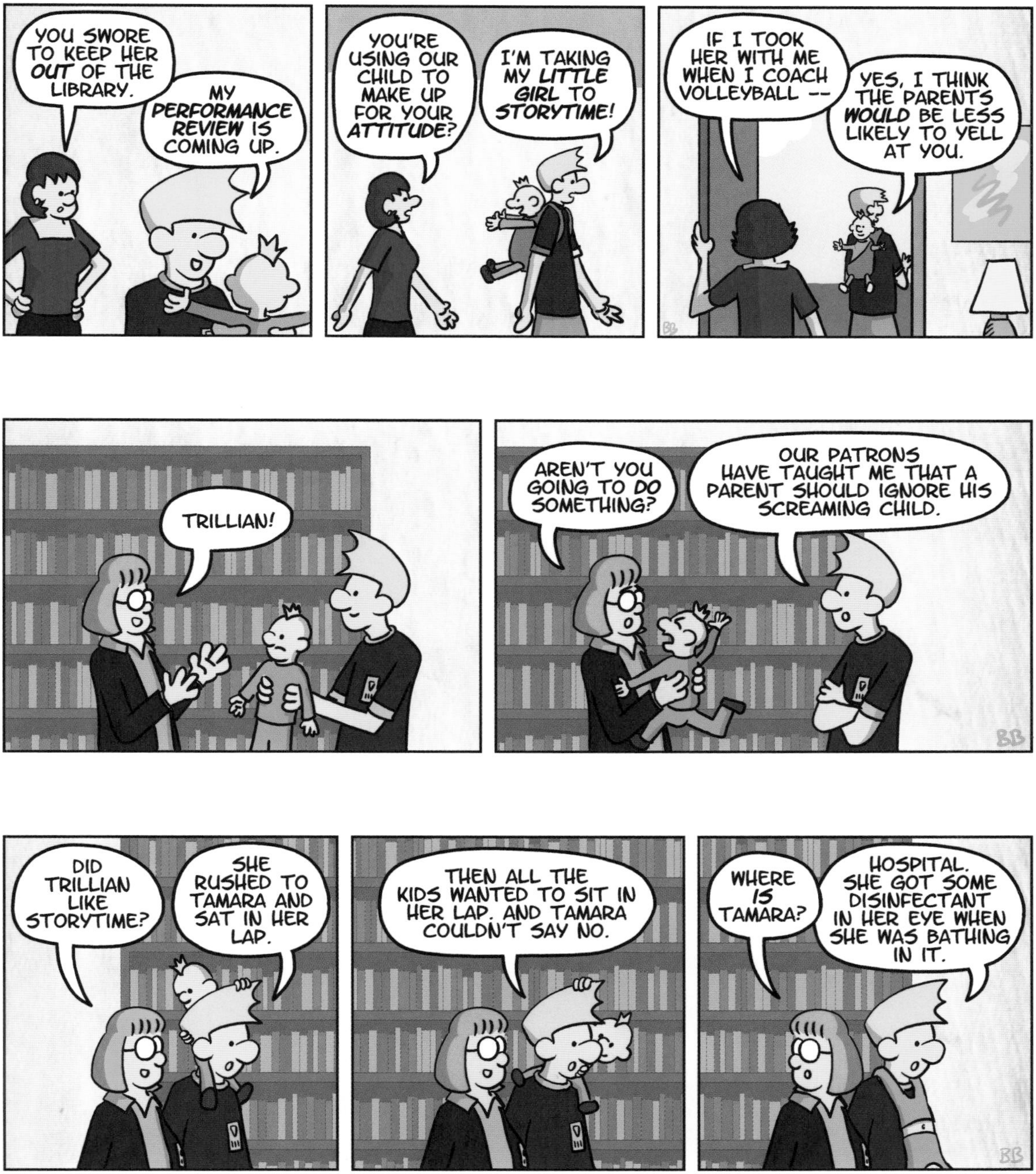

YOU SWORE TO KEEP HER OUT OF THE LIBRARY.
MY PERFORMANCE REVIEW IS COMING UP.
YOU'RE USING OUR CHILD TO MAKE UP FOR YOUR ATTITUDE?
I'M TAKING MY LITTLE GIRL TO STORYTIME!
IF I TOOK HER WITH ME WHEN I COACH VOLLEYBALL --
YES, I THINK THE PARENTS WOULD BE LESS LIKELY TO YELL AT YOU.
BB
TRILLIAN!
AREN'T YOU GOING TO DO SOMETHING?
OUR PATRONS HAVE TAUGHT ME THAT A PARENT SHOULD IGNORE HIS SCREAMING CHILD.
BB
DID TRILLIAN LIKE STORYTIME?
SHE RUSHED TO TAMARA AND SAT IN HER LAP.
THEN ALL THE KIDS WANTED TO SIT IN HER LAP. AND TAMARA COULDN'T SAY NO.
WHERE IS TAMARA?
HOSPITAL. SHE GOT SOME DISINFECTANT IN HER EYE WHEN SHE WAS BATHING IN IT.
BB

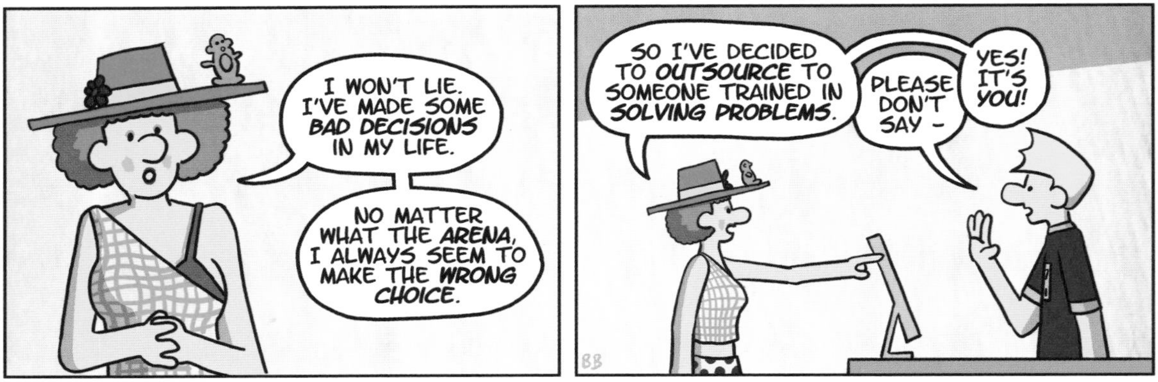
I WON'T LIE. I'VE MADE SOME *BAD DECISIONS* IN MY LIFE.
NO MATTER WHAT THE *ARENA*, I ALWAYS SEEM TO MAKE THE *WRONG CHOICE*.
SO I'VE DECIDED TO *OUTSOURCE* TO SOMEONE TRAINED IN *SOLVING PROBLEMS*.
PLEASE DON'T SAY –
YES! IT'S *YOU*!
BB

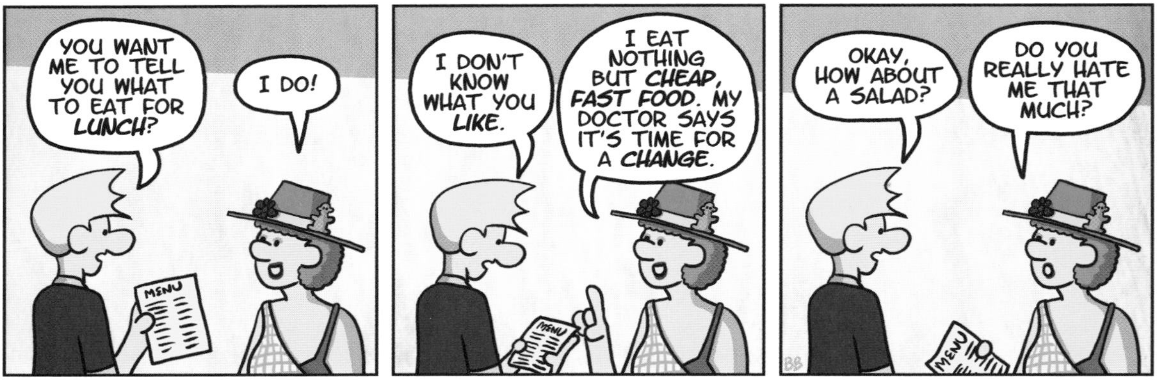
YOU WANT ME TO TELL YOU WHAT TO EAT FOR *LUNCH*?
I DO!
MENU
I DON'T KNOW WHAT YOU *LIKE*.
I EAT NOTHING BUT *CHEAP, FAST FOOD*. MY DOCTOR SAYS IT'S TIME FOR A *CHANGE*.
MENU
OKAY, HOW ABOUT A SALAD?
DO YOU REALLY HATE ME THAT MUCH?
MENU
BB

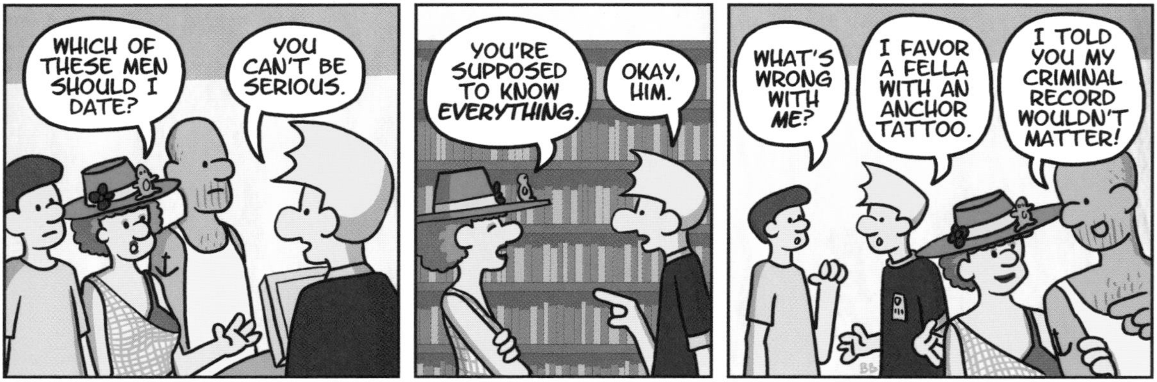
WHICH OF THESE MEN SHOULD I DATE?
YOU CAN'T BE SERIOUS.
YOU'RE SUPPOSED TO KNOW *EVERYTHING*.
OKAY, HIM.
WHAT'S WRONG WITH *ME*?
I FAVOR A FELLA WITH AN ANCHOR TATTOO.
I TOLD YOU MY CRIMINAL RECORD WOULDN'T MATTER!
BB

Bibliovores

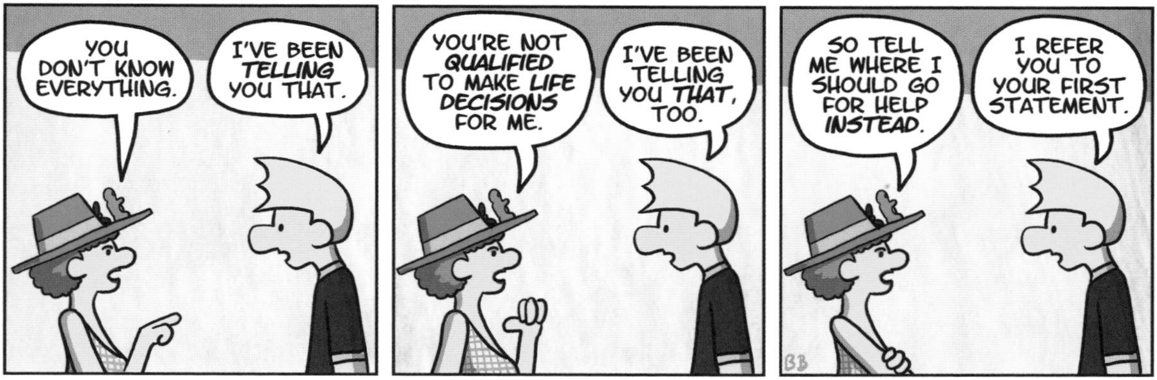

YOU DON'T KNOW EVERYTHING.
I'VE BEEN TELLING YOU THAT.
YOU'RE NOT QUALIFIED TO MAKE LIFE DECISIONS FOR ME.
I'VE BEEN TELLING YOU THAT, TOO.
SO TELL ME WHERE I SHOULD GO FOR HELP INSTEAD.
I REFER YOU TO YOUR FIRST STATEMENT.
BB

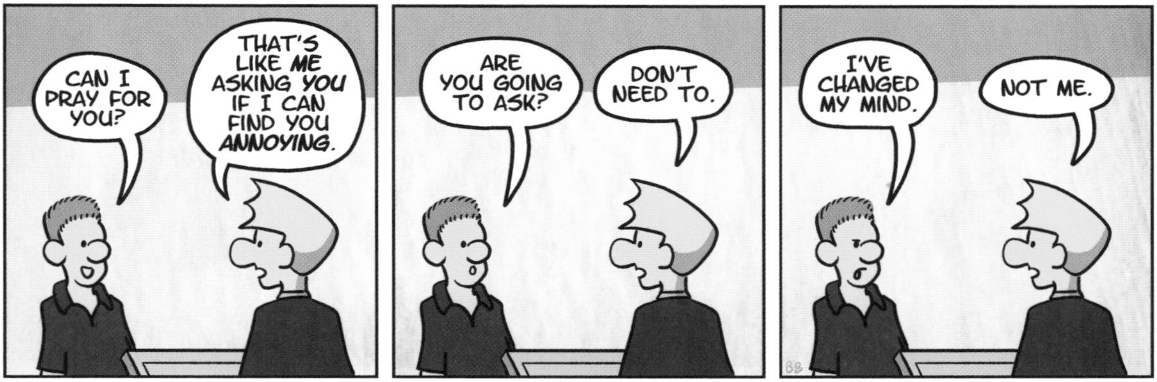

CAN I PRAY FOR YOU?
THAT'S LIKE ME ASKING YOU IF I CAN FIND YOU ANNOYING.
ARE YOU GOING TO ASK?
DON'T NEED TO.
I'VE CHANGED MY MIND.
NOT ME.
BB

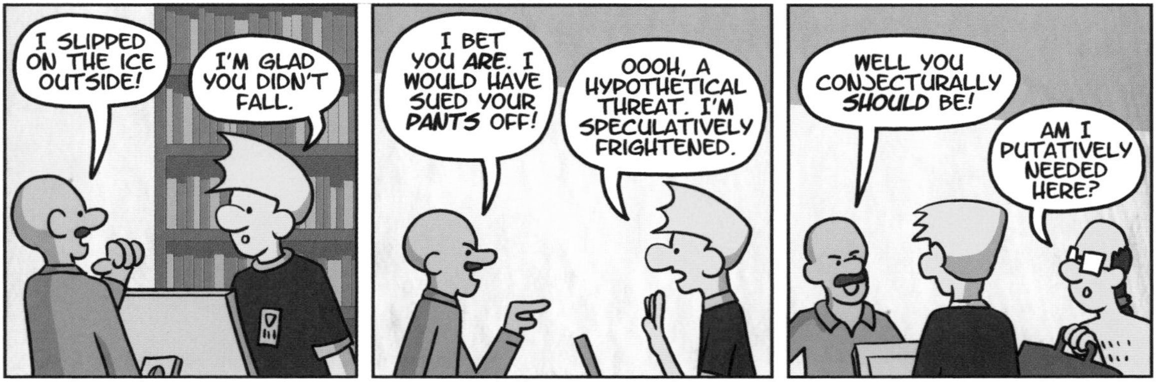

I SLIPPED ON THE ICE OUTSIDE!
I'M GLAD YOU DIDN'T FALL.
I BET YOU ARE. I WOULD HAVE SUED YOUR PANTS OFF!
OOOH, A HYPOTHETICAL THREAT. I'M SPECULATIVELY FRIGHTENED.
WELL YOU CONJECTURALLY SHOULD BE!
AM I PUTATIVELY NEEDED HERE?

IT'S TIME TO TURN IN YOUR *SELF-ASSESSMENTS!*

STAFF TRAINING

THIS JUST HAS THE WORD "AWESOME" SCRAWLED ACROSS ALL THE FIELDS.

TOO MODEST?

I DON'T KNOW HOW TO SUMMARIZE A YEAR OF DISPARATE CUSTOMER INTERACTIONS SO I'M ENUMERATING ALL OF THEM.

I'M MY OWN WORST CRITIC. BUT I'M ALSO MY OWN BIGGEST FAN. SO I KEEP RATING MYSELF AS "AVERAGE".

LET'S TRY THIS AGAIN. FOLLOW THE DIRECTIONS ON THE SELF-ASSESSMENT.

STAFF TRAINING

COULD YOU TELL ME HOW YOU RATED *YOUR* WORK ETHIC? I NEED TO UNDERSTAND THE SCALE.

I BELIEVE IN PRESERVING EVERYONE'S PRIVACY, INCLUDING MY OWN.

SHE GAVE HERSELF THE HIGHEST RATING.

WHY SHOULD YOU AND I GO ANY LOWER?

SINCE YOU FAILED TO LOOK INWARD, I WANT YOU TO RATE EACH OTHER.
STAFF TRAINING
I'LL RATE YOU "EXCELLENT" IF YOU RATE ME "OUTSTANDING."
DONE.
NO COLLUSION!
THAT LOST HER AT LEAST A POINT IN MY ESTIMATION.
MINE, TOO!
DO WE HAVE TO WORRY ABOUT TAMARA?
NO. SHE'S INCAPABLE OF SAYING NEGATIVE THINGS ABOUT ANYONE.

WHY CAN'T YOU BE MORE COOPERATIVE? I'M TRYING TO FIGURE OUT WHAT TRAINING YOU NEED!
STAFF TRAINING
NO MATTER WHAT WE SAY, YOU'LL MAKE UP YOUR OWN MIND AND SEND US TO CLASSES WE DON'T NEED.
WE'LL SIT IN THE BACK ROW MAKING FUN OF THE INSTRUCTOR.
DRINKING FREE BUT SUBSTANDARD COFFEE.
I LIKE TRAININGS!

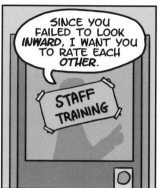

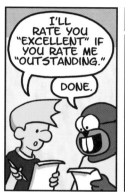

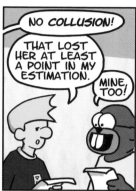

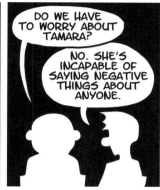

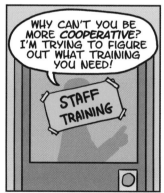

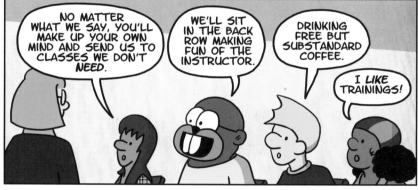

More UNSHELVED by Gene Ambaum & Bill Barnes

Unshelved

What Would Dewey Do?

Library Mascot Cage Match

Book Club

Read Responsibly

Frequently Asked Questions

Reader's Advisory

Large Print

Too Much Information

Books by Gene Ambaum

Poopy Claws (with Sophie Goldstein)

Fifty Shades of Brains (as BF Dealeo)

 **by Bill Barnes**

Runtime Error

Upgrade Path (with Jeff Zugale)